Multiplatform Media in Mexico

Paul Julian Smith
Multiplatform Media in Mexico

Growth and Change Since 2010

Paul Julian Smith
Latin American, Iberian, and Latino Cultures
The Graduate Center, CUNY
New York, NY, USA

ISBN 978-3-030-17538-2   ISBN 978-3-030-17539-9 (eBook)
https://doi.org/10.1007/978-3-030-17539-9

© The Editor(s) (if applicable) and The Author(s), under exclusive licence to Springer Nature Switzerland AG 2019
This work is subject to copyright. All rights are solely and exclusively licensed by the Publisher, whether the whole or part of the material is concerned, specifically the rights of translation, reprinting, reuse of illustrations, recitation, broadcasting, reproduction on microfilms or in any other physical way, and transmission or information storage and retrieval, electronic adaptation, computer software, or by similar or dissimilar methodology now known or hereafter developed.
The use of general descriptive names, registered names, trademarks, service marks, etc. in this publication does not imply, even in the absence of a specific statement, that such names are exempt from the relevant protective laws and regulations and therefore free for general use.
The publisher, the authors and the editors are safe to assume that the advice and information in this book are believed to be true and accurate at the date of publication. Neither the publisher nor the authors or the editors give a warranty, express or implied, with respect to the material contained herein or for any errors or omissions that may have been made. The publisher remains neutral with regard to jurisdictional claims in published maps and institutional affiliations.

Cover illustration: Gabriel Perez/Moment/Getty Images

This Palgrave Macmillan imprint is published by the registered company Springer Nature Switzerland AG
The registered company address is: Gewerbestrasse 11, 6330 Cham, Switzerland

Preface

This book is dedicated once more to the faculty and students of the (recently renamed) Latin American, Iberian, and Latino Cultures Program at the Graduate Center, City University of New York, who have provided such a fruitful place to teach and write over some ten years. My thanks are also due to the scholars who kindly invited me to speak in Europe and the Americas, thus providing the initial impetus to write some chapters of this book. Collaboration on the annual conferences jointly organized with Nancy Berthier, Álvaro Fernández, and Antonia del Rey Reguillo was especially important.

Earlier versions of parts of Chaps. 2, 3, and 8 were first published in *Film Quarterly*, where I remain, as continuing columnist, deeply indebted to my editor B. Ruby Rich. The wholly new sections of star profiles included in each chapter were researched at the Centro de Documentación of Mexico City's Cineteca, where I am most grateful as ever to its director Raúl Miranda. I was honored to be invited to the festivals at San Sebastián and Guadalajara, the former as juror. Paula Astorga generously received me at the Cineteca, when she was its director, as did Claudia Prado Valencia at the Centro de Capacitación Cinematográfica. It was a privilege to meet documentary directors María José Cuevas and Maya Goded. I am most grateful for the helpful suggestions of the expert anonymous reviewers of my manuscript. At Palgrave Macmillan, Shaun Vigil was the Senior Editor every author hopes for and Glenn Ramirez was admirably fast and efficient. Finally, I thank exemplary film critic Fernanda

Solórzano for much kind and expert conversation, and Guillermo Orozco Gómez for his inspiration as a pioneering scholar of Mexican television. My thanks are due finally to the anonymous readers of the MS for their helpful comments.

New York, NY, USA
2018

Paul Julian Smith

Contents

1 Introduction   1

Part I Cinema   11

2 Two Film Festivals: San Sebastián, Guadalajara; Two
   Institutions: Cineteca, Centro de Capacitación
   Cinematográfica   13

3 Sex Docs: *Bellas de noche, Plaza de la Soledad*   27

4 Post-Homophobic Comedy: *Macho, Hazlo como hombre*   45

Part II Television   61

5 Women-in-Prison TV Drama: *Capadocia, Vis a vis*   63

6 Anthology Dramas: *La rosa de Guadalupe, Como dice el dicho*   77

7 New Platforms, New Contents: *Run, Coyote, Run*   99

Part III Transmedia — 125

8 Two Media Crossovers: Cinema and Television for Day of the Dead; Live Theater Versions of TV Shows — 127

9 Earthquake Media — 151

10 Essay Film, Network Narrative, Streaming Series: *Vive por mí, Sincronía* — 173

11 Conclusion: Netflix and the New Telenovela — 195

Index — 201

List of Illustrations

Illustration 2.1	The Cineteca Nacional in Mexico City	20
Illustration 3.1	*Bellas de noche* (María José Cuevas, 2016)	28
Illustration 3.2	*Plaza de la Soledad* (Maya Goyed, 2016)	32
Illustration 4.1	Miguel Rodarte in *Macho* (Antonio Serrano, 2016)	47
Illustration 4.2	Mauricio Ochmann (left) in *Hazlo como hombre* (Nicolás López, 2017)	52
Illustration 5.1	Ana de la Reguera (right) in *Capadocia* (HBO Latin America, 2008–12)	66
Illustration 6.1	*La rosa de Gualalupe* (Televisa, 2008–present)	84
Illustration 6.2	*Como dice el dicho* (Televisa, 2011–present)	88
Illustration 7.1	Harold Torres (left) in *Run, Coyote, Run* (Fox Networks Group Latin America, 2017–present)	114
Illustration 8.1	Promotional material for *Romeo contra Julieta*, starring Angélica María (Julián Soler, 1968)	136
Illustration 8.2	Polo Morín in *Mi corazón es tuyo* (Televisa, 2014–15)	141
Illustration 9.1	*El día de la unión* (Kuno Becker, 2018)	158
Illustration 10.1	Martha Higareda in *Vive por mí* (Chema de la Peña, 2016)	178
Illustration 10.2	María Rojo in *Sincronía* (Blim, 2017)	188

1

Introduction

Cinema, Television, Multiplatform Media

Multiplatform Media in Mexico is the first book to treat the interconnected fields of cinema, television, and transmedia in Mexico over the last decade and the new audiovisual trends to which they have given birth. The book combines industrial analysis of a major audiovisual field at a time of growth and change with close readings of significant texts on all screens: big and small; theatrical, broadcast, and digital. It is also based on local reporting on the ground, as in the chapter documenting media response to the 2017 earthquake. For the first time, the book also draws throughout on star studies, tracing the distinct profiles of actors who migrate from one medium to another. I return to star studies in the second half of this Introduction.

In extended and more theoretical chapters at the end of each of its three parts, *Multiplatform Media in Mexico* also addresses three broad questions relevant beyond Mexico: what does it mean for a newly tolerant society to have a self-proclaimed genre of post-homophobic film comedy? Do changes in TV distribution (such as new streaming platforms) lead to changes in content (new types of series)? And how do established cinematic genres such as the essay film and network narrative translate to newly formed internet fiction forms? In a further attempt to structure and integrate the diverse material, each chapter (except for Chap. 9) treats two texts or phenomena, comparing and contrasting them. While media convergence is acknowledged in the abstract, it is less acknowledged in the concrete. One rare precedent devoted to film reception in a Mexican context is Juan Carlos Domínguez Domingo's

Las nuevas dimensiones del espectador (2017), which situates the new cinema spectator within a variety of contexts, from media market preferences to "cultural rights."

Mexican film studies in English tend to focus on accounts of a small number of contemporary internationally distributed features and auteurs or on consecrated historical periods such as the Golden Age of the 1940s (one notable exception is Sánchez Prado [2014], who addresses commercial cinema in a period just before my own). In Mexico itself, where film studies is mainly historical and TV studies mainly quantitative, there is little tradition of close textual analysis. This book attempts to shift and expand the focus of research in that, beyond auteur cinema and television statistics, it addresses a wide range of media and texts from the last decade and offers close analysis of specific texts. Although it does examine some international critical favorites, such as the genre of ground-breaking documentary features which play the festival circuit, it mainly pays close attention to what the great mass of Mexicans themselves prefer to watch, from mainstream film comedy to popular daily TV drama and web series. This book treats very recent material, which is often well known to modern Mexican audiences but unfamiliar to foreign scholars and has yet to receive academic attention. *Multiplatform Media in Mexico* thus aims to satisfy the interests of not only specialists but also non-Spanish-speaking readers interested in Latin America's second biggest economy and most dynamic media market. To this end the book combines industrial and textual analysis throughout.

Part I of *Multiplatform Media in Mexico* addresses cinema. The opening chapter on film explores the industrial context: two festivals (the first, San Sebastián, a "bridge" between Spain and Latin America; the second, Guadalajara, the main industry event in Mexico, just as Morelia is the main art cinema forum [Smith 2014, 30–7; D'Lugo 2018]); and two of Mexico's public film institutions located in Mexico City (the Cineteca Nacional, or National Film Institute, and the Centro de Capacitación Cinematográfica or CCC, one of the two official film schools). By focusing on production, distribution, and exhibition, this reportage sets the scene for the more textual chapters that follow. This chapter includes a review of a representative fiction feature directed by a graduate of the CCC and produced by and starring Harold Torres, a respected actor who is further treated in Chap. 7.

Chapter 3 ("Sex Docs") contrasts two documentaries by first-time female filmmakers, widely shown at international festivals, which focus on the unexplored topic of sex and aging: *Bellas de noche* ("Beauties of the Night," María José Cuevas, 2016) and *Plaza de la Soledad* ("Solitude Square," Maya Goded, 2016). Additionally, it offers an archive-based star studies account of the *vedettes* of the first film, showgirls of the 1970s such as Lyn May and Wanda Seux who boasted surprisingly durable careers.

The third, most extended chapter on cinema treats a recent trend in Mexican mainstream film, comedies in which it is not the homosexual but the homophobe who is the butt of the joke. The films here are *Macho* (Antonio Serrano, 2016) and *Hazlo como hombre* ("Do It Like an Hombre [sic]," Nicolás López, 2017). This chapter interweaves this sexual theme with that of urban space, arguing that the city is inextricable from new gender identities. The stars examined here are Miguel Rodarte and Mauricio Ochmann, previously and incongruously known for their unrepentantly macho and heterosexual romantic roles, respectively.

Part II shifts to TV fiction. The first chapter on television charts the emergence in Mexico of a genre that is well established elsewhere, the "WIP" or women-in-prison drama. As a control, it contrasts the Mexican series *Capadocia* (HBO Latin America, 2008–12, available for streaming in the USA from Amazon Prime) with a Spanish version of the same theme, *Vis a vis* ("Locked Up," Antena 3, 2015-present, also streaming on Amazon), which was shown free to air on Mexico's national network Azteca. The performers studied here are Mexicans Dolores Heredia and Ana de la Reguera, who play the prison director and main inmate respectively (de la Reguera also takes a campy cameo as herself in comedy *Macho*). The high-profile producer of the Mexican series, Epigmenio Ibarra, is himself a media figure with far-reaching influence in Mexico.

The second TV chapter is on anthology dramas (called in Mexico "unitarios" or "one-offs"), a genre which is often overshadowed by the better known genre of telenovela. It analyzes two daily series broadcast in the early evening which are massively popular with Mexican youth audiences and much despised by critics: *La rosa de Guadalupe* ("The Rose of the Virgin of Guadalupe," Televisa, 2008–) and *Como dice el dicho* ("As the Saying Goes," Televisa, 2011–). Arguing that they serve a pedagogic function in working through urgent social issues for their young viewers, the chapter also traces how the series have, over some 1000 episodes, functioned as a school for novice actors who are a focus for fans on social media.

The final, longest chapter on TV, "New Platforms, New Contents," is devoted to *Run, Coyote, Run* (Fox Latin America, 2017), the first series made by the Fox network in Mexico, a comedy that treats the potentially traumatic topic of people smuggling and the border wall. It argues that the novel format of the series, which is quite distinct from the coarse free-to-air sitcoms and sketch shows commonly aired by Televisa, is inextricable from its new distribution on pay-TV and by app. The stars studied are Luis Gerardo Méndez (a versatile actor who is the protagonist of Netflix's first series in Mexico) and Harold Torres of *Run, Coyote, Run* (who was previously known as a featured player in Leftist and indie filmmaking).

Part III is devoted to multiplatform media. The first chapter is based once more on on-site reportage. It treats two examples of media crossover, focusing in each on two texts. In the first half of the chapter, we see how film and TV production is crafted to coincide with the Mexican calendar and its unique Day of the Dead festivities. The texts examined are horror feature *Espectro* ("Demon Inside," Alfonso Pineda Ulloa, 2013) and (more incongruously) *No se aceptan devoluciones* ("Instructions Not Included," Eugenio Derbez, 2013), a film comedy inseparable from its director-star's ubiquitous work on television.

In the second half of the chapter, live theater shows recreate TV successes in provincial Mérida, Yucatán, and metropolitan Mexico City. The shows are, respectively, musical talent contest *Parodiando* ("Taking Off," or "Impersonating," Televisa, 2015–) and telenovela *Mi corazón es tuyo* ("My Heart Is Yours," Televisa, 2014–15), itself a Mexican remake of a Spanish TV series. Adaptations from small screen to stage thus span diverse genres. The stars examined here are veteran Angélica María, a favorite icon for drag queens, and Polo Morín, a telenovela juvenile with a controversial past. Both serve as images of and for teenagers in very different decades.

The second multiplatform media chapter is called "Earthquake Media." This chapter is also based on reportage, beginning as it does with an account of television coverage minutes after the massive earthquake on September 20, 2017, and continuing with a survey of media on the anniversary of the disaster one year later. The chapter tracks how film institutions, TV programming, and social media tackled the aftermath of the tragedy. It focuses especially on the charity drive set up by transnational superstar actors Gael García Bernal and Diego Luna, whose press profiles are studied at the end of the chapter, and also mentions the role of the presenters of Televisa's long-running morning show *Hoy* ("Today," Televisa, 1998–), which is so integrated into the daily lives of Mexican viewers. Normally devoted to celebrity gossip and trivial banter, in these special circumstances, the performers either left the studio to participate in rescue work or chaired unaccustomed and uncomfortable discussions with visiting seismologists or trauma specialists.

The final chapter on multiplatform media (and of the book) is on the genre known as network narrative. It deals with feature film *Vive por mi* ("Live for Me," Chema de la Peña, 2016; released in Mexico in 2017) and, at greater length, web series *Sincronía* ("Synchrony," Blim, 2017). A genre well established in Mexican film since at least the first features of Alejandro González

Iñárritu, the network narrative boasts multiple plot strands and a diverse cast who intersect after a random event. The chapter also engages with the essay film as a further discursive context, arguing that, like the essay film (which is generally identified with documentary) the fictional network narrative can also serve as a form of social and even personal commentary. Of the two texts featured here the dramatic feature stars Martha Higareda (previously known for romantic comedies with a fluffier tone) and the first drama series made for Televisa's internet platform features María Rojo (a long-established and distinguished film actress with a high political profile).

Confirming once more my suggestion that new platforms produce new contents, *Sincronía* has a radically new structure in that viewers are encouraged to view its episodes in any order they choose. It is perhaps significant, then, that it is the most marginally distributed work treated in this book (a web series on the belated digital platform associated with the much-despised heritage network Televisa) that boasts the most experimental formal innovation in its audiovisual text. Clearly, *Multiplatform Media in Mexico* will end up in unexpected locations. And the book's Conclusion examines, among other recent and contradictory phenomena, Netflix's third Mexican series, black dramedy *La Casa de las Flores* ("House of Flowers," 2018) and the streaming platform's award-winning auteur feature *Roma* (Alfonso Cuarón, 2018). It also mentions the case of Karla Souza, at once the biggest grossing actress in Mexico and the first and unexpected high-profile accuser in the country's incipient and faltering #MeToo movement.

At several points *Multiplatform Media in Mexico* uses Spain as a control to set against Mexico's specificity and as a prime source of transnationalism for its former colony. Thus Chap. 2, on film festivals, begins by showing how San Sebastián presents itself as a European showcase for the Latin American cinema that is also promoted at home in Guadalajara. In Chap. 5, Mexico's first women-in-prison TV drama is set against the Spanish version that followed it in the same genre. Or again, in Chap. 6, the popular daily television series that treat and target Mexican teens are explored via reference to a book-length investigation of their Spanish opposite numbers, a study that does not exist for Mexico itself. Finally, in Chap. 8, a Spanish star headlines a horror feature made for that most Mexican of holidays, the Day of the Dead; and in Chap. 10 a Spanish director helms a network narrative that is inextricable from the urban geography of Mexico City.

More importantly, perhaps, I have chosen not to update chapters that draw on reportage, as they testify to unique historical moments. This criterion applies to festival reports (2013, 2014), profiles of film institutions (2012, 2015), snapshots of media crossovers (2013, 2015), and responses to the earthquake and its aftermath (2017, 2018). The remaining chapters, more focused on audiovisual texts than on events or institutions, are written in a more timeless mode. And the reader is brought up to the date at the time of writing in my Conclusion.

Revisiting Mexican Star Studies

It seems fair to say that star studies has been relatively little treated by scholars of Mexican film, whether inside or outside Mexico. More common than Julia Tuñón's extended and erudite feminist rereading of "women of light and shade" and "faces of a myth" in the Golden Age (1998, 2000) are Carlos Monsiváis' lavishly illustrated and evocative but sketchy tribute to the "faces of Mexican cinema" (1993) or the fetishistic compilation of glamor shots in the special issue of *Artes de México* also devoted to the iconic actors of Churubusco (2001).

Yet there are signs, both industrial and critical, of growing interest in the area for both contemporary and historic periods. For the first time in 2016, the *Statistical Yearbook of Mexican Cinema* compiled by the Ministry of Culture and Mexican Film Institute published figures for the highest grossing actors of the year (interestingly, 12 of the top 20 are women and only 8 are men) (Secretaría de Cultura and IMCINE 2017, 108–9). And a recent encyclopedic collection of scholarly essays in two volumes includes several on the Mexican "star system," female and male, from periods earlier than my own (de los Reyes García Rojas 2016). Star studies thus potentially offers scholars of Mexican media a new approach to addressing the contemporary audiovisual field and one which, like this book, overflows the industrial or textual barriers between cinema, television, and multiplatform media.

In her review of a cluster of monographs launched by Palgrave Macmillan in 2012 to inaugurate a collection in the area (which included volumes devoted to Brigitte Bardot, Elizabeth Taylor, and Nicole Kidman), Niamh Thornton notes that the discipline rejects "uniformity in format and approach." Moreover, she claims, it has experienced "peaks and troughs" in its academic fortune, sometimes being despised by those scholars who believe that a concern for surfaces must itself be superficial (2014, 216).

Beginning her piece with Martin Shingler's *Star Studies: A Critical Guide*, Thornton traces the discipline back to French semiotician Roland Barthes, pioneering queer British scholar Richard Dyer, and Hollywood icon Bette Davis, the last a star with a "unique style and performance" (2014, 216). The initial, central insight, however, is from Dyer who proposed a critical strategy of "structured polysemy." The latter's aim is defined as "not to determine the correct meaning of the stars but rather to expose the variety of meanings that a star has for different types of audiences." The range of concepts treated by Shingler, according to Thornton's review once more, are wide, suggesting a broad horizon and diverse wealth of topics for my own book: "marketing, audience reception, celebrity, physicality and physical attractiveness, accent, the public/private divide, acting, voice and how [stars] function as auteurs, workers, and entrepreneurs." Moreover, Shingler's detailed attention to Indian film (a Bollywood star is even featured on his book's cover) "de-privileges Hollywood," shifting the parameters of debate beyond the USA (2014, 216).

Not coincidentally, Thornton is herself one of the very few scholars to treat Mexican stars in a more than superficial way. In two major articles, she addresses, first, iconic women and then (more rarely) men from the Golden Age of Mexican cinema, focusing on their multiplatform media afterlives on the internet. First in "YouTube: Transnational Fandom and Mexican divas," Thornton analyzes fan videos of María Félix and Dolores del Río (2010). On the one hand, she writes, the videos serve multiple purposes for their makers: the celebration of the idols themselves, the connection with a transnational audience, and the creation of a (fan) self. On the other, they blur textual boundaries between genres, mixing the techniques and images of classical film with the duration and aesthetics of the modern music video.

Thornton's second article (2017), on three male stars of the same period, "YouTube as Archive: Fans, Gender, and Mexican Film Stars Online," is included in a volume called *Revisiting Star Studies: Cultures, Themes, and Methods*. According to the editor's Introduction to this volume, which inserts the Mexican material into a broader transnational context, Thornton writes that fans are "creators" and "curators" of star discourse and that the "transient fan archive" of YouTube, once more, enables them to reconstruct star images. Crucially, on comparing the two articles, she discovers that male stars receive less attention from fans on the internet and the curation of their lasting legacy is less creative and more respectful (Yu 2017, 12).

But my main precedent for Mexican star studies is Olivia Cosentino. In her article on squeaky clean singing star of the 1980s Lucerito (2016), Cosentino stresses for the first time the multiplatform nature of stardom in Mexico: "a constellation of interlocking media products" (38). Discovered by dominant broadcaster Televisa, Lucerito (who later transitioned to the more adult "Lucero") embodied the "horizontal" integration of the threatened Mexican cinema industry as she migrated from TV shows to pop music and (Televisa-produced) family-oriented feature films (39), which proved more popular than their Hollywood competitors.

Beyond multiplatform media, Cosentino insists also on national specificity. The dazzlingly blond Lucero cannot be inserted into US-style methodological paradigms of the racialized and sexualized female figures familiar from Latinx studies (40). Nor was she one of the transnational stars (such as Dolores del Río in an earlier period) who still monopolize the attention of English-language scholars. Following Cosentino's lead, then, I focus on Mexican stars whose stardom is "an internal phenomenon" (41) (the exceptions are Gael García Bernal and Diego Luna), just as I limit myself to multiplatform texts whose audience remains overwhelming within Mexico itself.

Taking my cue from Thornton's and Cosentino's account of the now established discipline of star studies and from their revisiting of it for Mexican film studies (albeit in a different period from my own), I propose in this book to "de-privilege Hollywood" also by taking the Mexican star system, across all media, seriously, and to pay equal attention to less-studied male actors as well as their more visible female counterparts. Among the few contributors to this area are Sergio de la Mora (2006), who provides a scholarly precedent for the analysis of male stars of the Golden Age, and Ignacio Sánchez Prado (2013), who examines the transnational Gael García Bernal as "neoliberal" star. While internet sources with their active possibility of curation by fans are of course central to this investigation, print remains vital for still recent periods, as past press coverage is generally inaccessible on the web. I have thus drawn for most of my analysis on the invaluable files of press clippings held by the Cineteca in Mexico City.

Stars treated in this book thus range from a dramatic veteran and politician (María Rojo) to a comic ingénue (Martha Higareda), and from a politically committed art house stalwart (Harold Torres) to a "Kids' Choice Award"-winning telenovela juvenile (Polo Morín). Seen in this new perspective of star studies, then, marketing and audience reception come together in the common crafting and curation of personae by both artists and fans working near simultaneously in the audiovisual field. With Latin American film studies still focused primarily on cinematic auteurs, I trust that my appeal to the unaccustomed discipline of star studies will add a new and valuable dimension to the analysis of the wide range of texts, producers, and institutions treated in *Multiplatform Media in Mexico*.

References

Artes de México. 2001. Special issue: "Revisión del cine mexicano."
Cosentino, Olivia. 2016. Televisa Born and Raised: Lucerito's Stardom in 1980s Mexican Media. *The Velvet Light Trap* 78 (Fall): 38–52.

D'Lugo, Marvin, ed. 2018. Special dossier on Morelia International Film Festival. *Studies in Spanish and Latin American Cinemas* 15 (3).

de la Mora, Sergio. 2006. *Cinemachismo: Masculinities and Sexuality in Mexican Film*. Austin: University of Texas.

de los Reyes García Rojas, ed. 2016. *Miradas al cine mexicano*, 2 vols. Mexico City: Secretaría de Cultura.

Domínguez Domingo, Juan Carlos. 2017. *Las nuevas dimensiones del espectador*. Cuernavaca: UNAM.

Monsiváis, Carlos. 1993. *Rostros del cine mexicano*. Mexico City: CONACULTA/IMCINE.

Sánchez Prado, Ignacio. 2013. The Neoliberal Stars: Salma Hayek and Gael García Bernal and the Post-Mexican Film Icon. In *Latin American Icons: Fame Across Borders*, ed. Diana C. Niebylski and Patrick O'Connor, 147–156. Nashville: Vanderbilt University Press.

———. 2014. *Screening Neoliberalism: Transforming Mexican Cinema 1988–2012*. Nashville: Vanderbilt University Press.

Secretaría de Cultura and IMCINE. 2017. *Anuario estadístico de cine mexicano 2016*. Mexico City: IMCINE.

Smith, Paul Julian. 2014. *Mexican Screen Fiction: Between Cinema and Television*. Cambridge/Malden: Polity.

Thornton, Niamh. 2010. YouTube: Transnational Fandom and Mexican Divas. *Transnational Cinemas* 1 (2): 53–67.

———. 2014. Review of *Star Studies: A Critical Guide*, by Martin Shingler et al. *Celebrity Studies* 5 (1–2): 216–219.

———. 2017. YouTube as Archive: Fans, Gender, and Mexican Film Stars Online. In *Revisiting Star Studies: Cultures, Themes, and Methods*, ed. Sabrina Qiong Yu and Guy Austin, 205–224. Edinburgh: Edinburgh University Press.

Tuñón, Julia. 1998. *Mujeres de luz y sombra en el cine mexicano: la constucción de una imagen (1939–52)*. Mexico City: Colegio de México.

———. 2000. *Los rostros de un mito: personajes femeninos en las películas de Emilio Indio Fernández*. Mexico City: Arte e imagen and IMCINE.

Yu, Sabrina Qiong. 2017. Performing Stardom: Star Studies in Transformation and Expansion. In *Revisiting Star Studies: Cultures, Themes, and Methods*, ed. Sabrina Qiong Yu and Guy Austin, 1–24. Edinburgh: Edinburgh University Press.

Part I

Cinema

2

Two Film Festivals: San Sebastián, Guadalajara; Two Institutions: Cineteca, Centro de Capacitación Cinematográfica

San Sebastián International Film Festival, 2013; Guadalajara International Film Festival, 2014

The 61st festival held in San Sebastián (or Donostia, the city's Basque name) ran in 2013 from September 20 to 28. The weather, unseasonably sunny for the damp and chilly northern region, seemed to signal a shift. And respected festival director José Luis Rebordinos said that his aim was to re-orientate the festival to Latin America as a "meeting point" between Spain and the continent that his predecessor had called "the future of cinema" (García 2013).

But was this pivoting a choice or a necessity? While many Latin American economies continue to grow, Spain remains mired in crisis. According to the Spanish producers' association, audiovisual production fell by 15% in 2012, even as exports rose by 13% (Smith 2017, 31–33). The industry thus lapped up the support from the festival which selected four local candidates for the Golden Shell prize in the Official Section and a co-production with Argentina (Juan José Campanella's animated *Futbolín* ["Foosball"]) as the opening film. As *Variety* noted, at this, "the most important festival in the Spanish-speaking world" (Hopewell and Barraclough 2013), films helmed by Spaniards or Latin Americans make up a higher proportion of titles at San Sebastián than French features at Cannes or German at Berlin. Moreover, bowing the week after the much bigger Toronto, San Sebastián has its work cut out in the brutal fight for world premieres. A rare success was the securing of the closing film: Jean-Pierre Jeunet's picture book replaying of Americana, *The Young and Prodigious T. S. Spivet*.

© The Author(s) 2019
P. J. Smith, *Multiplatform Media in Mexico*,
https://doi.org/10.1007/978-3-030-17539-9_2

In keeping with this vision of the festival as an encounter between two Spanish-speaking regions (not to mention as a springboard for Toronto's titles into Europe), Rebordinos has beefed up the industry section with the festival daily eagerly announcing foreign sales and a burgeoning Spanish-Latin American development workshop held for the second year (De Pablos and Hopewell 2013). The opening animated co-production was exemplary of this collaboration. Released under the title *Metegol* in Latin America, it boasted soundtracks in Peninsular Spanish, the director's own Argentinian dialect, and a so-called neutral Spanish version that was in fact dubbed by a well-known Mexican cast, featuring established actors such as Alfonso Herrera and Irene Azuela.

Pan-Hispanic boosters must have been pleased by the festival's outcome. Spain's main newspaper *El País* covered the closing ceremony under the telling headline "Cinema in Spanish Sweeps the Boards" (García and Belinchón 2013). The jury for the Official Selection (led by respected American director Todd Haynes) passed over established auteurs like Atom Egoyan to give the main prize to *Pelo malo* ("Bad Hair," Mariana Rondón), a low-budget plea for tolerance and an indictment of homophobia from a first-time woman director from Venezuela, a territory hardly prolific in filmmaking. The jury's special prize went to *La herida* ("Wounded," Fernando Franco), another debut project this time from Spain, an austere drama on self-harming (the protagonist won best actress too). Best director went to Mexican Fernando Eimbcke for his third picture, the coming of age story *Club Sandwich*. Breaking the mold, the New Directors jurors (led by Marina Stavenhagen, former director of IMCINE, the Mexican Film Institute) went to the Icelandic debut *Of Horses and Men*.

I myself was invited as a juror in the Latin Horizons competition, in a team led by Chilean producer Bruno Bettati. The 11 films we saw were remarkable for their variety in both national origin and cinematic genre. Mexico boasted two very different films on the same theme of the train ridden by immigrants from Central America to the USA: a worthy drama played by youthful non-professionals (*La jaula de oro* ["The Golden Cage," Diego Quemada-Díez]) and an uneasy mix of documentary and fiction starring Mexican transnational celebrity Gael García Bernal (*¿Quién es Dayani Cristal?* ["Who is Dayani Cristal?," Marc Silver]) (I examine the star profile of García Bernal in Chap. 8 of this book).

Uruguay offered a charming animation on a palindromic child (*AninA* [sic], Alfredo Soderguit) and a droll dramedy on a divorced father on holiday with his teenage daughter (*Tanta agua* ["So Much Water," Ana Guevara, Leticia Jorge]). Argentina, a more prolific territory than its neighbor, was represented by *Wakolda* ("The German Doctor," Lucía Puenzo) a polished historical piece on Mengele in Patagonia, and *Pensé que iba a haber fiesta* ("I Thought It Was a Party," Victoria Galardi), a morose contemporary drama on housesitting and infidelity. Brazil, isolated in spite of its size by the Portuguese language, fielded a well-intentioned denunciation of the country's legal system (*De Menor* ["Underage," Caru Alves de Souza]) and a searing drama on a child's kidnapping (*A Lobo Atrás da Porta* ["A Wolf at the Door," Fernando Coimbra]). The latter, which was awarded the prize in its section, combined kinetic photography in authentic Rio locations with a labyrinthine plot and shattering central performances. It could hardly be further from the contemplative, minimalist films promoted by Mexico's Morelia and often selected from Latin America for festivals in Europe and the USA (see Smith 2014).

One trend of the festival, then, was this burgeoning of Latin American, and especially Mexican, influence, both artistically and industrially. *Variety* once more wrote, "San Sebastián's large merit this year was to consolidate its position as a must-attend event for a broad base of players in the Latin American arthouse and crossover business" (Hopewell and Barraclough 2013). Yet this transnational focus remains firmly and proudly rooted in the local. Impressively long lines of San Sebastián residents (known as Donostiarras) preceded screenings of even the most difficult titles at the least propitious times. The opening ceremony (and, indeed, the festival as a whole) switched effortlessly between the Basque, Spanish, and English languages. Basque cuisine, a key attraction of the region's tourism, was featured in a rare section called "Film and Gastronomy." The Basque cinema section, called "Zinemira," boasted an impressive eight features in both drama and documentary. Even local fashion took its turn, with models twirling each night on the red carpet, alongside Hollywood stars like Hugh Jackman and Annette Bening.

This synergy between cultural industries (film, food, fashion) is echoed by a second trend in the festival, after the pivot to Latin America: television. Spanish public broadcaster Radio-Televisión Española remains the main corporate sponsor of the festival (although fast fashion brand Desigual was also ubiquitous). In interview, jurors repeatedly cited the growing influence of the medium. Todd Haynes, who scored such a success with *Mildred Pierce* for HBO, told the festival daily that much of the energy of indie cinema was now flowing to cable. Marina Stavenhagen is working on projects for long-scorned Mexican television. My co-juror, Spanish actress Adriana Ugarte (mobbed by fans whenever she set foot outside), effortlessly combines film, theater, and TV, saying that the last medium is the best for storytelling. Her new series, *El tiempo entre costuras* ("The Time in Between," Antena 3, 2013–14) would be a period piece shot on location in Morocco, a high-budget project difficult to imagine as a feature film in Spanish cinema's current straitened circumstances. RTVE itself sponsored a

"TV gala" at the festival, promoting its lavish India-shot drama on real-life humanitarian activist Vicente Ferrer. When the lifetime achievement award was given to Carmen Maura (the actress best known abroad for her collaborations with Almodóvar), the clip tape of her lengthy and distinguished career reminded Spanish viewers that her success had begun in television. Maura had recently also begun to make a parallel career in features in Mexico.

In her acceptance speech, Maura noted somewhat ruefully that she was the first Spanish woman to receive a prize hitherto handed to foreigners. And a final mini-trend of the festival was the increased presence of female and queer artists. As noted earlier, the main prize of the Golden Shell went to a first-time woman director. The established Other Look prize (presented to a film addressing the "feminine world") went to François Ozon's *Jeune et Jolie* ("Young and Beautiful"). The local queer paper also gave out several awards. I was privileged to accept myself, on behalf of Mexican director Roberto Fiesco, best Latin LGBT prize for *Quebranto* ("Disrupted"), his moving documentary on a former child star who became a transgender woman.

But perhaps the film that best embodies the festival trends is one starring Maura that played out of competition in the main section. Given the unfortunate English title *Witching and Bitching*, the original *Las brujas de Zugarramurdi* invokes a location long famed for witchcraft, the equivalent of Mexico's Veracruz. Director Álex de la Iglesia tackles Spain's financial crisis directly: a band of Madrid living statues (a silver Christ and green G. I. Joe) are forced to rob one of the pawn shops suddenly ubiquitous in the capital and head north to de la Iglesia's native Basque Country. Insistently local in its references (the film features songs in Euskera), it is also global in its reworking of the transnational genres of horror and comedy and use of American-style quick cutting and frenzied lensing. The motley male crew (including Spain's biggest TV star, Mario Casas) prove no match for the coven who, in an impressively realized sequence, raise a monstrous Great Goddess. Cannily combining auteur and genre film, *Witching* used San Sebastián as a launch pad to take the number one slot at the Spanish box office the weekend after the festival.

The 29th Guadalajara International Film Festival (known by its Spanish acronym as FICG) took place during March 21–30, 2014, with Quebec as guest nation. It featured special tributes to two icons of Mexican Golden Age cinema: singing star María Victoria (who thanked the local Virgin of Zapopan for her good fortune) and the deceased Sara García (the so-called grandma of Mexico, veteran of innumerable classic comedies and melodramas). Boasting an academic conference and book launches in which I myself took part, FICG also hosts a thriving LGBT strand, known as "Maguey" (a pun on the name of the tequila-producing agave cactus typical of the region and the Spanish pronunciation of "gay").

While its main Mexican rival, Morelia, is known for fostering rigorous art film and documentary, the FICG is acclaimed as the main market for Latin American film (an honor also sought, as we saw, by San Sebastián). The festival features an industry Forum for Mexican Cinema, which this year revealed mixed emotions. One panel mourned the 20 years since the introduction of the North American Free Trade Agreement, in which Mexico (unlike Canada) failed to insist on a cultural exception for film, with reportedly disastrous results for the distribution of local pictures. Another hailed new forms of consumption of Mexican cinema, claiming that movie theater attendance (which is still increasing year on year) and rising internet streaming (as yet hobbled in Mexico by limited access to broadband) are not in conflict but are, rather, mutually reinforcing.

Three of my favorite features from the huge program look likewise forward and backward in Mexican film history and treat a common and sadly topical theme: crime and punishment. *Los años de Fierro* ("The Years of Fierro") is directed by first-timer Santiago Esteinou, who trained at the Mexico City state film school Centro de Capacitación Cinematográfica (studied later in this chapter) and Philadelphia's Temple University. It is a somber documentary on the oldest Mexican on death row in the USA, César Roberto Fierro, a petty criminal convicted of murder back in 1979 on the basis of a coerced confession (the Ciudad Juárez police, closely collaborating with their El Paso colleagues, abducted the suspect's mother). *Días* takes a leaf from another recent documentary on an apparent travesty of justice, the glossy, audience-friendly *Presunto culpable* ("Presumed Guilty"), which became one of the biggest grossing features in the history of Mexican cinema. The photography is thus eerily handsome with frequent shots of the red desert at dawn and dusk. And the inmate's only relation, his homeless brother, beds down in picturesque squalor at an old-time fairground.

Heart-breakingly handsome, as shown in family photos, as a young man, the now mature Fierro proves astonishingly composed in interview (the director was permitted only 45 minutes with the condemned man every three months). Esteinou paces his story well, avoiding the perils of stasis inherent in his narrative, cannily weaving together the two strands of his plot: the personal and the legal. And only at the end do we learn that, in spite of repeated appeals when the proof of coercion was unearthed, Texas has refused to reopen the case. Moreover it claims, as a state, not to be subject to international conventions signed by the USA which would bring about the captive's release. Fifty more Mexicans remain on death row in Texas, tried like him illegally without the benefit of assistance from their consul.

Fierro's years thus have no happy ending. And nor do the days recounted in the best Mexican fiction feature I saw, Damian John Harper's *Los Ángeles*, which won its director the festival prize for first film. Although named for the US metropolis, this German-funded drama takes place entirely in a remote village in Oaxaca and, most unusually for a Mexican film, is spoken mainly in an indigenous language, in this case Zapotec. Things begin grimly with main character Mateo, a young man anxious to emigrate to the USA, receiving a beating from the gang he wishes to join for protection. But Harper avoids the pornographic violence of much recent Mexican drama, no doubt because of his intimacy with and respect for the indigenous cast (all non-actors) with whom he has cohabited from some 14 years. Documentary-like shooting sticks close to the locals as they negotiate the pleasures and perils of life in a village which, refreshingly once more, is not shown as a hell hole, in spite of its pervasive poverty.

We are thus presented with a moving anthropology of rural life and labor, where patriarchs' privileges are threatened by the youthful gangs (mainly Spanish-speaking, having cast off their native language) and dogged shawled women are the courageous backbone of the community. There is also a touching love story, with the shy Mateo chastely wooing a young woman (in a typically sweet detail, they whistle to each other to set up their meetings). When ordered to carry out a murder as an initiation rite, Mateo defies the gangsters. And his story (like Fierro's) remains open at the end of the film. But the importance of *Los Ángeles* is that it refutes the unthinking equation of Mexico and brutal violence purveyed by such recent festival hits as Amat Escalante's *Heli* (2013). Rather, rural women, still supported by strong social bonds that resist the narcos' encroachment, comment with horror on the dangers to be found on the other side of the border. Los Angeles, they fear, is like "a cage of wild animals," a deadly trap for their vulnerable migrant sons.

A different, but related, kind of trap is dramatized in *El puño de hierro* ("The Iron Fist"), a rare fascinating silent from 1927, restored by the Filmoteca of the UNAM (National Autonomous University) and given a free open-air screening at the festival with live musical accompaniment by Nortec, Mexico's best known techno band. A rare and fascinating curio shot in tropical Veracruz (which never even made it to Mexico City on first release), *El puño* is a crazy, drug-fueled mash up, a Mexican ancestor of *Reefer Madness*. The little-known director Gabriel García Moreno sets his lush melodrama among the gilded youth of the lush provinces, decked out as they are with panama hats and parasols. He begins with his hero, a dandyish morphine addict, fondly embracing a donkey, to the disgust of his girlfriend, a formidable horsewoman. When she takes him to be cured by a famous doctor, the twist doesn't take long in coming. The respectable medic is in fact the kingpin dealer in the region, running a decadent dive where young men lounge languidly on mattresses in thrall to the demon drugs he has supplied them with.

This narco narrative (a salutary reminder that illegal substances are hardly new in Mexico, as elsewhere) is combined with multiple, hallucinatory plotlines. For example, a masked highway man called The Bat joins forces with the dealer at one point; and a pipe-smoking child detective attempts to solve the sprawling mystery. But the most delightful thing about the film is its eroticism. García Moreno stages sexual encounters through shots of feet, with male and female shoes approaching and intertwining. In the drug dive handsome youths stroke the legs of an older addict, naked except for a loin cloth and wreath of flowers. Yet there are disturbing moments too. Apparent cinema vérité footage shows dope fiends imprisoned in strait jackets in an asylum and deformed children, supposedly the offspring of user mothers, receiving similarly tough treatment. The cruelty of *Los días de Hierro* and *Los Ángeles*, with their beatings and shootings mitigated only by vulnerable familial and social ties, is here presented in a fragmentary and yet more frightful form.

Finally, however, what these three Mexican features have in common, across genre and period, is a particular model of crime and punishment. *Fierro* praises brotherly bonds where policing is corrupt and justice absent. *Los Ángeles* likewise invokes communal structures of lawmaking in the absence of state police: the village possesses an indigenous local council which struggles to keep order in rapidly changing circumstances. And the titular "iron fist" of the silent refers not to the forces of law and order, which are nowhere to be seen, but to the tenacious grip of morphine and cocaine over young users. Twenty years after NAFTA, it would appear that cross-border trade flows more freely in narcotics than in film, given the barriers to entry erected by the US industry to foreign features. But if natural justice is hard to achieve, in legal process as in cultural exchange, then the Mexican films in this year's FICG show that a rich national cinema can still be achieved in the shadow of inequality and exploitation.

Cineteca Nacional, The Mexican Film Institute (2012); Centro de Capacitación Cinematográfica, The Mexican State Film School (2015)

A sultry spring afternoon in Mexico City and the Cineteca Nacional (film archive and theater) is already teeming. Young people loll on the new lawns or sample excellent ice cream under the spectacular white latticed dome that filters the harsh light. And screenings at the ten theaters have yet to begin.

Illustration 2.1 The Cineteca Nacional in Mexico City

Today is an important day. Workers clip vegetation and polish pathways in anticipation of a visit by a delegation from Conaculta, the national council for the arts which is the supervisor of the Cineteca. The civil servants have come to see the almost completed extension of the complex, now claimed to the biggest cinematheque in the world and the brain child of Paula Astorga, the energetic director general (Illustration 2.1).

Things were not always so sunny at the Cineteca. Founded in 1974 as the national film repository, it was gifted first to the brother of one president and then to the sister of another. Its darkest day, and proof of criminal incompetence, was a fire in 1982 in which irreplaceable holdings, on celluloid and paper alike, were consumed. With the end of the 71-year regime of the PRI (the Institutional Revolutionary Party) in 2000, new possibilities emerged. One director previous to Astorga was Leonardo García Tsao, a distinguished critic. Astorga herself has survived even a renewed change of government, with the PRI, now returned to power, allowing her to remain in place to finish the job. Given the history of clientelism in Mexican arts administration, this is something of a miracle.

It seems plausible that former President Felipe Calderón's rash of funding for large cultural projects at the end of his period in office (a lavish new National Library has also just been completed) resulted from a desire to leave a legacy more lasting than a failed and deadly war on drugs. Whatever the case, the Cineteca expansion, with its two new vaults for film storage, restoration lab, and four additional screens, marks a welcome contrast with the retrenchment of arts institutions in Europe and elsewhere. Certainly the facilities now surpass New York's Film Society at Lincoln Center and London's BFI South Bank. Astorga herself explains in interview the institutional context. Four state bodies support Mexican film: Churubusco Studios (also upgraded) produces; the Centro de Capacitación Cinematográfica (CCC) (public film school) trains (see the next section in this chapter); IMCINE (the national film institute) regulates; and the Cineteca conserves and exhibits. More than an "extension," the current project is a "refounding" of an institution which Astorga conceives as a center for "thought." Along these lines, in-house researchers at the Cineteca's indispensable library ("Centro de documentación"), headed by Raúl Miranda, have begun a new journal, *Icónica* (I myself gave a lecture in the library and contributed to the first issue of the journal). Abel Muñoz, the editor of *Icónica*, has also co-edited a recent book published by the Cineteca of "reflections on contemporary Mexican cinema," whose contributors are restricted to young critics and academics (Curiel de Icaza and Muñoz Hénonin 2014).

This emphasis in scholarly activities on youth is echoed in exhibition. While the Cineteca continues to schedule seasons of historic Mexican cinema, it now also presents itself as the sponsor of a new generation of local directors (Astorga mentions Nicolás Pereda here). As the one-time organizer of Mexico City's now defunct international film festival (FICCO), Astorga is well placed to engage with contemporary filmmakers whose work did not always appeal to previous occupants of her position (García Tsao was known for some scathing reviews of Mexican films in *Variety*). And while, under Astorga, much programming remains mainly scholarly, focusing on both historic and current art film, it also boasts a populist strand that may prove controversial to old-school cinephiles. Open-air screenings, staged in a grassy space that was formerly an arid parking lot, were inaugurated with a classic Mexican film of the Golden Age and a new print of Spielberg's *Jaws*.

Astorga explains her strategy of audience creation. With Mexico, a young nation demographically (much more so than Europe or even the USA), youth is her key target. And with one of the biggest cities in the world (some 26 million people) lacking a circuit of alternative distribution, exhibition space for young Mexican film is a priority. Like television broadcasting (still dominated by Televisa and Azteca), movie exhibition is a duopoly in Mexico, with chains Cinemex and Cinépolis regularly accused by locals of kowtowing to Hollywood producers (it has to be said, however, that Cinépolis, as well as supporting the Morelia festival, has recently opened its own art house strand for independent film in selected theaters). And if the Cineteca is situated in the comfortable southern suburb of Coyoacán (best known to tourists as the site of Frida Kahlo's house), still it seeks to welcome in general audiences from, say, the staff of the hospital that stands next door.

Increasing access is thus a main theme of the Cineteca's refounding, just so long as this does not come at the expense of quality. One of the most intriguing of these access initiatives is a "memory archive" composed of digitized home movies submitted by private citizens. Moreover, venturing out from the soft south, Cineteca has just opened a branch in the gritty city center: the large Cine Teresa, a notorious and ruinous porn theater, has been refurbished and is now devoted to Mexican film.

Having completed my research at the library and interview with the director general, I take in a movie at one of the new screens. Everardo González's beautiful and disturbing documentary *Cuates de Australia* (a non-fiction prize-winner at the Los Angeles Film Festival) is typical of the films by young directors to find a home at the Cineteca that they would be hard pressed to gain on the commercial circuit in their home country. Given the depressingly literal English title of *Drought*, the original name repeats the picturesque and enigmatic toponym of its location (literally "Australian Buddies"), an arid and impoverished settlement in Mexico's distant northeast, a world away from the booming capital. Subsisting on their livestock, the inhabitants are forced each year to move temporarily to a marginally more pleasant location, as the pathetic water hole on which humans and animals alike depend progressively and distressingly dries up.

Now, the documentary genre has made a huge contribution to the revival of young Mexican cinema in the past decade. Indeed Roberto Hernández's and Geoffrey Smith's mesmerizing *Presunto culpable* ("Presumed Guilty," 2008), briefly banned by the courts, is one of the biggest grossing local films of recent times. González's contemplative style and leisurely pace, however, are clearly less audience friendly. Yet with five features to his credit, González has established himself as an important voice. And in spite of the grimness of the film's theme (at one point we watch as a young foal collapses and dies), the film's satisfying aesthetic and narrative structure renders it relatively accessible to the new non-cinephile audience to which the Cineteca is successfully reaching out (audiences have already greatly increased compared to previous years).

Thus *Cuates de Australia* begins with a scene of equine sex graphic enough to satisfy erstwhile patrons of the Cine Teresa, before cutting to the hospital room where a young couple view with touching delight the ultrasound image of their unborn child. And it ends with the closure of this natural cycle: the child is safely born, albeit undernourished, and the rains finally fall causing the bleak desert to start into verdant life. While there is always a risk of aestheticizing deprivation in such films, the director lived in the tiny community for some three years; and his handsome cinematography (which often appear to be monochrome, given the location's lack of color) gives rise to haunting effects which serve to reinforce, rather than distract from, the evidence of grinding poverty to which *Drought* attests. Here's hoping that the Cineteca will long screen and promote such films; and that its successful refounding will serve as an inspiration to cinematheques elsewhere.

It is hot and noisy on teeming Calzada de Tlalpan in southern Mexico City. But, just off the busy boulevard, all is cool and calm in the state film school officially called "Centro de Capacitación Cinematográfica" ("Film Training Center") but universally known as "CCC." Nestling next to legendary Churubusco Studios, where Dolores del Río and María Félix once walked the soundstages, the CCC shares its handsome Mexican modernist quarters (in shades of day-glow pink and orange concrete) with government-funded academies for theater and dance. The location is appropriate. The CCC is both proud of its connections with the industry, boasting that it is "natural" for its graduates to find jobs there, and devoted to artistic innovation.

It might be said that the CCC, which was founded in 1975, has sometimes been in the shadow of its rival public film school, the CUEC ("Centro Universitario de Estudios Cinematográficos" or "University Center of Film Studies"), which claims to be the oldest in Latin America. After all, the Oscar winners director Alfonso Cuarón and cinematographer Emmanuel "El Chivo" Lubezki matriculated there (although Cuarón did not graduate). However 2015 is something of a banner year for CCC, with students who have not yet completed their degrees receiving the highest of honors. Thus one student film was chosen for Sundance's fiction short competition (*Primavera* ["Spring"] by Tania Castillo) and another (Gabriel Serra's *La parka* ["The Reaper"]) for the short documentary competition at the Oscars.

The CCC's deputy director of Outreach and Research Claudia Prado Valencia kindly gives me a guided tour of the facilities, state of the art in both digital and film formats. In one editing suite we see a new student documentary being cut. It traces the history of Mexico City's dilapidated bathhouses, once intended for families without the luxury of plumbing and now patronized by clients that include gay men with thoughts other than cleanliness on their minds. (Dalia R. Reyes' *Baño de vida* ["Bath of Life"] would be premiere at Guadalajara in 2016.)

Prado Valencia next offers me some facts. The school, which boasted Luis Buñuel as its first honorary president and is now celebrating its fortieth anniversary, offers three academic programs (a bachelor degree in filmmaking and courses in screenwriting and production) and accepts 15 students in each strand, including a maximum of two foreigners. Fiction feature graduates include recent art house auteurs Matías Meyer (*Los últimos cristeros* ["The Last Christeros," 2011]) and Michael Rowe (*Año bisiesto* ["Leap Year," 2010]) and more commercially minded helmers Carlos Carrera (*El crimen del padre Amaro* ["The Crime of Father Amaro," 2001]) and Sebastián del Amo (*Cantinflas*, 2014). Maryse Sistach (*Perfume de violetas* ["Violet Perfume," 2001]), one of the tiny number of Mexican career directors to be a woman, also got her start here.

The burgeoning documentary sector includes such festival favorite alumni as Everardo González, Eugenio Polgovsky (who, sadly, was to pass away in 2017), and Juan Carlos Rulfo. And if the CUEC takes credit for nurturing cinematographer El Chivo, the CCC can boast Rodrigo Prieto of *Amores Perros* (Alejandro González Iñárritu, 2000) and *Brokeback Mountain* (Ang Lee, 2005). Screenwriting graduates have scripted the most innovative corpus of drama in Mexico today, the quality TV series of public Canal Once. And as a producer of some 15 shorts and three features a year, the CCC has also made some of my favorite films: from Jorge Michel Grau's cannibal horror *Somos lo que hay* ("We Are What We Are," selected for Cannes in 2010) to Tatiana Huezo's devastating documentary on genocide in El Salvador, *El lugar más pequeño* ("The Tiniest Place," shown in Venice in 2011).

As these varied titles suggest, the CCC is committed both to training students for the job market and to serving the public interest. Current Director General Henner Hofmann stresses to me the school's notion of service and accessibility: tuition fees are around 1000 dollars a year for the lucky local students who pass highly competitive admission exams. And, seeking to counteract the perennial bias toward the capital, the CCC promotes film education outside Mexico City and for the general public, including children. Recently they offered courses to indigenous students in the distant and impoverished states of Oaxaca and Chiapas.

Finally, the CCC has since 1998 offered a program called "Ópera prima," co-financed with IMCINE (the Mexican Film Institute), which gives students the chance to make a first feature. In spring 2015 one film that benefited from this scheme secured theatrical release, albeit two years after its premiere at the Morelia International Film Festival. As we shall see, it embodies some of the strengths of the CCC, without which it would not exist (it is co-produced with a government fund for quality filmmaking). I caught it at the Cinépolis Diana, in the heart of the capital, where Mexico's most powerful exhibitor has set aside a screen for its "Art House" brand.

González: falsos profetas ("González," 2014) by Christian Díaz Pardo (who studied cinematography at CCC and screenwriting at CUEC) stars the compellingly handsome Harold Torres, cast somewhat implausibly as a neglected nonentity in what the synopsis calls "the largest city in the world." In his loneliness, the banally named anti-hero is reduced to touching women's hair on night buses. *González* begins, then, as an aesthetically crafted study in urban alienation. Torres' dapper figure, clad in the formal suit and tie with which he hopes to luck into employment, is shot consistently from above (lost in the megalopolis) or, alternately, atop perilously tall structures (the high-rise housing project where he broods in a room dominated by a wide screen TV). Stylish noir cinematography follows González into the hellish subway and the hostile workplaces where he is ritually humiliated.

This would appear, then, to be an exercise in existential ennui familiar from much slow cinema around the world. But, like the CCC, Director Díaz has a social conscience. On the television that taunts him with its vapid consumerism, González glimpses a charismatic preacher in whose church he later gains a precarious job as a call operator. Becoming adept at fleecing the desperate flock for their few remaining pesos (he explains that God needs their money to know they love Him), González is now ready to challenge his boss, the media-savvy pastor. Hitherto leisurely paced (some local critics complained about this slowness), *González* now kicks the rhythm up a notch, shifting into thriller mode. There is a near rape, a kidnapping, a speeding car, and a body in the trunk. Existential ennui yields suddenly to spectacular violence.

How does *González* relate, then, to the culture of the CCC I examined earlier? Written as well as directed by alumni of the school, the film is stylish and professionally made, rejecting the minimalism which can serve as an alibi for filmmakers less thoroughly trained than Díaz. And it boasts recurrent striking shots of its high cheek-boned star looming out of the infernal city night.

Yet, beyond industry and aesthetics, *González*'s major innovation is its subject matter. Mexican Catholics have long been deserting their heritage faith for the more inclusive evangelical churches. While Torres (who for the first time takes a producing credit) has stressed that the film attacks not Protestantism itself but the abuse of religion to exploit the vulnerable, this is to my knowledge the first Mexican feature to call attention to this urgent social issue, which remains little known abroad.

The noir or thriller elements of *González*'s second half are thus perhaps intended to sugar the pill for the Mexican public and to better communicate to them a timely warning on the subject. Certainly other genre movies by CCC students, such as Jorge Michel Grau's *Somos lo que hay*, also carried barely hidden messages about the deadly effects of exploitation in contemporary Mexico. Michel Grau's ravenous cannibals are thus the unlikely siblings of Díaz Pardo's bloodsucking preachers. But finally *González* is not just exemplary of the CCC's twin mission of professional training and public service. It is also evidence for a national institution's success in exporting its culture internationally: *González* won its director the award for best first film at the Montreal World Film Festival.

References

Curiel de Icaza, Claudia, and Abel Muñoz Hénonin, eds. 2014. *Reflexiones sobre cine mexicano contemporáneo*. Mexico City: Cineteca Nacional.

De Pablos, Emiliano, and John Hopewell. 2013. San Sebastián Boosts Biz. *Variety*, September 27. https://variety.com/2013/film/global/san-sebastian-boosts-biz-1200673390/

García, Rocío. 2013. Amor eterno al cine latinoamericano. *El País*, September 19. https://elpais.com/cultura/2013/09/19/actualidad/1379582244_042249.html

García, Rocío, and Gregorio Belinchón. 2013. El cine enespañol arrasa. *El País*, September 28. https://elpais.com/cultura/2013/09/28/actualidad/1380394246_678327.html

Hopewell, John, and Barraclough. 2013. *Bad Hair* Tops San Sebastián Fest. *Variety*, September 28. https://variety.com/2013/film/global/pelo-malo-wins-at-san-sebastian-1200676894/

Smith, Paul Julian. 2014. Following Festivals. In *Mexican Screen Fiction: Between Cinema and Television*, 30–46. Cambridge/Malden, MA: Polity.

———. 2017. Madrid de Cine: Spanish Film Screenings. In *Spanish Lessons: Cinema and Television in Contemporary Spain*, 30–41. New York/Oxford: Berghahn.

3

Sex Docs: *Bellas de noche, Plaza de la Soledad*

By happy coincidence, Mexico produced in 2016 two expert and moving documentaries on women, sex, and aging: María José Cuevas's *Bellas de noche* ("Beauties of the Night") and Maya Goded's *Plaza de la Soledad* ("Solitude Square"). Both are first-time features by female directors. And both are twin attempts to reclaim previously neglected subjects: showgirls of the 1970s and sex workers in their seventies, respectively. Moreover lengthy production processes in which the filmmakers cohabitated with their subjects have resulted in films that are clearly love letters to their protagonists.

Widely shown at festivals and beyond, *Bellas de noche* won best documentary at Morelia, long Mexico's key showcase for the genre, and was picked up by Netflix in the USA. *Plaza de la Soledad*, meanwhile, earned plaudits at Sundance (Rich 2016) and a theatrical release in its home country in May 2017, a rare opportunity for a documentary. Its touching tagline was "We are all looking for love," a sentence that in the original Spanish (*Todas buscamos amor*) is emphatically feminine.

Twilight of the Vedettes

I caught *Bellas de noche* at the Casa del Cine, a small independent art house in Mexico City's Historic Center. It was an intimate screening and, by the film's moving finale, there was not a dry eye in a house made up, nonetheless, of hardened cinephiles such as myself. Testifying to its wide appeal, *Bellas de noche*'s credits acknowledge support from not only TV network Televisa (which provided sequin-strewn vintage footage from its variety shows) but

Illustration 3.1   *Bellas de noche* (María José Cuevas, 2016)

also from government cinema and culture agencies IMCINE and CONACULTA, which might once have turned up their noses at such an apparently populist project. The production process thus suggests a reevaluation of the *cine de ficheras* (the original popular films on cabaret girls), long despised by the film establishment (Illustration 3.1).

In an evocative pre-credit sequence, a raven-tressed siren (later identified as Lyn May) is seen writhing seductively on a silver chair as drapes billow purple and pink around her. Cuevas cuts to period footage testifying to the contested definition of the term *vedette*, a Mexican Gallicism which roughly translates as "showgirl." One enthusiast of the time claims the voguish figures are "authentic stars in the true meaning of the word"; but another opines more skeptically that they are simply strippers.

After this preamble the five principals of *Bellas de noche* (little known to most modern Mexicans) are helpfully introduced with on-screen titles. Their exotic stage names are Olga Breeskin, Lyn May, Rossy Mendoza, Wanda Seux, and Princesa Yamal. And the original conflict between stardom and stripping is now complicated by a new and jarring contrast between past and present versions of the aging women. Yet there are continuities. The mature Wanda is first shown managing, still, to maneuver a huge orange headdress, a testimony to the enduring showgirl fetish for feathers. She reassures us that the peacocks that gave their plumes did not suffer painful plucking but rather naturally molting (in her current incarnation Wanda will prove to be an animal rights activist).

Throughout, Cuevas will tell her tale through the technique of contrastive editing, juxtaposing past glories with present indignities. Thus at a modern-day photo shoot for one *vedette*, the small crew are encouraged to recite somewhat half-heartedly, "We all want Olga." The film then cuts to a vintage number from the star's heyday, complete with silver sci-fi costumes and decor, but this time with a massive audience chanting the same talismanic words. Olga's gimmick was an incongruous violin. Her dry comment is typical of the showgirl survivors' disenchanted verdicts on their truncated careers: there were few opportunities, she says, for female classical musicians.

It is not surprising, then, given the disadvantages they faced, that *vedettes* actively participated in the crafting of their public selves. One claims explicitly that her role was to "create characters." Yet Lyn May, who boasts the most altered face and implausible sex life (she advocates intercourse in trees), claims simply, "I'm normal." Similarly, in vintage footage, the girl who took the shamelessly unlikely name of Princesa Yamal is interviewed with her dowdy family in tow, testimony to the everyday life that even the most glamorous *vedette* could not quite shake off. And it is love between mothers and daughters that will prove to be the most durable, surpassing the fickle affections of male admirers. A lasting life in the spotlight thus did not come easy: one showgirl insists on the inner strength needed for a half-naked woman to control a crowd of men who were watching her so closely (too closely).

Cuevas' shooting style recreates that minute visual attention with tight close-ups that emphasize her subjects' psychological complexity. And although her questions are heard only off screen, we are sometimes given evidence of the presence of the filmmaker, identified informally by her first name. For example, the former Princess remarks nonchalantly to a friend on the phone: "I'm filming with María José." And the women have reason to be grateful to the director who shared their daily lives during the lengthy shoot. Cuevas generously includes musical numbers from her stars, whether in period footage (glamorous or grainy) or in performances restaged for the documentary in full costume and make up and with variably proficient back up dancers and bongo players.

Most poignant perhaps are the everyday settings chosen for informal musical numbers. In *Bellas de noche*, *vedettes* sing and dance, one more time, in beauty salons, cars, and kitchens, or to an audience now composed only of cherished canine companions. And, though faces and bodies may have changed, classic dance moves remain preserved in aspic. While some torch songs such as "Bésame mucho" are safely familiar, others prove more unsettling. In one number a naked Lyn May boasts "A mí me gusta lo que a ti te asusta" ("What I like scares you"), a defiant erotic challenge to the complacent male viewer. It is a phrase borrowed by Laura G. Gutiérrez for the title of her excellent article on the film, which builds on her earlier work on *cabareteras* or *ficheras* (Gutiérrez 2010, 2017).

With its five varied subjects, *Bellas de noche*, a documentary stranger than fiction, offers frequent surprises as its narrative develops. Rossy was crowned "Queen of the Tlacoyo," an endearingly humble staple of street food. Meanwhile Wanda, who sought to be a "real, quality actor," became an animal rights campaigner. Still she dresses in scarlet lurex for street demonstrations. And while one woman recounts the shock she felt when a long-lost boyfriend asked her to wash his socks, another (May) recalls how she slept for two months with the dead body of a beloved husband beside her. A third continues to see men through rose tinted glasses. Groping for an adequate word to describe the generous gifts of her male admirers in the period, she finally settles on "espléndidos" ("lavish"). Now, of course, along with the fake glitter, all that real gold is gone. Cuevas cuts for contrast once more here: as one showgirl recounts how "rivers of champagne" flowed, another (Seux) is shown flushing out a pet-soiled patio with copious buckets of water.

Vedettes thus enjoyed spectacular successes (Rossy is shown on the back of an elephant in a soccer stadium) and suffered equally notorious misfortunes (Princesa Yamal was imprisoned for the theft of antiquities from the Museum of Anthropology, an escapade later fictionalized as feature film *Museo* ["Museum," Alonso Ruizpalacios, 2018]). But most now maintain a modestly dignified afterlife. We see Wanda honored at a Mexico City shopping mall which hosts a bargain basement version of Hollywood's Walk of Fame. The small audience at the event is made up of diehard fans, mainly mature women (middle-aged Mexican men also shyly confirmed to me that the *vedettes* were once the stuff of their teenage dreams). Briefly back in front of her faithful followers, Wanda will boldly remove her flowing blond wig to reveal the skimpy tufts of hair beneath, an effect of the chemotherapy she describes elsewhere in the film.

Bellas de noche thus charts a kind of oblique history of modern Mexico. One showgirl even compares the deadly earthquake that hit the country in 1985 to her aborted career, which foundered around the same time (the night life of the capital would never regain its original splendor). But Cuevas, like her subjects, never settles for sentimentality or facile pathos. There is genuine emotion when Wanda coos heartbroken to a dying dog. Olga, meanwhile, now lives in the unexpected but surely appropriate location of Las Vegas and stars in a new kind of show. Clad in flowing white, but still clutching her violin, she is shown conducting a religious service for an evangelical congregation. She is the only one of the five subjects to have found Jesus. Cuevas cuts back to another showgirl visiting a fortune teller in Mexico City ("You will have a great success"); and to Lyn, the one-time sexual athlete, promenading oh-so-slowly with the aged pajama-clad sixth husband whom she claims as the love of her life.

But the tour de force of surprising endings is a final tearful monologue from Wanda straight to a mercilessly close camera in which she demands angrily "Who am I?"; and, gesturing to a ravaged body and face, "What's wrong with this?" It is a scene that might seem cruelly voyeuristic, were we not so aware of the showgirls' skill in self-fashioning for the benefit of an audience. Meanwhile Rossy has written a doorstopper of a book (its unlikely title: *Universes in Evolution*). And Yamal, now seen at the seaside, has a daughter who clearly adores her. She whispers with hard-won contentedness: "Life is as short as a sigh."

Bellas de noche thus ends optimistically with a paean to rebirth and freedom. And indeed the film itself ensured that its five heroines gained a certain renewed celebrity giving rise to a photo exhibition, public appearances, and sitcom cameos. Perhaps fame the second time around was more enjoyable than the first, when the women had supporting roles in exploitation movies with names like *El sexo sentido* ("The Sex Sense," Rogelio A. González, 1981). And a continuing connection with this cinematic past is clear. Cuevas' documentary even takes its name from the original *Bellas de noche*, a fiction feature from 1975 by prolific director Miguel M. Delgado, which stars the nearest thing to a male *vedette*, the fondly remembered muscle hunk Jorge Rivero (see de la Mora 2006, 116–17).

Solitary Sex Workers?

Showgirl celebrity, however tawdry, cannot compare with the dangerous and dirty lives of the working-class women of *Plaza de la Soledad*. I attended a screening of this second feature at New York's Museum of the Moving Image in Queens, where it formed part of a festival of the year's best Latin American films from enterprising distributor Cinema Tropical and was shown in the presence of director Maya Goded (Illustration 3.2).

Plaza de la Soledad was shot over three years in collaboration with its subjects and edited for a further year and a half. And it opens, like *Bellas de noche*, with music. Here the principals, five in number once more, have more commonplace names: Ésther, Ángeles, Carmen, Lety, and Raquel. They are first shown in a minivan singing along to "Amor de cabaret," a classic ballad that voices, in spite of the singer's bitterness and grief, an addiction to a love that

Illustration 3.2 *Plaza de la Soledad* (Maya Goyed, 2016)

is untrue, for one that is bought for money. The women sing their song and gently weep.

But, unlike in *Bellas de noche* (where the *vedettes* are barely seen together), there is here from the start a sense of long-lasting community. The next sequence shows a collective dinner outside the church in the titular plaza. Although unidentified at the start of the film, individuals will soon emerge from this initial festive group. However the fact that the women will be awarded on-screen titles only at the end of the feature means that Goded's stress remains more on the collective than on Cuevas' clearly differentiated individuals.

Plaza de la Soledad's technique is, however, similar to that of *Bellas de noche*: normally subjects simply respond to questions from the off-screen director. And occasionally, they refer orally to "Maya" as casually as they did in the previous film to "María José." One lengthy scene, however, shows the smiling filmmaker reflected in a mirror as she shoots a female couple in their hotel room. Goded thus acknowledges her own presence as observer and participant in the world she knows so well and records so beautifully. This sense of intimacy is enhanced by an nonintrusive crew of just two: the director-photographer herself (shooting with Canon Mark II and III cameras, known for low-light performance) and a sound engineer. As the author of a book and photo exhibition on the same subject before she made her film, Goded has a close connection with her admirable but vulnerable subjects.

Some of these women have harrowing backstories. Lupe, a young pregnant lesbian, recounts her rape. Later we will see her present her newborn son to a series of possible fathers, who are smiling but surely reluctant to take responsibility. Shockingly, a second woman was violently molested when she had just given birth. And a third had to leave her pueblo in shame when she was sexually abused as a child of only eight. If life is tough for independent women in the hostile city, then, it would seem hardly better for them back in the censorious village.

Yet, countering stereotype, these proud sex workers are rarely miserable. Even a trip to a rubbish-strewn cemetery is brightened by the presence of a bougainvillea and a heartfelt song to a missing mother. Soon pink blossoms will grace the pristine tomb. In this world of women, maternal bonds are, as in *Bellas de noche*, strong once more, even when as so often those mothers are remembered as neglectful or brutal. Elsewhere the all-female purification rituals of popular religion (known significantly in Spanish as "limpieza" or "cleansing") or simply warm hugs from girlfriends serve as compensation for past neglect or present distress. Conversely one woman seeks a cure for her woes with a Tarot reader who, blaming the victim, attributes illness "in female parts" to "resentfulness" against fellow women.

Like the showgirls, the sex workers are seen consciously creating personalities via elaborate makeup and costume. And like the *vedettes*, once more, they are not unreflecting victims but rather psychologically self-aware subjects. One confesses to seeking in older clients the father figure she never had as a child. Another tells her affectionate female friend: "This is the hug I needed from my mother." And Goded's women, even more so than Cuevas', are diverse in language and origin. Two migrants to the city speak in Mixteco, an indigenous language rarely heard on screen. Another is shown taking an outing beyond the city limits to float luxuriously in the river of her village. In a typically poignant detail, she keeps her precious wig on.

While men are near absent in *Bellas de noche*, in *Plaza de la Soledad*, they make frequent appearances. Unsurprisingly the sex workers' relations with their long-term male clients are ambivalent. One woman's regular partner is a street shoe shiner who seems sympathetic and declares his respect and love for his "stunning blonde" on camera. Both of them, he says, are wounded and despised by the world. Carmen, we discover, was lengthily married to a man who appears to be her pimp, although it should be noted that, unlike in the recent fiction feature *Las elegidas* ("The Chosen Ones," David Pablos, 2015), Goded shows no evidence of duress or trafficking in sex work. A third reminisces fondly of a policeman trick who turned out to be a transvestite and gave her a wig as a souvenir of their encounter. A fourth tolerates one very elderly client only to raise funds for her daughter's chemotherapy. In this case at least (as for one of *Bellas de noche*'s *vedettes*) maternal love is a constant and durable force.

But most moving are the scenes featuring Ésther and Ángeles, two passionate lovers who tell us they are forced to "hide from society," not because they are sex workers but because they are lesbians. Intimate, but not voyeuristic once more, Goded's camera lingers on the couple as they lie fully clothed on their shared bed, fingers entwined. When later they take to the street, however, the couple dare not hold hands. The pair will also take part in a collective discussion on whether women should allow themselves to feel pleasure in sex acts for which men have paid. This will prove to be an especial bone of contention for the lesbian partners.

Like Cuevas, Goded cuts for contrast once more. For example, a sequence of quiet and meticulous preparation for work at home segues into a noisy and chaotic nocturnal street scene. Yet the Plaza de la Soledad itself, with its colorful houses and circular fountain, is surprisingly calm and picturesque. And it stands in the shadow of one of the gorgeous Baroque churches that stud this popular market area (my own experience is that, in spite of the vibrant street life shown here, the surrounding streets are not so aesthetically pleasing). The so-called "Square of Solitude" belies its name, which is in any case taken from its church. The site of shared work, meals, and even funerals, this is hardly a lonely place. It comes as no surprise when one woman claims toward the end of the film, "This square is my home. These women are my family." And humor is their weapon of choice. Sitting familiarly by the fountain, a couple of sex workers talk back to unwelcome potential clients ("Keep on walking, old man") and keep up their spirits with jokes ("I'm as cold as a popsicle. I need a lick").

Like *Bellas de noche*, again, *Plaza de la Soledad* boasts several sequences of improvised or informal performance. One woman does a sexy dance which she specifies is for Goded's camera and her (female) partner, not for macho men. The pimp, who laments his inability to be faithful, sings with practiced skill a romantic ballad to his ex-wife, in an empty nightclub where both are dressed to kill. Heartfelt soliloquies by Goded's subjects are often accompanied by a delicate piano theme, a tender aural equivalent of the camerawork that frames her subjects with such respect and compassion.

Like *Bellas de noche* with its now incongruous piles of feathers and sequins, *Plaza de la Soledad* offers moments of pure visual pleasure that sometimes come close to the surreal. One woman's bedroom boasts twin altars: the first is made up of fluffy toys, the second of the images of the Virgin and Saint Judas, the patron of lost causes and a popular favorite in Mexico City. Amid the confusion of a market street, we suddenly come across an imposing statue of Santa Muerte, its flowing pistachio robe contrasting with a blood red artificial flower. As the women have their nails elaborately painted and eyebrows waxed, they are accompanied by disembodied mannequin hands, disconcerting displays for the manicurist's latest creations. *Bellas de noche* thus strays well beyond the degree zero of cinematic realism, offering a master class in film form as well as in social engagement.

Although the two directors know each other and were aware of each other's feature projects, it is surely a coincidence that these two similarly themed films appeared at the same time. After all, both spent years in pre- and post-production. Yet, as shown by the example of the prize-winning Tatiana Huezo (*El lugar más pequeño* ["The Tiniest Place"], 2011; *Tempestad*, 2016), documentary seems a more congenial genre for women in Mexico than fiction. It is telling that Mexican theaters are currently full of local romantic comedies whose target audience is young and female but whose directors such as Marco Polo Constandse and Antonio Serrano are exclusively male (I treat two such films, albeit with a queer spin, in the next chapter). Beyond gender, the question of age is vital here. After the Queens screening, Maya Goded said that the subject of her documentary is not so much sex work as the possibility of getting older and remaining sexually active. It is a combination that remains taboo in Mexico, as elsewhere.

Yet the final moral of both documentaries is quite simply love. The *ranchera* or classic ballad featured in the last sequence of *Plaza de la Soledad*, beautifully sung by Raquel, one of the film's more senior subjects, cites the strange effect that love has on people: they go to sleep praying for release from their beloved yet wake up longing to see them once more. In lyrics unheard in the film itself, the song goes on to say that lovers are at once slaves to their passion and masters of the universe. Complex and contradictory, like that final song, these twin films celebrate women whose lives may be limited by circumstances cruelly beyond their control but who are vital, still, in their quest for friendship and freedom.

Shooting Stars: Wanda Seux and Lyn May

We can turn now to the enduring star profiles of the only two *vedettes* from *Bellas de noche* who are considered worthy of press files at the Cineteca Nacional's archive: Wanda Seux and Lyn May. It is instructive to compare the recent documentary with the period reception enshrined in the clippings.

But first we should address the main question posed by the film itself within the discipline of star studies. Yu and Austin's recent volume, cited in the introduction to this book, makes surprisingly frequent reference to stardom and aging: to intrusive coverage in celebrity tabloids (2017, 35), to the double standards for male and female stars (2017, 150), to a classic narrative of midlife (professional) decline (2017, 166), and, conversely and finally, to the new concept of "successful aging" (2017, 175).

Most relevant here is Linda Berkvens' account of classic Hollywood movie star Barbara Stanwyck as a "mature role model" (2017, 147–61). A figure as strong and durable as Cuevas' beauties of the night, Stanwyck contrived career longevity in part through her latter choice of a new genre (the Western) that allowed her to show off her continuing physical dexterity, a characteristic considered "unfeminine" (2017, 158). And one particular physical feature proves central to this defiance: the prematurely gray hair, which she refused to dye (2017, 150). When Stanwyck moved to television, as host of her self-named show in 1961, she even called attention to her refusal to hide and go back to her (once) natural color. And in a series of publicity articles of the time, Stanwyck was promoted (promoted herself) as an icon of naturalness and maturity, more accessible to female fans than conventional glamor. They are two qualities that, writes Berkvens, "complemented each other" (2017, 151).

We shall see shortly that for Wanda Seux, a less likely example of naturalness and authenticity, hair also holds special significance (in Lyn May's case, it was to be not the hair but the eyes). But unlike the veteran Hollywood actress whose skill was securely established, Mexican *vedettes* benefited and suffered from a more modest star system in which sex was at once idealized and denigrated. Hence the relative absence of Seux, Lyn, and their colleagues in the national film archive, in spite of their prolific cinema credits.

I will argue that, as is already suggested by Cuevas' documentary, from these unpromising beginnings, the *vedettes* laid claim to new forms of agency and community, before and after the career revival produced by *Bellas de noche*. And in their press files, the *vedettes* offer a surprisingly explicit commentary on cinema as sex abuse and on the complicit role of labor unions in that process. Seux and May also stage two distinct modes of exoticism, in which the other is precariously combined with the same: although each is identified problematically as of foreign origin (Argentinian and Chinese, respectively), still they seek to distance themselves from their American peers and lay claim to Mexicanness. (We might compare the classical *rumberas* of an earlier era, such as the Cuban Ninón Sevilla, who also made their home in Mexican cinema.) And, finally, the two showgirls provoke (procure) two kinds of displacement from a vision of erotic ecstasy that is perhaps too scary to endure, namely, beloved pets and equally loyal husbands.

As suggested by their English name, showgirls were transmedia phenomena *avant la lettre*: even when they appear in feature film, they are often shown performing on stage to what passes for a live audience. Yet they have extensive curricula in Mexican national cinema, albeit during a period when that cinema was perceived as being in decline and in a genre (the *fichera* film) that remains widely despised and is only now beginning to be reclaimed. For example, Wanda Seux booked small parts in popular features whose sexual content was flagrantly signaled even in their titles by the word "golfa" or "slut" (*La golfa del barrio* ["The Neighborhood Slut," Rubén Galindo, 1982]; *Oficio: golfa* ["Profession: Slut," Francisco Sánchez, 1990]). Calling attention to the fetishistic nature of her mane of hair, in one she plays a character identified only as the "blonde lover" of the protagonist (*La hora del jaguar* ["Hour of the Jaguar," Alfredo B. Crevenna, 1978]).

Yet Seux's career has been more continuous on television than in a film medium that was already in crisis when she began to work. *Variedades de media noche* ("Midnight Follies," Televisa, 1977) (at the height of her fame) was a TV version of Seux's more raunchy stage reviews in which she shared top billing with fellow *vedettes* and comedians, including long-time friend, the comic, Carmen Salinas (later a politician). *Alcanzar una estrella* ("Reach For a Star," Televisa, 1990) is a fondly remembered musical youth telenovela (it is even name checked in Netflix's modern comedy *Club de Cuervos* [2015–present]). And unmentioned by IMDb is *40 y 20* (Televisa, 2016–17), a successful late-night sitcom created by movie director Gustavo Loza, who will prove to be a key figure in this book.

As hinted at by its enigmatic and laconic title, this last comedy is on the theme of aging. A middle-aged dad (played by Jorge "El Burro" Van Rankin, a veteran of Televisa's morning talk show *Hoy* ["Today"]) is partial to young girls, while, less conventionally, his immature offspring favors the more mature woman. Seux's guest-starring role in 2017 (shortly after the career boost of *Bellas de noche*) was as a visiting old flame of the father who proves unsettlingly attractive to the son. Although there is some very broad comedy here (when Seux's character falls asleep, the men fear that she has died), the episode challenges still the double standard of aging for male and female stars, offering up Seux as a mature role model who remains physically attractive some 40 years after her prime. This episode has of course an added meaning for Mexican audiences of a certain age, who will be more familiar than their children with the seductions of Seux's now distant showgirl past.

In *40 y 20*, as in *Bellas de noche*, Seux's persona is one of forthright defiance. And even in press clippings from decades earlier, she contested her and other women's role as objects of sexual exchange. In one interview from 1987, she is cited as protesting that "In cinema they want to strip women naked for pennies" (more graphically in the original Spanish, "sueldos de hambre," or "hunger wages") (Galeana 1987). Fully conscious of her worth, Seux claims that producers now pay less for nude scenes, obliging young neophytes to parade around fully naked throughout a film for just 200,000–300,000 pesos. She attacks the injustice here for established actresses such as herself who have "struggled for many years" to achieve not just fame but also "good salaries" in film, theater, television, and personal appearances.

Referencing her foreign status, the journalist mentions that Seux has been based in Mexico for 11 years and cites the title of her current review (which is touring the provinces) "Che, México, gracias," whose first word cites a stereotypical Argentine exclamation. (Seux does not however boast the very recognizable Buenos Aires accent, as she was born in Paraguay and raised in northern Argentina.) This long-term resident of Mexico will soon take her "international" show to Miami. At once exotic and familiar, then, she also remains, we are told, unmarried and thus available for erotic reverie from her fans.

We have seen that the focus in *Bellas de noche* is on the still-single Seux's cohabitation with a spectacularly large number of beloved fluffy dogs. And through much of her career, these canine companions served as a kind of public alibi to protect a personal life that remained unseen. As we shall see, in 2018, it was not human partners but pets that stood in most poignantly for their missing mistress. But we remember that in *Bellas de noche*, Seux defiantly revealed her chemo-affected hair, so different to the signature blonde tresses of her youth. This was a more poignant version of Stanwyck's prematurely gray mane, but one that staked a similar claim to successful aging, even while openly surviving cancer.

One year later Seux suffered a massive stroke. Her Twitter feed, tended in her enforced absence by her sole relative in Mexico, a godson, became testimony to her continuing fame and fandom. Following tweets and retweets celebrating Seux's return to TV in the aforementioned *40 y 20* (@wandaseux_ofi, November 29, 2017) came bulletins on the star's health status in Xoco General Hospital, which coincidentally is located next door to the Cineteca Nacional in the southern borough of Coyoacán (@wandaseux_ofi, January 27, 28, 2018). As proof of the intimacy with her subjects as displayed in *Bellas de noche*, director María José Cuevas takes charge of Seux's social media, confirming the veracity of the star's official Twitter feed which was of course no longer curated by the *vedette* herself (@mariajosecuevas, February 1, 2018).

But in first place come the dogs. A benefit for the star held in the knowingly named Teatro El Vicio ("Vice Theater," a center for new cabaret, also located in Coyoacán) encourages fans to bring biscuits for the neglected pets, who are always referred to in an affectionate diminutive as "perritos" (@wandaseux_ofi, February 2, 2018). Announcements of a further benefit event to be held at the Cineteca Nacional itself are illustrated alternately by a star-spangled Seux in her seductively blonde-tressed heyday and, more defiantly, in her recent chemo-tufted hairdo (@wandaseux_ofi, February 4, 6, 2018). A third event consisted of a donation of dog biscuits scheduled to be held in a park (@wandaseux_ofi, February 10, 2018). Under the headline "Wanda and her doggies need you," it is illustrated by a vintage press clipping (one of so many absent from the Cineteca archive) in which the blonde bombshell exclaims poignantly: "I like animals because they are understanding." Once more *Bellas de noche* supports its star, tweeting a gif of the mature Wanda fiercely advancing toward the camera in her towering, orange headdress (@bellasdenoche_, February 19, 2018). The film's feed also documents the attendance of her fellow *vedettes* Lyn May and Princesa Yamal at the benefit for the still gravely ill Seux held at the Cineteca Nacional (also @bellasdenoche_, February 19, 2018).

This dramatic health narrative continues on social media. Transferred to a distant Acapulco hospital for rehabilitation, Seux makes a video from her hospital bed thanking *Ventaneando* ("Peeping," 1996–present), Azteca's gossip show; Pati Chapoy, its notorious host; and Wanda's "great friend" Carmen Salinas (@wandaseux_ofi, March 19, 2018). Here the hashtag translates as "#YouSawItOnVentaneando." Salinas would subsequently donate a walker and wheel chair to her friend, also pictured on Twitter (@wandaseux_ofi, March 24, 2018). A week later #WandaNeedsYou would more queasily appeal for gifts for post-stroke therapy sessions, costing a modest 400 pesos (some 20 dollars) (@wandaseux_ofi, April 1, 2018). Finally Wanda's return to Mexico City was celebrated with a striking photo: the bed familiar from the film, once shared with 20 dogs, is now crowded with human friends, including a smiling Cuevas. The convalescent Wanda, we read, is "surrounded by love" (@wandaseux_ofi, April 11, 2018).

There are of course multiple ironies here. Seux has now achieved renewed celebrity status, including access to Mexico's highest rated gossip TV show, only through grave illness. And where once she offered the promise of ecstasy in the loved and despised figure of the *fichera*, now as an invalid she gives rise to wholesome community and affection, bonding with her audience through a shared love of pets and the collective prestige of Mexican cultural institutions. Even in extremis, then, Seux and her surrogates have clearly curated her narrative in the mass and social media. And the foreign sex symbol, barely acknowledged by the Cineteca Nacional's archives, is now (finally) gifted with a starry tribute at that same prestigious film institution.

Lyn May charts a different and more fully documented path from scandalous notoriety to the warm embrace of public affection. Like Seux, May appeared in a TV variety show in 1977. But unlike Seux, she has a more extended career in feature film, beginning with period comedy *Tívoli* (Alberto Isaac, 1975). This film's premise may have been emblematic, however. Perhaps May's sole feature with aspirations to quality, *Tívoli* focuses on the titular burlesque house which is threatened with closure by the corrupt mayor of Mexico City (May takes the undemanding role of principal showgirl). The film thus reads as an allegory of the then-current decline of Mexican cinema.

May later appeared in the sequel to the original *Bellas de noche* (Miguel M. Delgado, 1977), whose title, as mentioned earlier, Cuevas borrowed for her documentary. And titles such as *Noches de cabaret* ("Cabaret Nights," Rafael Portillo, 1978) and *Chile picante* ("Hot Chili," René Cardona Jr., 1983) are self-explanatory. After the success of the documentary, however, May, like Seux, returned to TV in a guest-starring appearance in the post-news bulletin slot Televisa reserves for adult sitcoms. May's show was *Nosotros los guapos* ("We Handsome Guys," 2016), where she shared a scene with the popular character known as Albertano, one of the dumb male would-be cuties of the title.

May's extensive press file tells a more complex story than her list of credits. The Cineteca's first item, a typewritten publicity release, calls her the "Queen" (exotically misspelled as "Reyna") of strip-tease but stresses, on the verge of the premiere of *Tívoli*, a tireless work schedule that combines the film shoot with daily dates in cabaret and at the storied Esperanza Iris Theater in downtown Mexico City. Here she has been dubbed by the audience the "Goddess of Love" (*Boletín de Radio y Televisión* 1974). A second press release says that, after the success of the feature film, May will return to the stage in a review also titled *Tívoli*. In the piece the star, invariably described as "statuesque" ("escultural"), stresses, in what will prove to be a leitmotif, her rigorous professional preparation, citing her "intensive" courses in dramatic art (*Boletín de Prensa* 1975). Still she tends to be described in terms not used for the more reassuring Seux: "exuberant and disturbing" ("inquietante").

The daily *El Nacional* reported from the set of her second feature *Noches de cabaret* (Mapero 1974). Seeking to unveil her true self, the journalist has May saying that she is secretly "romantic" and proud of her achievements, coming as she does from a dirt-poor background. May praises her faithful audience, claiming that the men come to admire her accompanied by their wives. And she proves self-aware, saying that she serves as an "escape valve" for people's problems. But the journalist insists on the ordinariness of this Goddess, calling attention to her "small eyes" (a loaded racial epithet) and saying she is more of a provincial girl than a femme fatale. The exotic and familiar thus go hand in hand once more.

Ten years later the "girl" gets married, as recounted in an unusually lyrical piece in *Sol de México* (Ramírez 1986). Identified here by her real (and very Mexican) name of Lilia Guadalupe, the white-gowned May is said to be "serene and happy" playing her part in the "beautiful story" she always dreamed of. Yet not all weddings are "the same." Lyn's is different because of her "oriental figure." Meanwhile her groom is said to be "quite the gentleman": even his "slanted eyes" are not able to hide his happiness. Later at the reception "exquisite Chinese dishes" were served to the sound of "tropical music," a "beautiful union of two different worlds." Yet this romantic dream (described in racist terms) was also oriented to the mass media: among the guests is the same professional gossip Pati Chapoy to whom Wanda Seux would speak from her hospital bed so many years later.

The world of work was less exotic, less beautiful. No longer the blushing bride, May soon denounced to new Leftist daily *La Jornada* the collusion between impresarios and delegates of the actors' union ANDA, who forced female novices to agree to sex or be fired (the verb May uses here for sexual activity is *fichar*, which is of course cognate with the *fichera* film genre in which she had starred) (Vega 1987). Now May reveals that she has always had to put up with "anger, shame, and loss." As an active union member, she trusts that her vote will finally elect a more honest representative who will "change things." That same year, however, we are told "Lyn May will leave the cinema because she doesn't want to strip any more" ("Lyn May se alejará del cine" 1987). Yet still she defends a recent topless appearance on Televisa, which brought her press criticism, appealing somewhat unconvincingly to "freedom of expression in the mass media."

As years passed, May became yet more vocal in criticizing sexual abuse in her workplace. One profile in *El Universal* is oddly insistent on her supposed oriental origins, implausibly invoking the trade with China that followed Marco Polo and first brought Asian immigrants across the Pacific to Mexico (Ruiz 1989). Male fans, the journalist writes, believed that her "slanted eyes" looked out at them lovingly from the pages of men's magazines. But May is no "stereotype." She criticizes the *ficha* "openly and directly" with a "sense of trade union [solidarity]" that is fit for the First of May (Labor Day in Mexico). And, repeating a cliché of press coverage, the journalist says that she is no femme fatale but rather "shy and domesticated," even an "exemplary mother."

Later May, more political and less domestic, will attack her union ANDA once more for not protecting the women who work at table dances (the phrase is given in English). This is a new phenomenon that has sprung up since the closing of the old cabarets and which exposes working girls to degradation and even disease for the sum of just 200 pesos (Quiroz 1994). And unlike the more creative *vedettes* of May's earlier era, these new girls, who cannot aspire to professional pride, do not invest in their own costume and makeup.

With the turn of the millennium, May was eager to tell her full story as "the little girl who showed off her body" (Almazán R. 2007). Now she claims that, unable to attend school, she was forced by her parents to sell tourist trinkets on Acapulco beach at the age of six and that she ran off with the boy who gave her two daughters at just 14. When a TV producer saw her go-go dancing in a nightclub, he took her off to the capital.

After that affair ended, and still only 17, May began to work the cabarets and theaters of Mexico City. Her priority was to raise money to support her daughters, but the crude comments of men in the audience made her "cry in her dressing room." When she finally achieved success, her notoriety became such that May felt obliged to send her daughters away to school abroad, so they would not be ashamed of their mother. As for the "cine de ficheras," which was held to have finished off the Mexican film industry, May claims it was ruined not by the performers but by the producers who skimped on the budgets and were content to make trash ("porquería").

May herself, however, remains a survivor with a ferocious work ethic and the lust for self-improvement also shown in *Bellas de noche*. We learn that her daily ballet class starts at 6 a.m. and her gym class lasts for four hours in the afternoon. Thirty years after she began to perform, May, then, remains, against all the odds and according to the press coverage that she (like Seux) appears to curate herself, a definitive "legend of the night" (Camacho Villanueva 2005).

Imitation of Life

The *vedettes*, still clinging in their old age to grease paint and feathers, seem unlikely candidates for naturalness and maturity. They embody rather a continuing quest for glamor and artificiality. But they would agree with Barbara Stanwyck that there are "no good screen roles for attractive but mature women" (cited in Berkvens, 150). And, before the documentary at least, their careers manifest the negative characteristics found by scholars of star studies around the topic of aging: intrusive tabloid coverage, double standards (only "male stars go on and on," as Stanwyck laments once more), and midlife decline.

Yet finally the showgirls have achieved successful aging. Seux's fiercely defiant image is softened by infirmity, May's disturbing eroticism by family (loyal husbands and daughters). Recent press interviews confirm that the *vedettes'* cinematic work, which involved *fichando* so as not to be fired, was perhaps not so far as it seems from the travails of the working-class women documented in *Plaza de la Soledad*. Sadly it was not always only on screen that the showgirls were obliged to play prostitutes. May's early life story has some similarities with that of the protagonists of Goded's film. And we could hardly expect the subjects of either documentary to solve the conundrum of women, sex, and aging, which appears to be so ubiquitous. However the history of the *vedettes* is also a hidden history of Mexican cinema. And both stars studied here proved to have a vigorous life after a media death that had been so long foretold.

References

Almazán, R. Jorge. 2007. Lyn May, la jovencita que mostró su cuerpo. *Esto*, February 12. Sección Espectáculos, 5.
Berkvens, Linda. 2017. 'When Barbara Strips Off Her Petticoats and Straps On Her Guns': Barbara Stanwyck, Maturity and Stardom in the 1950s and 1960s. In *Revisiting Star Studies: Cultures, Themes, and Methods*, ed. Yu Sabrina Qiong and Guy Austin, 147–161. Edinburgh: Edinburgh University Press.
Boletín de Prensa. 1975. Lyn May reaparece como vedette con una revista musical titulada 'Tívoli'. January 22.
Boletín de Radio y Televisión. 1974. Lyn May, la reyna del strip-tease y 'Tívoli'. July 19.
Camacho Villanueva, Roberto. 2005. Lyn May, leyenda nocturna. *Unomásuno*, January 18. Sección Espectáculos, 24.
de la Mora, Sergio. 2006. *Cinemachismo: Masculinities and Sexuality in Mexican Film*. Austin: University of Texas.
Galeana, Edgar. 1987. Dice Wanda Seux: 'En cine quieren desnudar a una por sueldos de hambre', *Ovaciones*, May 19. Sección Espectáculos, no page.
Gutiérrez, Laura G. 2010. *Performing Mexicanidad: Vendidasy Cabareteras on the Transnational Stage*. Austin: University of Texas Press.
———. 2017. I Like What You Dislike/I Like What You Fear: On Vedettes, Nightlife, Beauty, and Aging in Bellas de noche/Beauties of the Night (María José Cuevas, 2016). http://reframe.sussex.ac.uk/mediatico/2017/03/14/i-like-what-you-dislike-i-like-what-you-fear-on-vedettes-night-life-beauty-and-aging-in-Bellas-de-noche-de-noche-beauties-of-the-night-maria-jose-cuevas-2016/
Lyn May se alejará del cine porque ya no quiere desnudarse. 1987. *El Nacional*, March 29. Sección Espectáculos, no page.
Mapero [sic]. 1974. Lyn May tiene dos personalidades: íntimamente soy romántica, dice. *El Nacional*, October 20, no page.

Quiroz, Macarena. 1994. Lyn May en contra del 'table dance' y lamenta que la ANDA no tome cartas en el asunto. *Últimas noticias*, February 7.

Ramírez, Oliva. 1986. Casó Lyn May. *Sol de México*, December 7. Sección Espectáculos, no page.

Rich, B. Ruby. 2016. Sundance 2016. *Film Quarterly* 69 (4): 112.

Ruiz, Andrés. 1989. Lyn May. *El Universal*, September 18. Sección Espectáculo, no page.

Vega, Patricia. 1987. La vedette Lyn May denuncia: Coludidos, empresarios y ANDA obligan a 'fichar'. *La Jornada*, November 23, 27.

Yu, Sabrina Qiong, and Guy Austin, eds. 2017. *Revisiting Star Studies: Cultures, Themes, and Methods*. Edinburgh: Edinburgh University Press.

4

Post-Homophobic Comedy: *Macho, Hazlo como hombre*

Sexes and the City

In 2016 and 2017, just months apart, two film comedies set in Mexico City were premiered, treating the novel theme of post-homophobia. Producer-director Roberto Fiesco (the winner of multiple Ariel awards) told me in an interview that for some time, the open expression of hate toward LGBT people is no longer acceptable in the Mexican audiovisual realm (Smith 2017, 3). These features, however, take a further step, in that they propose that it is homophobia, not homosexuality, that provokes laughter in the characters and audience. They also appeal to metropolitan locations as metonymies of a new culture of urban tolerance.

The first film is *Macho* by Antonio Serrano. Taking as its point of departure the so-called sexy comedy *Modisto de señoras* ["Ladies' Dressmaker"] (René Cardona, 1969), *Macho* refashions the figure of the fake queen or "mariquita" who takes advantage of his overt effeminacy to seduce the married women who are his customers. The difference in this new version of an old topic is that it is now the revelation of the main character's heterosexual preferences that provokes a scandal. Moreover, obliged by his publicist to feign a relationship with a false boyfriend, the dress designer ends up having sex with him, an act which (filmed illicitly by the documentary crew that is following him everywhere) is shown on a big screen to the delight of all present in his next fashion show. Homosexuality and the city thus serve as mediatized settings in which queerness is literally projected into public space, thus confirming a new social contract among progressive citizens.

The second feature is *Hazlo como hombre* by Nicolás López. While the urban setting is here less glamorous than in *Macho*, *Hazlo como hombre* does not fail to offer Mexico City locations that are inextricable from the film's post-homophobic vision of a new Mexican masculinity. In this case the main character becomes the object of everyone's ridicule by rejecting his best friend, who has just come out of the closet, and trying to convince him that he is not really gay. This is an unacceptable position within the world depicted within the film, which is characterized by privileged and gay-friendly urban spaces such as the gymnasium, the nightclub, and the bar. The final reconciliation of the two friends (the repentant homophobe and the unrepentant gay) is based on both the main character's learned rejection of machismo and homophobia and a common choice to continue living (together) in the city, a unique place of acceptance and tolerance.

A preliminary conclusion would thus be that the moral of these two films, both of which were sizeable box office hits, is that urban space and metropolitan culture are necessary, if not sufficient, causes for the elaboration of new forms of subjectivity and sexuality. These innovations somehow managed to connect with the broader Mexican public, which is more conservative than the very particular cast of characters represented on screen. But to test this hypothesis, let us look more closely at the reception and textual detail of the two films, examining in turn their twin, linked themes: sexuality and urbanism.

Macho: From Time to Space

In the case of *Macho* (directed by veteran Antonio Serrano), it is significant that all critics cite the precedent of Mauricio Garcés' *Modisto de señoras*, still a staple of Televisa's heritage channel, which is also available on multiple YouTube sites. In addition quality Leftist monthly *Proceso* cites *Macho* as "necessary" at the present moment when "diversity" is making itself felt in contemporary culture, although the film is clichéd and superficial (Ponce 2016). Moreover its genre is confused, veering between social critique, farce, and romantic comedy (Illustration 4.1).

Cinephile website *Enfilme* claims that even 40 years after *Modisto*, *Macho* can give us only a vulgar commentary on diversity and identity (Galván 2016). And it relates the problematic genre of the film to the lachrymose melodrama exemplified by its director's celebrated earlier *Sexo, pudor, y lágrimas* ("Sex, Shame, and Tears," 1999). *Macho*'s vision of effeminacy is "grotesque," and its treatment of female characters (whether objectified for the straight male viewer or vilified as unfaithful wives or superficial models) is

4 Post-Homophobic Comedy: *Macho, Hazlo como hombre* 47

Illustration 4.1 Miguel Rodarte in *Macho* (Antonio Serrano, 2016)

appalling. Popular monthly *Cine Premiere* also stresses genre, noting that unexpected dramatic elements will "surprise" viewers expecting pure comedy (2016). Yet, it writes, *Macho* does not yet offer a "three dimensional" approach to its topic.

For skeptical critics, then, the film is anachronistic: contemporary in its theme but as retrograde in its treatment of that theme as a sexy comedy of the distant 1970s. I will suggest, however, that it is precisely this intermittence (at once temporal and generic) which is of significance. And that we should shift critical focus from the element of time to that of space or place, which will prove more productive, if equally fluid and conflictive.

Surprisingly, perhaps, the production team of *Macho* stressed their film's serious intent. In a promotional video for critical aggregator *Tomatazos* (Ortiz García 2016), director Serrano denied the connection with *Modisto de señoras*, citing the originality of respected screenwriter Sabina Berman's script and even invoking Homer's *Odyssey* and Molière's *Tartuffe* as high culture precedents for the protagonist's "journey" and the film's critique of hypocrisy, respectively. Star Miguel Rodarte, similarly, invoked positively the quality most attacked by critics, namely, the film's blend of comedy and drama, which he said he sought to express in his character's development. The contemporary relevance of the piece was inadvertently heightened by the fact that as *Macho* appeared in theaters, marriage equality, proposed by the president, had just been rejected by parliament, a real-life development branded also as "retrograde" by a cast and crew eager to present themselves as progressive.

The film's poster suggested a less earnest register, with a bare-chested Miguel Rodarte in gold swimming shorts miming showy shock with an open mouth as he is protectively pawed by Aislinn Derbez (who plays his married lover, Vivi) in a black bikini and thigh-high boots. Veteran Cecilia Suárez (his business manager) and novice Renato López (his pretend boyfriend) are seen precariously peering out from behind. The tagline, "Una comedia sin etiquetas" ["a comedy without labels"], features an unchallenging pun on the "labels" of sexuality (which the film claims to disdain) and those of fashion brands (which it celebrates). The casting reinforces the generic expectations of Mexican audiences familiar with big and small screens: as we shall see late in this chapter, Rodarte is known for preening (but safely heterosexual) machos in *Salvando al soldado Pérez* ["Saving Private Pérez"] (Beto Gómez, 2011) and *Héroes del norte* ["Heroes of the North"] (Televisa, 2010–12), on film and TV, respectively; Derbez is of course a scion of Mexico's most successful and ubiquitous comedy dynasty (she will also take the female lead in *Hazlo como hombre* just months later).

Confirming its producers' avowedly serious intent, somewhat at odds with its stars' profiles and within a tradition of studied superficiality, *Macho* begins with an onscreen Wildean epigraph, which claims that beneath the mask is just another mask. As we shall see this jibes with its reverse closet premise, whereby the protagonist, when outed as straight by the press, undertakes an odyssey from fake effeminacy to authentic polyamorous identity. He does so via an experience of gay lovemaking that belies a showy homosexual panic that, it is finally revealed, protests too much. As we shall see in the close analysis that follows, this play of inside and outside consistently links sexuality and urbanity throughout a film generally thought to be discontinuous, even incoherent.

The location of the first sequence is the unestablished interior for a fashion show, which is later identified as New York. With flagrant anachronism, models are seen go-go dancing in 1960s' Courrège-style mini-dresses in primary colors. Fat-shaming Aislinn Derbez, the client and secret lover who is here a star model unable to fit into her dress, designer Evo chokes on a bread roll as he takes his call (Mauricio Garcés' "D'Maurice" character is similarly humiliated in the opening fashion show of *Modisto*). Over a brief aerial shot of lower Manhattan from Evo's private plane, we learn that (like D'Maurice once more) what the designer fears most is Mexican criticism. The conflict between international (external) renown and national (internal) contempt is thus established from the very start.

Mexico City is (apparently) shown briefly through the limo windows on the posse's ride from the airport. But the film's main location is a glossy

4 Post-Homophobic Comedy: *Macho, Hazlo como hombre* 49

modernist edifice in glass and concrete with Le Corbusian pillars on the outside and white spiral staircases inside. This is a hybrid home-work space for Evo, where he is attended by a retinue of workers and clients whose transport arrangements go unspecified. Where once town planners conceived parks and gardens as a country in the city (*rus in urbe*), this is a city in the country (*urbs in rure*), where metropolitan sophistication is recreated in a low density Eden. The geographical location of this studio remains unclear: we first glimpse only trees from its ample windows, but more distant mansions later come into shot. Subsequently an equally glossy fancy restaurant (where Evo asks incongruously for tacos) will also prove hard to place. Its exterior features generic office towers, as in Mexico City's Santa Fe business district. But a driving shot shows palm trees, hardly typical of the capital.

Two other lavish residences reveal the importance (and ambivalence) of architecture in the film. When Evo visits the home of Sandro (the gay assistant with whom he is feigning an affair and whom he insists on calling "Sindy"), he finds that it is similar to his own, but more private and domestic. Nestling in nature once more (the designer complains it is "a mile from the road"), this time the house boasts a wooden veranda over a babbling brook, reminiscent of Frank Lloyd Wright's Falling Water. A subsequent sketching party in the forest around the house, far from the merciless metropolitan critics, turns into a *déjeuner sur l'herbe*, as Evo sketches a shirtless Sandro over a picnic and finds unexpected inspiration in birds and beetles. It is in this rural idyll that Evo, previously a victim of homophobia (Sandro's affection provokes him to flight or fight), will first succumb to the pleasures of gay sex. It is an experience facilitated by the location's isolation, although it will be secretly shot by the documentary duo that trail the designer everywhere.

The third spectacular domestic space is Evo's mother's home, which is half buried in a verdant garden: the real-life curving Casa Orgánica ("Organic House"), designed by the Gaudí-influenced National Autonomous University of Mexico's (UNAM) architect, Javier Sanosiain. This is a rare case where the location can be positively established. Apparently isolated once more, it is in fact in Naucalpan, a town in Mexico State that has long been part of the greater Mexico City conurbation. Once more this location marks a carefully contrived blurring of country and city and one to which Evo retreats after a montage sequence of heterophobia: urban gay activists are furious at his supposed betrayal of their cause. The return to the mother is thus also the return to that most intimate and interior of spaces, the womb (Sanosiain [n.d.] cites the fetus and uterus as the primal relation he seeks to reestablish in his organic architecture). And it is only by regressing to childhood (Evo projects home movies of himself playing with dolls on the curving walls) that the adult can come to acknowledge what he (and we) will finally take to be his true, homophilic sexual self.

Spatiality and sexuality are thus braided together throughout the film, albeit with variations of the theme. Evo's flagrant effeminacy is contrasted with Sandro's modest dignity (he is in mourning for a much-loved husband). Performative exaggeration thus rubs up against a naturalistic style of authentic feeling, required by a film that makes homophobia, not homosexuality, the butt of its joke and is thus required to represent its gay characters in positive terms. Similarly Ana de la Reguera (to whom I return in the next chapter) plays a hyperbolic version of herself as a sex-crazed "superstar" customer, but Celia Suárez as Evo's sensible business manager suggests throughout that her boss' gay panic is ridiculous (like Humberto Busto in *Hazlo como hombre*, whose role is somewhat similar, Suárez is a respected veteran of serious art movies). The film's chronological and geographical indeterminacy are thus echoed in the inconsistency of its performance styles.

But it is the film's last act that best conjugates comedy and drama, space and place, gay panic and gay pleasure. Evo finally leaves his mother's house to arrive at a severe industrial building hung with drapes: it is the setting for his latest show in an "International Fashion Week" that comes complete with a Karl Lagerfeld look-alike in the audience. The collection, completed by Sandro and Vivi in Evo's absence, is comprised of armored beetle-women and feathered bird-men: nature once more is reinscribed in the city.

To the surprise, shock, and delight of all, a screen behind the models shows lyrical footage of lovemaking between two men (Evo and Sandro), blue lit and romantically scored. This climax is applauded by the metropolitan crowd, now reassured of the designer's queer allegiance. Watching the secretly shot footage, Evo murmurs in wonder: "¡Soy yo!" ("It's me!"). But it is typical of the film that the revelation of this gay identity is mediated by technology, seen on the biggest of screens and in the most public of settings. Sex and location are thus made to rhyme. And a new lightened sexuality ("without labels") is confirmed in a final scene of renewed placelessness, moving from the country in the city to the city in the country. At an idyllic tropical beach, with palm trees and a turquoise sea, *Macho* climaxes with a polyamorous three-way wedding between Evo, Sandro, and Aislinn Derbez's Vivi in front of an adoring metropolitan crowd. It is a conclusion consistent with a speech in praise of gender fluidity and mutability given to Sandro after he has first made love with Evo. This climax is capped by a final onscreen title claiming that the film is "inspired" by Oscar Wilde and other writers who treat themes of identity, hypocrisy, and disguise.

It is perhaps no accident, then, that *Macho*'s vision of Mexico City is also disguised. The credits mention only the state of Guerrero as a shooting location (Evo visits the cliff-top Acapulco mansion of one lascivious female client), and there is just one scene recognizably of the capital, when the towers of the grand avenue of Reforma form a backdrop as a jealous husband threatens to shoot the designer on a high-rise rooftop. And, starting with one fashion show in New York and ending with another in Mexico City, the film shuffles between international and domestic brands: from MAC and Timberland to Pineda Covalin and Gianfranco Reni, the local designer who created the on-screen collections. Likewise *Macho* references Compra Moda Nacional, the real-life online platform for Mexican fashion, even as it takes care to establish from the very start its fictional designer's prestige in New York. Sexual and national location are thus equally mobile and flexible, both resistant to labels.

Yet Bourdieu has written precisely on the necessity of the label to fashion, comparable to that of the signature to a painter and magically conveying as it does cultural distinction to the previously undistinguished garment (1996, 171). Likewise the disavowed markers of gay identity and geographical place reassert themselves intermittently in the film (Evo exclaims "It's me!" and asks for hyper-Mexican tacos) only finally to be spirited away in the alibi of a polyamorous wedding outside the city. It proposes this fantasy even as marriage equality for everyday homosexuals, already a reality in the capital, was rejected for the nation in the Mexican parliament. In spite of its creators' critique of a "retrograde" Mexican society, then, a comedy that claims to celebrate sexual diversity cannot participate in the real-life political drama in which it found itself enmeshed on its release.

Hazlo como hombre: From Comedy to Drama

Beyond the rarified world of fashion, my second film, *Hazlo como hombre* (by Chilean director Nicolás López), comes closer to approaching everyday urban life, even as it distances itself once more from political agency. And, rejecting *Macho*'s fluidity, it takes sex labels seriously, even as it stages the conflicts produced by such labels, at once comic and dramatic once more, in city spaces that are yet more fluid and ambivalent (Illustration 4.2).

Let us start once more by examining *Hazlo como hombre*'s reception. *Tomatazos*' website offers a useful press survey of what was at that time the biggest grossing Mexican film of 2017 (even *Macho*, considered a relative failure, reached 700,000 viewers in its first weeks) (Martínez Pintos 2017). "Lukewarm" is the key response here. Respected reviewer Ernesto Diezmartínez

Illustration 4.2   Mauricio Ochmann (left) in *Hazlo como hombre* (Nicolás López, 2017)

(in *Cine Vértigo*) complains that the film won't criticize its gay characters "with even a rose petal," thus making them "mortally boring." Conversely the gay man's jilted fiancée Nati, played once more by Aislinn Derbez, is so hysterical that she should be confined to a lunatic asylum (he notes that, surprisingly, the film is co-produced by Derbez's own company). *EnCine* laments, as in the case of *Macho*, an inconsistent tone, fluctuating between comedy and drama; while Excelsior critiques anal sex jokes and "local references." *Tomatazos* asks a final question: "Is Mexico getting the cinema it deserves now?" Here once more the question of a national cinema (that of space) is combined with that of contemporary issues (time).

In a promotional video (Videocine 2017) Alfonso Dosal (who plays the gay character, Santiago) calls attention, like the cast and crew of *Macho*, to his film's supposed contribution to current debates on the issue it treats. He claims that the original title "Amigo Gay" was ditched, as it would not connect with the "retrograde" audience (those clinging to a traditional sense of what it means to be a man) who most needs to see the film.

Strikingly *Hazlo como hombre*'s poster, the main way in which the makers would connect with that potential audience, is very similar to that of *Macho*, showing four figures once more on a neutral background. The central macho is conspicuously troubled (hand theatrically held to forehead), while his varied friends pose behind. The casting no doubt helped with the resounding box office success. Derbez, once more, is cast in this case with her real-life partner, telenovela heartthrob Ochmann (the couple are a staple of gossip magazines).

4 Post-Homophobic Comedy: *Macho, Hazlo como hombre*

Meanwhile Alfonso Dosal is one of the tiny number of openly LGBT Mexican actors, having come out as bisexual (he is married to a woman but acknowledges past affairs with men).

Yet while *Macho* proposed a Wildean fluidity and superficiality (beneath the mask is just another mask), *Hazlo como hombre* assumes stable and definitive identities. With the tagline "su mejor amigo salió del clóset… Y el hará todo para regresarlo" ("His best friend came out of the closet… And he'll do anything to push him back in"), it appeals to the familiar spatial metaphor of the internal and external, even as the actual urban locations are blurred in the film itself. *Hazlo como hombre*, then, does not reject labels. Indeed its mock-solemn epigraph is styled after a public health warning: "Advertencia: El protagonista es un machista, homofóbico, retrógrado. Rogamos no repetir su comportamiento en casa." ("Warning: the main character is macho, homophobic, reactionary. Don't try this at home.") Yet if, as the film shows, the homophobe is instantly recognizable, loutish homosociality blurs boundaries between different types of male physical intimacy.

The credits show an interior by day, the relatively modest home shared by Ochmann's Raúl and his long-suffering pregnant wife. A slow pan over framed photos establishes the straight couple and their three male friends: macho (Raúl), gay (Santiago), and a third guy, the metrosexual hipster hairdresser. Already there is a retrograde gender divide established in domestic space. The three men play loud video games, jammed together on a coach in the lounge enjoying an unconscious homosocial physical intimacy. The two women are relegated to preparing lunch in the kitchen (a garden is glimpsed behind), although in a nod to modernity they are given some graphic dialogue on the rival merits of oral and anal sex.

The cinematography soon breaks out of this hermetic domestic space, however. Vertiginous aerial shots show mid-rise apartment buildings and verdant tree medians, which are typical of upmarket *colonias* such as la Condesa, although the character's neighborhood is never established. While the use of drones (restrictions on the use of which are regularly announced by the Mexico City film location office) has clearly made such shots simpler and cheaper to include, they seem to signal here a privileged perspective of the city which diminishes and relativizes the limited point of view of the macho and homophobic protagonist.

Thus, in spite of the initial domestic location (a place which will itself later be split when the wife moves out), the film favors more liminal spaces, between public and private. The still-closeted gay guy and his unknowing fiancée meet at an outdoor café by a store selling paper wedding napkins that "look just like cloth" (once familiar heterosexual markers are now fake). The friends' gym features open showers, the sign of an intimacy in public once thought to be safely masculine and now infiltrated by the promise or threat of gay eroticism. Raúl's corny soap joke (he fears to bend over) is less funny after Santiago chooses to come out precisely here, where the three men are naked and vulnerable. Further discussion in a bar over beers and tequila features some graphic and intimate sex talk once more: Santiago says that his first "close encounter" with a man included rimming ("chupar el culo").

What is also contemporary in the mise-en-scène is that wardrobe and performance style are allocated in non-traditional ways. In *Macho* only the straight sissy got to wear the gold shorts. Here the gay guy dresses in modest hoodies and carefully curated T shirts (the first bears the image of David Lynch). And, like Raúl's tolerant wife, he is consistently sober in his demeanor (critics called him boring).

Conversely the extravagant exaggerations of the unsympathetic homophobe and the jilted fiancée contrast with the naturalistic performance style of newly gay Santiago, Raúl's sensible wife, and the hipster barber friend (who everyone assumes is gay himself). The latter are thus Molière-style "honnêtes gens," supporting characters who throw into focus the comic excesses of the deluded and obsessive protagonist and female lead. The straight men of this comedy are thus gay or feminized, while the comic foils are heterosexual. Once more urban locations make this contrast clear. Of the two workplaces we are shown, the hipster barber's is attractively modern, with its bearded staff and vintage wallpaper, while Raúl's car dealership lacks visual interest. Indeed it is already established that cars are just one of the trivial toys with which this immature male distracts himself from genuine feeling.

Next, however, Raúl is seeing a therapist who guides him in his book-lined office through the stages of mourning for a best friend that he now considers lost. Even the most farcical scenes here are made to carry some emotional or educational weight. When Raúl takes Santiago to an absurd "equine conversion therapy" location, a stable outside the city run by a Spanglish-speaking American huckster, the dialogue could not be more explicit. Discovering the purpose of the excursion, the gay friend angrily rejoins: "I can't be cured because I'm not sick." As in *Macho* once more, the third act of *Hazlo como hombre* shifts uncomfortably from comedy to drama, from sight gags to sentiment. Thus Raúl does not just tearfully mourn his best friend's loss, he is also (as his wife remarks) clearly jealous of Santiago's first boyfriend. The latter is a sexy celebrity chef ("the key ingredient is sweat"), who enamors the rest of the cast. Yet the chef's origins (born in Austin but "with a drop of Aymara blood") make him, like the American therapist, somewhat suspiciously cosmopolitan.

This modern ambience, newly uncomfortable for the macho, is exemplified in another urban location: the nightclub where the chef is launching his latest cook book. This features not only a dance floor full of muscled hunks but also an unlikely swimming pool where Raúl and his rival for Santiago's affections will stage a disastrous race.

This oddly liminal space marks the midpoint of the macho's odyssey. Soon, in scenes reminiscent of the breakups in straight romantic comedies, he is weeping in the shower, the gym, and at his therapist's over the loss of "the man of his life" and pleading on his knees for his wife not to leave him when she discovers evidence of his multiple infidelities on his phone. A montage sequence (also typical of the romcom) contrasts solitary straight and communal gay urban spaces: the gay couple dance ecstatically in a nightclub or enjoy an exquisite dinner at home, while the macho drinks alone in the bar, weeps in the arms of his trainer, and contemplates a burned barbecue in the garden. The therapist tells Raúl: "Now you are connected with your feelings." He replies more bluntly, "I'm fucked" ("Estoy jodido"). It is striking that it is only at this point, when Santiago has announced his intention of moving to Miami with his cosmopolitan boyfriend, that we are given the sole image of a recognizable building in Mexico City: an aerial shot of the twin round towers of Polanco that rise over Chapultepec Park. It is a sign that characters (and viewers) will remain at home and in the city.

In these final sequences, parallel plotting will reestablish the homosocial intimacy between the two friends. Thus Santiago discovers pictures of other lovers on his boyfriend's phone, just as Raúl's wife had on his. The difference here is that the cook defends polyamory, claiming in an argument reminiscent of *Macho*, that "relationships work better in threes" (the couple-centric *Hazlo como hombre*, unlike *Macho*, will not support this viewpoint). But just as *Macho* ended with male coupling reproduced on video, in *Hazlo como hombre*, male intimacy is reestablished through technology: the two play a long-distance video game together onscreen, but physically apart. This time the macho "monster," previously obsessed with winning, apologizes to the friend he still calls "puto" ("queer"), weeps, and lets his partner beat him. Even as he celebrates his renewed friendship and willingly loses the game, Raúl keeps up his anal-fixated dialogue, however, saying his old friend has managed to "split his ass" ("romper el culo").

But now the macho is tamed. Returning to the privileged place of urban male socialization, Raúl proudly presents his bottom to his gay friend when he drops the soap in the communal shower. And a final pan over new photos of family and friends, rhyming with the opening sequence, reveals a revised domestic arrangement: Raúl and his wife are still living apart, but sharing the care for their new baby. Meanwhile the gay guy has a more attentive boyfriend. And the barber has taken up with Raúl's formerly hysterical fiancée, who has now also learned her lesson. In this newly flexible domestic space, no longer gender-segregated, relationships are being remade. Raúl asks his wife out on a "friendly" date. In a final twist the baby rejects the toy dinosaur offered by his father and cries for his favorite doll. Gender non-conformity will thus continue to reproduce itself within the heart of the home.

Two Stars, Two Masculinities: Miguel Rodarte and Mauricio Ochmann

The question to be asked now, then, is to what extent the distinct star profiles of Miguel Rodarte and Mauricio Ochmann, who both enjoy lengthy careers on TV and in film, inflect the post-homophobic comedies that each so showily headline. Although their roles are similar, the professional histories of the two performers are very different.

Fleshy and hairy, Miguel Rodarte was not a good fit for the wave of film romantic comedies that hit Mexico in the first decade of the millennium, although, safely shaven, he had a supporting role as one of the heroine's several suitors in *Cansada de besar sapos* ("Tired of Kissing Frogs," Jorge Colón, 2006). But, like other actors at the time, he had sufficient dignity and professionalism to be enlisted in the prestige period productions in film and TV that marked the bicentennial of Mexico's independence in 2010 such as *Gritos de muerte y libertad* ("Cries of Death and Liberty," Televisa) and *Hidalgo, la historia jamás contada* ("Hidalgo, The Untold Story," by *Macho*'s Antonio Serrano).

Rodarte's breakthrough came the next year, however, as the lead in the biggest grossing live action film of 2011: so-called narcomedia *Salvando al soldado Pérez* ("Saving Private Pérez," Beto Gómez). Citing and farcically revising Spielberg in its title and plot, the premise here is that Rodarte's Mexican drug baron travels with his comic posse to distant Iraq (which he believes is "somewhere near Holland") to free his brother who has been captured after enlisting in the US army.

Rodarte gives a finely modulated performance in this big-budget comedy from Lemon Films, a rare Mexican company devoted to high quality genre movies. In his pointy snakeskin boots and purple paisley shirts, he looks the part of a parody mafia boss from the north of Mexico (Rodarte was himself born in Sinaloa). But his character's devotion to his ailing mother, missing brother, and mismatched comrades is palpable. And when he emerges dripping wet in a skimpy suit from the palm-shaped swimming pool on his lavish estate, he is a more frankly erotic presence than any other Mexican comic actor. At the same time Rodarte also served out three seasons in a TV comedy helmed by the ubiquitous Gustavo Loza, *Los Héroes del Norte* ("Heroes of the North," Televisa, 2010–13), where he played another regional stereotype in a big sombrero, in this case a country singer heading a further band of misfits.

Press coverage confirms the precarious equilibrium between dignity and comedy which Rodarte would also exploit in the more farcical *Macho*. His official biography in the Cineteca Nacional press file that is dedicated to him begins by stating that he trained as an actor in Mexico City's prestigious Foro Teatro Contemporáneo, under the Polish theater director, Ludwin Margules (Cineteca Nacional n.d.). And a major interview in *Esquire Latinoamérica* starts by defining him as "multifaceted" (Pérez-Guevara 2015). Here Rodarte stresses that his then current project was not a "common or garden romantic comedy," and that when faced with an acting challenge (such as playing a police officer), he will carry out research to give the character "the realism he deserves."

When asked what he likes most about Mexican cinema, Rodarte replies that it is the "complicity" between its characters and its audience. Moreover humor is not trivial. Rather it is a "tool to carry on … to keep moving forward in your life." In spite of his appearances in dramas, then, Rodarte considers that comedy as a genre "comes closer to real life." This statement is an implicit defense of the *Macho* which, he notes here, is scripted by the established playwright Sabina Berman and treats the weighty theme of "sexual diversity."

As we have seen, Mauricio Ochmann headlined the other post-homophobic comedy whose release was near simultaneous with that of Miguel Rodarte. Yet his star profile could hardly be more different. Handsome-faced, floppy haired, and with his smooth chest often bared for the still or movie camera, Ochmann was initially a romantic hero of traditional telenovela who could be defined in one headline as "uncomplicated" (Del Río 2004). A classic early role of his was in *Amarte así, Frijolito* ("Loving You This Way, Frijolito," Telemundo, 2005), where he played a cute doctor finally reunited in the whitest of weddings with the humble cleaning lady who had secretly borne him the charmingly nicknamed child ("Little Bean") of the title.

But even while working within the heritage genre of serial melodrama, Ochmann's roles slowly became darker. *Victorinos* (Telemundo, 2009) featured three men of the same name and different social classes. Uncharacteristically, Ochmann's character is the working-class thug with an unflattering razored haircut. *El clon* ("The Clone," Telemundo, 2010), a transgenerational romance, dealt with drug trafficking, Islam, and (as the title suggests) the novel and disturbing theme of cloning, offering Ochmann a double characterization. In spite of such newly challenging roles, given his conventional good looks and winning charm, Ochmann had little trouble making the leap to mainstream film romantic comedy. In the formulaic *A la mala* (Pitipol Ibarra, 2015), he costarred (as later in *Hazlo como hombre*) with his real-life partner Aislinn Derbez and their mediatized romance served to fuel publicity for the movie.

Yet in the meantime, Ochmann's public image had become more nuanced. Where once he was obliged to answer questions on what it felt like to be a "galán" ("heartthrob"), a somewhat dismissive term (Del Río 2004), now he confessed to have experienced bullying in the workplace (Rangel 2010) and to have suffered drug addiction and suicidal tendencies. These were experiences that he wished to use in his future acting work, such as the starring theater role of the psychologically troubled youth in *Equus* (Rangel 2013).

Miguel Rodarte's studiously serious approach to comedy prepared audiences for the more sentimental moments of *Macho* and its relatively novel approach to social issues. In the same way Mauricio Ochmann's slow shift from fairytale romance to psychological drama no doubt facilitated the willingness of his more fervent fan base (who tweet as the punningly named @ochfans) to accept the odyssey of his *Hazlo como hombre* character. As we have seen he travels from boorish masculinity to hard won sensitivity via tearful breakdown, treating all the while the challenging topic of the gay-straight alliance. Both actors, although physically so different, thus chart in their linked film and TV appearances and in the media coverage which is inseparable from those roles, a plausible evolution in what it means to be macho in Mexican media, in what it means to do it like a man. They thus confirm what Richard Dyer suggested: "Stars embody values that are to some extent in crisis" (cited by Cosentino 2016, 47).

Changing Cities, Changing Sexes

To return to the two films, what is missing in both of them is social context. As in *Macho*, but now with less justification, there is little trace of social or urban space in *Hazlo como hombre*. The latter, unlike the former, is shot in Mexico City, but shows no monuments or even streets: characters favor the individualized transport of cars and scorn mass transport. While this is typical of Mexico City's middle class, the lack of workplaces beyond the car showroom and barber's is also telling. Moreover the director is Chilean and brings with him Ariel Levy, the Chilean star of his earlier heterosexual romcom trilogy that began with *Qué pena tu vida* ("F*ck My Life," 2010) (Levy plays the cosmopolitan lover with an "unclassifiable accent"). This blurring of national boundaries suggests a certain cultural displacement in a film that is a Mexican-Chilean co-production and must sell itself to a non-metropolitan audience (outside Mexico City, outside Mexico). The latter may be reluctant to attend a film at first called "Gay Friend" and resistant, initially at least, to the modern modes of post-macho and post-homophobic society.

Where *Macho* magics away sexual and spatial difference with a utopian three-way wedding by the ocean, *Hazlo como hombre*, to its credit, acknowledges the continuing power of labels (whether homophobe or homosexual) and situates domestic or lived spaces within planned or conceived urban vistas. The characters' limited points of view on the ground are thus qualified by the omniscient, inhuman perspective of the repeated aerial shots. *Hazlo como hombre* thus plots a plausible odyssey for its protagonist from insufferable macho to sensitive new man, or from comedy to drama. And it does so in recognizable but versatile and liminal urban spaces of diversion: the outdoor café, the gym with its teasing open showers, the nightclub complete with swimming pool.

For Henri Lefebvre (from whom I take the distinction between lived and conceived spaces), the defining condition of the city is historically not labor but leisure: it is only when workers had established sufficient surplus value that they could afford festivity and urbanity (Lefebvre 1991, 262). In spite of their inevitable gaps and compromises, then, it is significant that these two Mexican films that address social changes and attract mass audiences should be not worthy dramas but festive comedies, taking a changing city as the location for a changing society and pitching an urban sensibility to a wider audience beyond the tolerant metropolis.

References

Bourdieu, Pierre. 1996. *The Rules of Art: Genesis and Structure of the Literary Field*. Cambridge: Polity.
Cine Premiere. 2016. Macho. November 3, 2016. https://www.cinepremiere.com.mx/macho-critica-61201.html. Accessed 17 June 2018.
Cineteca Nacional. n.d. Miguel Rodarte. Press file. Expediente no. E-06368.
Cosentino, Olivia. 2016. Televisa Born and Raised: Lucerito's Stardom in 1980s Mexican Media. *The Velvet Light Trap* 78 (Fall): 38–52.
Del Río, Taydé. 2004. Sin complicaciones. *Reforma*, September 26. Sección Top Magazine: 40–2.
Galván, Luis Fernando. 2016. Macho. *Enfilme*, November 7. https://enfilme.com/en-cartelera/macho. Accessed 17 June 2018.

Lefebvre, Henri. 1991. *The Production of Space*. Oxford: Blackwell.
Martínez Pintos, Ruben. 2017. Hazlo como hombre ya tiene calificación en el Tomatómentro: la comedia mexicana es la más exitosa en lo que va de 2017. August 28. www.tomatazos.com/articulos/279155/Hazlo-Como-Hombre-ya-tiene-calificacion-en-el-Tomatometro. Accessed 17 June 2018.
Ortiz García, Eric. 2016. Macho: entrevista con Aislinn Derbez, Miguel Rodarte y Antonio Serrano. November 13. www.tomatazos.com/videos/221444/Macho-entrevista-con-Aislinn-Derbez-Miguel-Rodarte-y-Antonio-Serrano. Accessed 17 June 2018.
Pérez-Guevara, Jacqueline. 2015. Los tiempos de Miguel Rodarte. *Esquire Latinoamérica*, March 5. no pages.
Ponce, Fausto. 2016. Macho: superficial y aburrida. *Proceso*, November 18. https://www.proceso.como.mx/462646/macho-superficial-aburrida. Accessed 17 June 2018.
Rangel, Rocío. 2010. Mauricio Ochmann: Sufrió acoso laboral. *Excelsior*, May 6. Sección Teve: 38.
———. 2013. Mauricio Ochmann: Plasmará vivencias. *Excelsior*, May 23. Seccion Teve: 24–5.
Sanosiain, Javier. n.d. La Casa Orgánica. www.arquitecturaorganica.com/casa-orgaacutenica.html. Accessed 17 June 2018.
Smith, Paul Julian. 2017. *Queer Mexico: Cinema and Television since 2000*. Detroit: Wayne State University.
Videocine. 2017. Hazlo como hombre: entrevista con el elenco. August 12. https://www.youtube.com/watch?v=a5fHN-XR3Sw. Accessed 17 June 2018.

Part II

Television

5

Women-in-Prison TV Drama: *Capadocia, Vis a vis*

Antiheroines

It seems plausible that television series are a more welcoming medium for women than feature film. Yet the focus of much popular and academic writing remains limited in this area, as elsewhere, to well-known productions in the USA. Hence the importance of the recent book *Television Antiheroines: Women Behaving Badly in Crime and Prison Drama*. Edited by Milly Buonanno (2017) of Rome's La Sapienza University, this book boasts an admirably international scope of primary texts from Italy and France to Scandinavia, Australia, and Brazil.

In her introduction, Buonanno writes that since the "beginning of the 2010s … truly uncommon and unconventional depictions of womanhood [are] being offered by twenty-first-century television" (2017, 3). Not just the "cosmetic updates of villainess figures" or the "strong female leads" seen earlier on TV, these international series offer "dark sides of human personality and behavior, moral ambiguity, damaging flaws, enduring strength and nuanced, despica-ble and admirable antiheroic figures." Crucially this trend "transcended … niche subscription-based TV channels and on-demand platforms [to include] broadcast networks [that brought] 'antiheroine television' to life and to a wider audience" (2017, 4).

An ever-curious scholar, Buonanno expresses her "surprise" that this "antiheroic creative turn" has radically revised the existing "heroine television" (Charlotte Brunsdon's term) in which sympathetic female protagonists negotiated femininity while trying to cope with contradictory demands made on women. She dates the new phenomenon back to 2013 and the incipient fall of the predominantly male antihero lead in American "quality TV" (a term she calls into question). This "sense of an ending" was marked symbolically by the death of James Gandolfini, the publication of Brett Martin's *Difficult Men*, and the finale of *Breaking Bad* (2017, 5–6). It was, she writes, a moment when the "gender bias in the acclaimed antihero storytelling epitome of quality TV" became clear. Series featuring such men may have acquired the status of art forms, but only by participating in "processes of cultural legitimization of television that implied exclusionary practices and discourses along gender lines" (2017, 7). As critic Emily Nussbaum asked in her essay on "Difficult Women": "Where is the female Tony Soprano … the female Walter White?" (2017, 8). Buonanno writes once more that "worthiness assessment and canon-building [were] premised on heavily gendered criteria."

Since that date, continues Buonanno, women in the business of crime have promoted a "changing representational politics of femininity" (2017, 10), challenging what Bourdieu branded the "symbolic machine" of patriarchy. These newer shows subvert the supposed norms of womanhood ("innocence, goodness, nurturance and social conformity") and disrupt the order of things via "badly behaving women" who not only break social norms but also exhibit a "distinctive quality of liminality." Such "flawed protagonists" (once male, now female) had been described by Jason Mittell as characters who are "our primary point of ongoing narrative alignment but whose behavior and beliefs provoked ambiguous, conflicted or negative moral allegiance" (2017, 11).

Central here for Buonanno is the women-in-prison (WIP) subgenre which "counterpoint[s] the male-dominated underworld with the all-female world of the prison institution in which the heteronormative ideology of gender can be transgressed and overturned." Buonanno notes that "stories of organized crime have resisted feminization a great deal longer than other kinds of narratives" (2017, 13) as it was "not until the noughties [that] a wave of antiheroines 'good at being bad'" set themselves against the "myth of female innocence."

Buonanno further reads WIP protagonists as staging "triple transgressions against social norms (as law breakers), gender norms (as women behaving badly) and against the norms of the underworld subculture (as women in power within the masculinist crime organization)." And, rejecting the thesis of "double entanglement," according to which female roles are "challenged but not changed" in such series, she suggests, that what we find here are not "masculinized subjects … but recombinant genders" (2017, 14), which embody a logic of "inclusive distinction" or, more simply, of "both … and." At its best, TV's antiheroine storytelling thus embraces both "ongoing longing for moral ambiguity" and "feminist-inspired ideas of female self-determination and achievement." It is a historically specific structure of feeling of the kind

Raymond Williams once identified as "a certain kind of disturbance or unease, a particular type of tension" (2017, 16).

WIP drama had already been a focus of *Copycat Television*, in which Albert Moran (1998) examined examples of the subgenre produced in such little-studied countries as the Netherlands. The three contributions in Buonanno's volume range rather across English-language territories and platforms. The UK's *Bad Girls* (1999–2006) staged a lesbian love affair between prison governor and prisoner on top-rated private channel ITV. Australia's *Wentworth* (Foxtel SoHo, 2013–) was a more recent reimagining for premium cable of the classic *Prisoner Cell Block H* (1979–86), offering a more explicit depiction of female sexuality for a new niche audience than the original, which had been made for free-to-air Network 10. Most famously the USA's *Orange Is the New Black* (Netflix, 2013–present) adopted a tricky tone between comedy and drama and addressed questions of race and transgender, little treated before. These series as a whole rewrite "stock characters" of the subgenre listed by scholars Zalcock and Robinson as the "corrupt warden, naïve new inmate, mad/bad lesbian stirrer, [and] wise and worldly top dog who rules the roost" (185).

Buonanno's volume includes two excellent chapters on criminal women in Latin America. The USA's *La reina del sur* ("The Queen of the South," Telemundo, 2011), a co-production with RTI of Colombia, Argos of Mexico, and Antena 3 of Spain, offers a new telenovela protagonist: the female transnational narco boss. Brazil's *Salve Jorge* ("Hail George," Globo, 2012–13) proposes the similarly ambivalent figure of the human trafficker who sells her fellow women into sex slavery.

But *Television Antiheroines* does not include two major award-winning series, one of which anticipates Buonanno's trend: Mexico's *Capadocia* (HBO Latin America, 2008–12) and Spain's *Vis a vis* (Antena 3, 2015–present). These titles, like the essays in Buonanno's book, venture beyond the USA and all too familiar English-language television. But, unlike Buonanno's book, they place Spanish-speaking antiheroines in the special, sexually charged context of the WIP subgenre.

As we shall see, both series are national narratives that are internationally distributed; both extend the conventions of the subgenre in their varied content; and both pioneer quality (so-called cinematic) production values in their form. Moreover they are made by local independent production companies with a lengthy tradition in their respective countries and who here made risky innovations to their established practice. And, finally, these Spanish-language WIP dramas are the creative responsibility of reputed (male) executives, comparable to the more celebrated "difficult men" of US quality TV. The history of the WIP series, apparently a minor subgenre, thus opens out onto the wider history of television and changing social attitudes in Mexico and Spain, as elsewhere.

Capadocia: Inclusive Distinction

The enigmatic titles of the two series treated in this chapter testify in true Bourdieu-style once more to their bid for cultural distinction. "Capadocia," the name of the high-tech, private women's prison within the drama, is taken from the supposed home territory of the Amazons, mythical female warriors that anticipate the feisty prisoners. And the series' initial premise is of a middle-class housewife and mother (Ana de la Reguera's Lorena Guerra), the familiar naïve new inmate, who is locked up after accidentally killing her husband's lover. The opening scenes of the character's confrontation with her adulterous spouse and forcible separation from her young children could almost have been taken from traditional telenovela. However this familiar central figure is juxtaposed with a more unusual protagonist, the new governor of the prison (Dolores Heredia's Teresa Lagos). A criminologist fond of casual sex, her aim is to rehabilitate her charges. She is herself juxtaposed with an equally novel character: a ruthless gay entrepreneur who puts the prisoners to work sewing lingerie padded with illicit drugs (Juan Manuel Bernal's Federico Márquez) (Illustration 5.1).

Illustration 5.1 Ana de la Reguera (right) in *Capadocia* (HBO Latin America, 2008–12)

The personal plotline (of the housewife's transformation into the hardened top dog whose privileges include the services of a sought-after female lover) is thus interwoven with a political narrative (of the conflict between the representatives of penal reform and of inmate exploitation). And each episode introduces a further social issue into the mix. For example, in one a transgender woman requests a transfer from a male prison and in another a lesbian inmate seeks a conjugal visit from her partner. And as HBO's first series made in Mexico, *Capadocia* benefits from liberties of expression in graphic sex and violence hitherto impossible on the self-censoring broadcast networks, Televisa and Azteca. The very first scene is of naked inmates in the shower, one of whom, a recent mother, has milk leaking from her breasts. A later sequence in the opening episode expertly stages a massive bloody riot, instigated by a corrupt warden, that would put any feature film to shame. The ample budget afforded by HBO also allowed for the construction of a full-size set in the bowels of what had been Mexico City's bullring in the northern outpost known as Cuatro Caminos.

While all this might seem very new in the context of everyday Mexican television with its Cinderella-style serials, producer Argos had for some 20 years made transgressive telenovelas for free-to-air broadcasters, often with a feminist or queer twist. *La vida en el espejo* ("Life in the Mirror," 1999–2000) had focused on an unapologetic adulteress and featured the first positive gay character on Mexican TV. *Las Aparicio* ("The Aparicio Women," 2010) had climaxed with a lesbian wedding (it was later made into a feature film). And *El sexo débil* ("The Weaker Sex," 2011) had centered on Mexican machismo in crisis. It was not, then, so difficult to reconcile this quality broadcast tradition with that of niche subscription-based HBO. And, as we saw earlier, Argos was also to coproduce female narco drama *La reina del sur* for US network Telemundo.

Leticia López Margalli, a head screenwriter for many Argos titles, told me in an interview that the company refused to hire writers who already had experience in Mexican broadcast TV, preferring to mold independent talents such as herself (Smith 2014, 249–55). And Argos CEO Epigmenio Ibarra is a loud and proud Leftist who came to prominence as a journalist embedded with the Zapatista rebels in the 1990s. At the time of the series he remained an outspoken critic of President Peña Nieto and was soon to be an equally vocal supporter of then presidential candidate Andrés Manuel López Obrador. Argos (like mainstream network Televisa) even has its own acting academy where it trains young talents in a more realist mode of performance than that favored by the more melodramatic telenovela. In a nod to Frida Kahlo's "Blue House" (Casa Azul), it took the name CasAzul.

It is no surprise, then, that *Capadocia* boasts a roll call of distinguished female actors who constitute a kind of third way between broadcast and narrowcast. As we shall also see in the final section of this chapter, Ana de la Reguera, as the housewife cum killer, was previously a leading lady in romantic comedies. Conversely Dolores Heredia, who plays the criminologist-governor who uses one of her students as a sex toy, has a track record in indie drama and legitimate theater and is at the time of writing (2017) president of the Mexican Film Academy. In the disconcerting new structure of feeling pioneered by *Capadocia*, the liminal antiheroines such actors play embody Buonanno's "inclusive distinction": they can be both traditional and transgressive (housewife/murderer, professor/sexual predator).

Vis a vis: A Cocktail of Moral Ambiguity

Spanish producer Globomedia's *Vis a vis*, which premiered some seven years after *Capadocia*, has much in common with its Mexican predecessor. Here, once more, a naïve new middle-class inmate (played by newcomer Maggie Civantos) is forced to toughen up in a brutal institution, although in this case she has been sentenced not for murder but for embezzlement committed out of misplaced loyalty to her lover, the married male boss who betrays her. And while the Mexican housewife confronts (and eventually kills) the lesbian top dog, the Spanish office worker is set against the hardened inmate played by Najwa Nimri, who characteristically keeps a scorpion as a pet.

In the interests of realism, Globomedia mainly cast actors who are not only diverse in both ethnicity and body type but previously unknown to Spanish TV audiences. Thus protagonist Maggie Civantos, our identification character, had barely been seen on screen before. And Nimri, who is in real life half Arab and half Basque and habitually employs a menacing, whispery delivery, has a background not in television but in art cinema under such directors as Julio Medem and with her own rock band.

Vis a vis is a term used in Spanish for "conjugal visit." But the original French phrase implies a close confrontation between partners. And Globomedia brought cable-style in-your-face sex and violence to the mass audience of network Antena 3 (and indeed of Mexico's Azteca, which most unusually scheduled the Spanish show free to air in primetime). Viewers who saw the scene where Nimri threatened to amputate Civantos' nipples with scissors are unlikely to forget it. Aiming like *Capadocia* for cinema-style production values, *Vis a vis* was also shot in a full-scale location fashioned from a real place, in this case an abandoned factory. And a distinctive art design emphasized the incongruously sunny color of the inmates' signature uniforms. Fervent fans soon adopted the shade as their own, baptizing themselves "the Yellow Tide."

Yet, unlike Argos, its Mexican counterpart, Globomedia, the most successful producer in Spain, was known not for envelope-pushing dramas but rather for domestic dramedies. The title of the unthreatening *Médico de familia* ("Family Doctor," 1995–99) was self-explanatory; *Los Serrano* ("The Serranos," 2003–08) boasted an unlikely extended family, *Brady Bunch*-style; and *Águila roja* ("Red Eagle," 2009–16) was a period-set martial arts romance, whose titular hero was in fact a kindly schoolmaster and devoted single father. Recently, however, such warm and fuzzy premises no longer connected with Spanish audiences who had grown more sophisticated, with the result that Globomedia planned a radical change in production processes.

In an interview, Álex Pina, the principal screenwriter, stresses the novelty of the series for Globomedia, saying this is "Year One" of a "new Golden Age" for series that resist North American "colonization," and reveals that, in their quest for inspiration, the team screened WIP dramas from the around the globe. Finally it was not the USA's *Orange Is the New Black* but Australia's *Wentworth*, which came closest to the grim and gritty sensibility they sought for their new title (Jabonero 2015). And if, unlike Argos' Epigmenio Ibarra, Globomedia CEO Daniel Écija is no political radical, he is the nearest thing in Spain to an American-style showrunner, responsible over two decades for the creative direction (and redirection) of his production company. And to the credit of Globomedia, the one-time family-friendly firm, the central lesbian theme in *Vis a vis* is both tender and very tough. In the finale to the second season, a desperate spurned lover will arrange the murder of her beloved's new husband on the very day of the wedding. It is a fittingly ambivalent climax.

Such characters clearly qualify as Buonanno's "antiheroines," mixing as they do damaging flaws and enduring strength into a cocktail of moral ambiguity. And these two series expertly exploit the triple challenge of the WIP subgenre to social norms, gender norms, and underworld subculture. Moreover both leapt the scheduling fence that imprisons most Spanish-language drama to attract foreign audiences. Complete episodes of *Capadocia* were long been available informally on YouTube, where they attracted admiring international commentators, as well as of course to HBO subscribers by cable or, more recently, on the app HBO Go. *Vis a vis* (under the more prosaic English title *Locked Up*) was acclaimed when shown in Britain on Channel 4 and can be seen on Amazon Prime in the US. And when Antena 3 canceled the Spanish series, a campaign by the "Yellow Tide" of faithful fans led Fox to announce that it would pick it up for a third season, the US networks' first fiction series made in Spain (Hopewell 2017).

After reading Buonanno's invaluable book, we need no longer ask where the female Tony Sopranos or Walter Whites are. Wherever there is crime drama, female figures will now be behaving badly. But after viewing the examples of *Capadocia* and *Vis a vis*, we know also that, even as they are confined to prison cells, compellingly difficult women are speaking Spanish as well as English on TV screens around the world. We can now go on to examine the special role of two Mexican actors in their country's example of the high-profile WIP genre.

Stars as Auteurs: Dolores Heredia and Ana de la Reguera

Dolores Heredia and Ana de la Reguera play respectively the prison governor Teresa Lagos and the naïve new inmate Lorena Guerra in *Capadocia*. Both embody different ways of being difficult women in their professional careers and press profiles, as well as in the characters they play in Argos and HBO's landmark drama. And as female stars they still have to negotiate more finely than their male counterparts such questions as physicality and physical attractiveness and the public/private divide, even as they assert their new-found independence. As we shall see, not only do the two actors reveal different ways in actively exploiting visual attributes (including costume) off set, they also negotiate different relations to that most charged of values in their country's audiovisual sphere, Mexicanness. In doing so they assert their auteur status over lastingly durable careers.

Dolores Heredia's big breaks were in quality television series that were, like *Capadocia*, from Argos. Thus she played a cosmopolitan Roma widow in *Gitanas* ("Gypsy Women," 2004) alongside a more sultry Ana de la Reguera. Although Heredia's press profile is politically and socially engaged, in a curious contradiction, she has been long associated with religious roles, especially maternal ones. She lent her flowing black hair and high cheekbones to Mexico's Mother of God in miniseries *La Virgen de Guadalupe* ("The Virgin of Guadalupe," 2002), also from Argos. And in film feature *Santitos* ("Little Saints," Alejandro Springall, 1999) she had played a mother searching for her lost child, inspired by the popular religious figure of Saint Judas. Even in soccer comedy *Rudo y Cursi* ("Rough and Corny," Carlos Cuarón, 2008), she played the long-suffering mother of protagonists Diego Luna and Gael García Bernal.

Returning to marquee TV with Azteca's *Hasta que te conocí: Juan Gabriel, mi historia* ("Until I Met You: Juan Gabriel, My Story," 2016), a bio-series of the beloved singer songwriter, she was once more the stoic mother. In *Capadocia*, too, she was not only an idealistic professional, but also a concerned mother of two teenage daughters. It was a welcome twist in Heredia's persona that her character here, however, was allowed an active, even cynical, love life, using or abusing her much younger student as a boy toy. And it is striking that, successfully keeping the public/private divide, her own status as mother is rarely invoked in the press.

It is consistent with her roles that the press should speak of her "angelical beauty," albeit combined with a "strong character" (Uribe 2008). Journalists note also her elegant but unstarry wardrobe, calling attention to her black dresses and shawls (Hernández 1999), the latter an item of clothing charged with tradition in Mexico. Asked pruriently in the same early interview if she would agree to nude scenes, she replies (modestly? defiantly?) that she doubts she could "sell" a picture even if she did. The accompanying picture shows her with flowing black hair, radiant countenance, and handsome shawl once more (Hernández 1999). More typical articles of the decade have a strictly professional focus: "Dolores Heredia wants to make her mark" (Morales Martínez 1999); and "I want to be eighty and still be an actress" (Anonymous 1994).

Soon also Heredia identifies her career path with the vicissitudes of the Mexican film industry ("Dolores Heredia, a great actress, demands support for Mexican cinema" [Anonymous 2000]); and with feminism and resistance to gender violence ("Dolores Heredia committed to her status as a woman" [Garita Cervantes 2004]). Support for Mexico is complemented by a rejection of the USA. Unlike the great majority of Mexican actors whose press files I have consulted, she proclaims "Hollywood was never my dream" (Calva 2007). One final interview sums it up: "She loves cinema, loves Mexico" (Hernández 2007). Praising her homeland in unusually lyrical terms ("tall, wide, deep"), still she calls its problems here with sadness "an open wound."

If Heredia's nationalism is based on a rejection of the powerful foreign rival to the north, so her cinephilia is founded on a disavowal of cinema's stronger competitor, the television in which, nonetheless, she has so many credits. Typical later headlines read: "She makes television to develop her passion, cinema" (Salgado 2015) and "I quarreled with TV" (Castillo 2015). Elected President of the Mexican film academy (known by its Spanish acronym of AMACC) in the same year, she brought together her twin passions, national and cinematic: "Dolores Heredia wants to build bridges in cinema" (León Luna 2015). Proof of Heredia's canny ability to craft her professional narrative is that her personal positions as mother and expatriate (she spent some years working in theater in her Swiss husband's homeland) have not affected, positively or negatively, her public identification with an idealized maternity and love for her native land.

Combining beauty, sanctity, and political engagement, then, Heredia successfully presents herself as more than an actor, an auteur. One early interview cites her self-description as "a teller of stories" (Del Río 2002). It is an off-screen agency that reinforces her on-screen role in *Capadocia* as a strong and creative executive leader who also serves as a caring substitute mother for her charges. Indeed by the end of the first season, her character's own daughter will be confined to the prison where her mother is director after a botched jewelry raid.

In keeping with her more spectacular and sensually charged physicality, Ana de la Reguera's media profile is both more intense and more contradictory than that of her *Capadocia* costar. Yet she has much in common with her colleague. Long before *Capadocia*, de la Reguera featured in Argos' sexually charged telenovelas such as *Tentaciones* ("Temptations," 1998). And when Argos made an alliance with Telemundo for shows primarily for a US audience, she took a leading role in *Cara o cruz* ("Heads or Tails," 2001). As mentioned earlier, she co-starred with Dolores Heredia in Argos' *Gitanas*. And when the production company made a rare film spinoff of lesbian/feminist focused novela *Las Aparicio* (2015), it was de la Reguera who stepped in. She took the part of a sex therapist cum male brothel keeper when the original actress was not available for scheduling reasons. De la Reguera also took a rare producer credit for the film, which was shot (unlike the Mexico City-based original TV series) in her lushly tropical home state of Veracruz.

More sexually charged, then, than Dolores Heredia, de la Reguera is also less maternal and more international. Press clippings invariably present her as "la veracruzana," and she has been active in raising charity funds for the decayed historic port city (Ávila 2011) (Heredia, on the other hand, is rarely associated with her home state of Baja California). But de la Reguera has also made a series of big budget but critically and commercially unsung comedies in the USA, such as *Nacho Libre* (Jared Hess, 2006) and *Cowboys and Aliens* (Jon Fabvreau, 2011). One early report set her press narrative of independence and foreign residence. De la Reguera is quoted as saying that she doesn't want to be a "mommy" ("mamacita") and also that she has no plans to marry the partner with whom she lives at that time in the USA, Mexican-born American Jorge Ramos, perhaps the country's best known Latino journalist (Arellano Merino 2007).

De la Reguera's public image is thus that of the Mexican in Hollywood and it is one that (like that of her then partner) is increasingly politicized. In 2008 we are told simply that "her journey continues abroad" (Calderón 2008), but in 2009 that "she doesn't surrender her quest for the American dream," although she is a "victim of discrimination" in the USA (Reyes 2009). Conflating and confusing a film role with her private life, another headline reads "De la Reguera, undocumented in the United States" (Velasco 2009). In the interview she clarifies her position, saying that although she was "not illegal" when she arrived, she has great sympathy for her undocumented brethren. And defending Latinos abroad, she claims, "We make the United States better" (Franco Reyes 2009). Elsewhere we are told that "De la Reguera takes on [*asalta*] Hollywood," by increasing the importance of her character and even writing her own dialogue in Kevin Smith's forgettable comedy *Cop Out* (Badillo 2010).

This sense of professional agency abroad, parallel perhaps to Dolores Heredia's at home, is undercut, however, by the pressures typical of conventional female stardom: physical attractiveness and inoffensiveness. Unlike Heredia, de la Reguera is often shot in plunging necklines and soaring hemlines. One piece, allegedly self-written, claims that she fled the glamorous New York launch party for one of her films "like Cinderella" at midnight, obliged to hand back her Dolce & Gabanna gown and Bulgari jewels (de la Reguera 2010).

Such self-deprecation is a leitmotif of her press profile. She claims to have been "scared to death" as she started to shoot *Capadocia* for well-known film director Carlos Carrera, one of the three working on the series (Huerta 2008a); says she keeps getting tickets as she "can't understand" the rules of parking in the USA (Huerta 2008b); and avows, implausibly, that she "doesn't feel pretty" (Badillo 2010). As a Mexican star abroad, then, she must negotiate her local audience's ambivalent attitude to the USA by combining a measure of glamorous distance with a stronger dose of homely proximity. This strategy is on self-ironizing display in comedy feature *Macho* (treated in Chap. 4 of this book) where she plays a cameo character billed as "Superstar Ana de la Reguera," a celebrity who is, supposedly, as enamored of high fashion as she is of kinky sex.

Finally, then, de la Reguera's role in *Capadocia*, a mold-breaking series that sought to change TV fiction in Mexico, is anomalous for two reasons. First, she is initially presented as a loving mother and devoted housewife, shown making the breakfast in an enviable kitchen for her (erring) husband and cute kids in her very first sequence. And when she is led away by the police, after accidentally killing her husband's lover, the melodramatic and tearful farewell to the children could, as mentioned earlier, have come from the most traditional telenovela.

De la Reguera, loyal to Argos throughout her career, rarely made that kind of novela, however. And we have seen that in press interview she rejected the real-life role of "mamacita." And over the course of the first season of *Capadocia*, her treatment by the series becomes yet more transgressive in the context of her glamorous and sexy star profile. Brutalized by the hardened inmates, de la Reguera's submissive housewife finally fights back and in a shocking final episode kills her tormentor and inherits the prized female lover allotted to the prison's top dog. Most dramatically Dolores Heredia's prison governor has just procured for her a pardon which will of course no longer take effect. Even de la Reguera's ample physicality is changed here: suddenly skinny, she had lost five kilos during the grueling shoot (Huerta 2008a).

Playing with the two stars' personae, then, the creators of Argos' (and Mexico's) first collaboration with premium cabler HBO break with the established images of their protagonists. Dolores Heredia's prison director is not just characteristically serious and capable, but also openly sexualized, even sharing her young lover with her daughter. Ana de la Reguera's inmate, conversely, is desexed (heterosexually at least), literally slimmed down, and converted into a challenging antiheroine. Finally she commits the murder of her fellow inmate by bashing in the victim's head with the picture frame of her family photo, a symbolic farewell to patriarchy.

Argos' break with conventional television casting strategy in Mexico is thus very different to that of Globomedia with its Spanish WIP drama *Vis a vis*. The latter, as we have seen, packed its TV prison with unknown actors in order to reinforce its groundbreaking realism, with the sole exception of Najwa Nimri, whose star persona from earlier art movies was already disturbing and threatening to mainstream viewers. Conversely Argos' risky venture into the genre marked its much loved stars' rupture with the prison-like constraints of their previous media image, a metamorphosis for which they themselves deserve much credit as auteurs.

References

Anonymous. 1994. Dolores Heredia: quiero tener 80 años y seguir siendo actriz. No source given on clipping, August 4. Sección Espectáculos: 8.
———. 2000. Dolores Heredia, una gran actriz. Reclama apoyo para el cine mexicano. *El Sol de México*, August 3. Sección Escenario: 3.
Arellano Merino, J. Fabián. 2007. No quiere ser mamacita: Ana de la Reguera aseguró que no está en sus planes tener hijos y piensa continuar su ascendente carrera en Hollywood. *Ovaciones*, November 30. Sección Reflector: 8.

Ávila, Fabiola. 2011. Ana al rescate de Veracruz. *Excelsior*, December 16. Sección Función: 18.
Badillo, Juan Manuel. 2010. De la Reguera *asalta* [sic] Hollywood. *El Economista*, April 22. Sección Arte, Ideas y Gente: 38.
Buonanno, Milly, ed. 2017. *Television Antiheroines: Women Behaving Badly in Crime and Prison Drama*. Bristol/Chicago: Intellect.
Calderón, Lucero. 2008. Ana de la Reguera: Sus pasos siguen en el extranjero. *Excelsior*, May 22. Sección Función: 12.
Calva, Araceli. 2007. Dolores Heredia: Hollywood nunca fue mi sueño. *Milenio*, January 3. Sección ¡Hey!: 3.
Castillo, Ana Luisa. 2015. Dolores Heredia: Estuve peleada con la TV. *Excelsior*, September 24. Sección Teve: 56.
de la Reguera, Ana. 2010. Me fui de la fiesta como Cenicienta. *Reforma*, February 24. Sección Gente: 1.
Del Río, Taydé. 2002. Dolores Heredia: Contadora de historias. *Reforma*, January 13. Sección Magazine: 14.
Franco Reyes, Salvador. 2009. Ana de la Reguera: Los latinos hacemos mejor a Estados Unidos. *Excelsior*, April 17. Sección Escena: 4.
Garita Cervantes, Alejandro. 2004. Dolores Heredia, comprometida con su condición de mujer. *Excelsior*, November 27. Sección Espectáculos: 1E.
Hernández, Jesús. 1999. Si me desnudo, no vendo: Dolores Heredia. *Espectador*, August 28, 1999: 51.
Hernández, Ricardo. 2007. Ama al cine, ama a México: Descarta Dolores Heredia radicar en otro país. *El Sol de México*, January 15. Sección Espectáculosr: 8.
Hopewell, John. 2017. Fox Networks Group España to Produce Its First Series in Spain. *Variety*, July 6. https://variety.com/2017/tv/news/fox-networks-group-espana-first-fiction-series-in-spain-1202488462/. Accessed 28 July 2018.
Huerta, César. 2008a. Ana pasó la prueba con Carrera. *El Universal*, March 2. Sección Espectáculos: 4.
———. 2008b. Ana de la Reguera juega desde niña a ser artista. *El Universal*, October 14. Sección Espectáculos: 6.
Jabonero, Daniel. 2015. Entrevista: Alex Pina ('Vis a vis'): 'Clonar éxitos y hábitos del pasado a veces no sale bien.' *Blúper*, April 20. https://www.elespanol.com/bluper/noticias/alex-pina-clorar-exitos-habitos-pasado-veces-no-sale-bien. Accessed 28 July 2018.
León Luna, Ariel. 2015. Dolores Heredia quiere crear puentes en el cine. *El Universal*, December 28. Sección Espectáculos: E6.
Morales Martínez, Felipe. 1999. Dolores Heredia quiere dejar huella. *El Universal*, August 18, 1999: 1.
Moran, Albert. 1998. *Copycat Television*. Luton: Luton University Press.
Reyes, José Juan. 2009. No se rinde por conseguir su sueño americano: Ana de la Reguera, víctima de la discriminación. *Esto*, April 17. Sección Espectáculos: 2.

Salgado, Ivett. 2015. Dolores Heredia: Hace televisión para desarrollar su pasión, el cine. *Milenio*, January 24. Seccion Hey: 45.
Smith, Paul Julian. 2014. *Mexican Screen Fiction*. Cambridge: Polity Press.
Uribe, Adriana. 2008. Dolores Heredia: Sin temor a la televisión. *Excelsior*, August 21. Sección Teve: 47.
Velasco, Karina. 2009. De la Reguera, una indocumentada en Estados Unidos. *La Crónica de Hoy*, April 17. Sección Espectáculos: 31.

6

Anthology Dramas: *La rosa de Guadalupe, Como dice el dicho*

Amid the media chaos in the wake of the 2017 earthquake (which I treat at length in Chap. 8), one focus of news bulletins was a missing girl said to be called "Frida Sofía." When it was revealed that (unlike the many real-life child victims) this infant had never existed, social media exploded against Televisa, the still dominant but declining free-to-air network. And posters did so by repeatedly citing a popular anthology drama that airs daily at 7.30 p.m., *La rosa de Guadalupe* (El Diario La Prensa 2017). One wrote that Denise Maerker, Televisa's new and first female news anchor, was an "opportunist" and "trash," telling a story worthy only of the early evening drama; another that the news coverage was nothing but a "thirty hour" episode of the series; and a third that the broadcaster had made "tragedy" into *La rosa de Guadalupe*, a "sick-making reality show" of morbid fascination, sensationalism, and disinformation.

It is striking that at this time of national trauma, Twitter users were so vehement in their denigration of a TV fiction that was unrelated to the disaster and whose regular episodes had of course been canceled. And striking too that, among Televisa's innumerable dramas, they should all choose the same title. At first sight this hostility to *La rosa de Guadalupe* seems near ubiquitous in both popular and academic sources. Thus one dissertation (among many) titled "Qué no te eduque *La rosa de Guadalupe*!" (Gómez Parga 2014) is devoted to critiquing supposed gender stereotypes in the series. Beginning with an account of the situation of women in Mexico ("from gender discrimination to femicides," 2014, 1–8), it goes on to give a content analysis of the series through the "physical appearance" of the female characters, their professional status and family responsibilities, "women as victims and men as heroes" and, finally, the "normalization of violence" (2014, 54–69). The social world and the TV universe are thus held to be continuous. Indeed the latter, it is implied, is politically and ethically responsible for the former.

Yet this analysis is based on erroneous preconceptions. The author identifies the series as a "telenovela" (it belongs in fact to the rare genre of the anthology programs known in Mexico as *unitarios*, in which unrelated stories are complete in each episode); claims that *La rosa de Guadalupe* "attempts to portray Mexican society" (the producers emphasize rather their show's connection to its audience); and suggests that "it explicitly includes a catholic [sic] element that dictates moral values and behaviors" (in fact the series' morals often contradict Catholic teaching, especially with regard to still controversial issues such as teenage homosexuality) (2014, 17).

Ironically enough the more positive scholarly literature referring to *La rosa de Guadalupe* points rather to the possibilities it offers for TV pedagogy. One dissertation cites the series as evidence for "parent beliefs regarding defender behavior when children witness bullying situations" (Savard 2014) (we will see that bullying and witness to bullying are frequent themes of the program); or again, an article in *Qualitative Social Work* on "Developing Communication Activities for Drug-Prevention Intervention" (a wide range of illicit narcotics are another constant concern of *La rosa de Guadalupe*) cites a Latina mother from the South West of the USA who says "a lot of times I take the conversation [on drug use] from [*La rosa de Guadalupe*]" (Ayón et al. 2016). According to empirical studies, then, television initiates an educational process that real-life parents find difficult to deal with alone.

The longevity and increasing prominence of *La rosa de Guadalupe* in Televisa's schedule no doubt makes it a very visible target for critics. With over 1000 episodes at the time of writing, it has been continuously broadcast since 2008 on weekday afternoons (and more recently early evenings) in its home country, while in the USA it is held to be central to Univision's dominance over rival Telemundo, outperforming adults aged 18–34 by 38% (Business Wire 2018). *La rosa de Guadalupe* is the highest rated Spanish-language program in the USA when it comes to "stickiness," that is, viewers' commitment to watching the whole length of the show without changing channel (it runs for a full hour) (Multichannel News 2016).

Most recently special two-hour episodes, feature films in all but name, have played on weekends. According to OBITEL, the academic survey of Latin American TV fiction, the series was the second most seen in Mexico in 2016 and achieved the highest share of all: an extraordinary 30.03%, unprecedented for an *unitario* (Obitel 2017, 238). Providing evidence of its broad appeal, the show proves most attractive to the youngest and oldest demographics, those aged 4–12 and those over 40 (Obitel 2017, 242). It seems that mass audiences, unlike critics on social media or in academia, are uniquely devoted to *La rosa de Guadalupe* and cannot get enough of it.

Álvaro Cueva, Mexico's most conscientious TV critic, to whom I defer elsewhere in this book, is a perhaps unlikely booster of the series, to the consternation of some of the social media followers who doubt the seriousness of his praise. But Cueva's respect for the series is genuine. And in two valuable articles he expertly positions *La rosa de Guadalupe* within the industrial field of Mexican TV.

In 2016 he invokes precisely the pedagogy of the show, advising his readers to "learn from *La rosa de Guadalupe*." Cueva starts with three observations. First, that Televisa (now known simply as "Las Estrellas" ["The Stars"]) has replaced an outgoing telenovela with additional Sunday episodes of *La rosa de Guadalupe*, the title that is "so attacked by young people on social media." Second, that those episodes are now 120 minutes long, at a time when fickle, inattentive audiences are said to be seeking shorter contents. And third, that the series proved on its new day and in its new format to be a ratings bonanza. What Cueva explicitly calls the "lessons" in this case are at once financial (Televisa saves production costs by scheduling more of this relatively cheap title with its little-known actors) and creative (veteran screenwriter Carlos Mercado-Orduña carefully crafts the longer plots to engage audiences in the new time slot). Cueva's final moral is that the public is now rejecting both the old telenovelas and the new series (which I treat in Chaps. 5 and 7 of this book) for stories that "begin and end on the same day, stories that are simple, everyday, similar to real life." This opinion is of course precisely the opposite of that of critics who accuse *La rosa de Guadalupe* of sensationalism and stereotyping.

In a second article of 2017 Cueva grants the series the epithets traditionally lent the Virgin for whom it is named: "Queen of Mexico and Empress of America." Here he celebrates the one thousandth episode of *La rosa de Guadalupe* which he names in adjectives that mix once more the industrial and the creative "the most seen, most sold, most intelligent, most committed, most positive, [and] most successful" of all on free-to-air TV. For Cueva, this "modest anthology program," exported around the world, is (or should be) Mexico's "pride and joy" as a nation. How can this be case of a show "attacked by intellectuals, public opinion, and social media"? The highbrow critics, answers Cueva, never actually turn on the TV that they attack so vehemently; public opinion is profitable only if it is negative; and social media often makes mistakes.

There is a question of age here also. At a time when veteran professionals are being fired from the television industry, *La rosa de Guadalupe*'s producer Miguel

Ángel Herros is a "senior" whose show has managed to attract the attention of the teens and pre-teens who, supposedly, no longer watch TV. Cueva also calls attention to the thousands of journeymen actors, both veterans and novices, who have passed through the show (one is Polo Morín, whom I treat in Chap. 9). *La rosa de Guadalupe* is thus not just an example of "social responsibility," but an object lesson to a Mexican television industry that finds itself in crisis.

Attracting such intense praise and blame, then, *La rosa de Guadalupe* might seem to be unique. Yet it shares Televisa's own schedule with another long-running anthology series which has attracted much less attention, *Como dice el dicho*. As *Como dice el dicho* is secular in its premise (appealing to the homespun heritage of Spanish-language proverbs for its pedagogic plotlines), it can serve as an invaluable control that reveals what is truly distinctive about the nominally religious *La rosa de Guadalupe* and what is simply a function of both shows' relatively rare genre and their increasingly troubled broadcaster.

Unlike *La rosa de Guadalupe*, which begins again with each episode (even as familiar faces occasionally recycle through the series in new roles), the more domestic *Como dice el dicho* has a small regular cast that consistently recurs. Kindly and elderly "Don Tomás" (veteran Sergio Corona) is the owner of the titular café that is decorated with the successive proverbs assigned to each new episode painted on the walls. It is a welcoming workplace that he shares with a small group of young and equally supportive colleagues. The familiar colorful location appears every day, a homely rendezvous for cast and audience alike, as troubled characters seek reassuring guidance from the staff within it (the real-life location is on an unremarkable street in Mexico City's Anzures *colonia* near Chapultepec park). Yet it was *Como dice el dicho*, not *La rosa de Guadalupe*, that boasted a controversial scene for a show in its afternoon timeslot. The press wrote that a "gay kiss in Televisa telenovela (sic) provokes polemics: the series treats the social issues that today's youngsters experience" (La Opinión 2017).

In spite (or because?) of such occasional controversies, Mexican daily *El Universal* charts *Como dice el dicho*'s increasing connection with its target audience. First, the series was expanded to daily episodes (like *La rosa de Guadalupe*, which it generally precedes in the schedule in the 5.30 p.m. slot coinciding with children's return home from school) (*El Universal* 2016a). Second, *Como dice el dicho* "consolidated its hold on the taste of the audience" even as it expanded its supply (again like *La rosa de Guadalupe*) (*El Universal* 2016b). And third, "it tries to transmit positive messages" (*El Universal* 2017).

This last article is the most telling. Longtime producer Genoveva Martínez states here that television has a responsibility toward its audience. And if her series aims to entertain, she also says that its images and contents are "exemplary," even to the extent that the dishes served in the show's cafeteria are "natural and healthy." The fact that the location boasts a juice bar and not a cake display is in itself an attempt to promote a healthy diet in a country that, she says, is number one in juvenile obesity (*El Universal* 2017).

Unlike *La rosa de Guadalupe*, which often lightly fictionalizes specific recognizable events torn from the headlines, Martínez prefers to take the general temperature of society, its "tone and state of mind." This interview was given at a party (this time complete with cake) celebrating the seventh season of a show which had accumulated over 400 episodes since it bowed in 2011. In contrast, now threatened telenovelas barely reached a reduced count of some 80 episodes before their definitive ending, while new-fangled "series" (based on US formats) boasted fewer than 20.

We have seen that academic critics have tried to identify "stereotypes" in *La rosa de Guadalupe*'s characters: in their appearance, occupation, family status, and relation to the opposite sex and to violence. Such studies are generally based on a small corpus of episodes. What is lacking, however, is a thorough study of young people and television fiction in which, beyond simple content analysis, character traits are systematically related to plotlines, narrative style (format, perspective, and temporality), and TV technique (shooting style, editing, and use of music). Moreover the role of social media, alternately virulent and devoted in the case of *La rosa de Guadalupe*, is also inseparable from the production and consumption of the TV host text. Although such a study does not, to my knowledge, exist for Mexico, it does for Spain. My next section will thus give an account of this Spanish study, which will put into perspective the particularity of my Mexican series.

Identity Construction and Transmedia

In 2013 Charo Lacalle, leader of a research group at Barcelona's Autonomous University, published *Jóvenes y ficción televisiva: construcción de identidad y transmedialidad* ("Young People and Television Drama: Identity Construction and Transmedia"). Admirably comprehensive, the book covers all first-run drama programs in all genres from both national and regional broadcasters for the calendar years 2009 and 2010 and a huge range of web resources from 2011 (2013, 18). As its title suggests, this study, at once qualitative and quantitative, treats youth and identity as "constructions" inside and outside the TV text. And, unlike other accounts of the subject, does not assume an unmediated relation between fiction and reality, television and society.

In the introduction (2013, 11–27), Lacalle sketches a situation in Spain that is strangely similar to that in Mexico. She notes that studies on the influence of mass media, often based on critiques of stereotypes, have been consistently negative and that the "didactic" tendency of youth television has too often been obscured by the repercussions in public opinion of the most controversial depictions (2013, 11–12). These were associated with the themes of gender violence, drugs, teen pregnancy, immigrants, psychological disturbances, homosexuality, and disability, all questions, she says, inspired by the most highly topical social issues (2013, 16).

Lacalle confesses that her study began by taking for granted that almost all these critiques and complaints were justified, but later concluded that the "spectacular" nature of these negative elements had obscured the "sensitivity, tolerance, and social commitment" of many of the characters depicted in these dramas and, by extension, of the shows themselves (2013, 17). It was thus necessary for the scholarly team to avoid a priori "stigmatization" without falling into the opposite trap of indiscriminate "legitimization." It is a tricky balance that I will try to follow myself in what remains of this chapter.

In the body of her book, Lacalle provides a detailed template for the analysis of TV fiction. Thus her understanding of "character analysis" (2013, 29–138) is based on a wide range of elements: physical appearance; *protagonismo* (i.e. the extent to which a character takes a leading role); social class; health, complications, and addictions; friendship; work and studies; entertainment and leisure; sexual and sentimental relationships; and family. More complex are what she calls "roles": the *actancial* is when a narrator talks directly to the viewer; the "informer" and "observer" modes on the other hand inform and suggest the viewpoint to be adopted by the audience (99). "Semiotic" roles turn around three main meaningful themes, as enacted by characters: the conflict between good and evil, sexuality, and friendship (102).

Beyond the domain of characters, "narrative analysis" (139–62) examines audiovisual discourse, an aspect generally neglected by both popular and academic commentators. Clearly conventions of "format" and "genre" are essential. Less familiar are *temporalidad* (is the simulation of an instantaneous present and of linearity dominant?) and *aspectualidad* (how does the story develop within respect to its beginning and end?). The latter is clearly most important for *unitarios* or anthology dramas, complete as they are in one day. Beyond storytelling, we also need to ask about audiovisual technique: what is the function of the shooting style? How are subjective and objective cameras used?

Finally the lengthy account of "user feedback" (201–56) examines a huge range of blogs, forums, and social media. Here questions include the structure and development of the posts; references made to plotlines, characters, and actors (the latter much less frequent than the characters they play [222]), and settings. More complex once more are *extimidad* (defined in the introduction as "the exhibition of one's private life [*intimidad*] on forums and social media" [26]); and *autorreflexión* ("how users see and live the drama, transforming the 'aesthetic object' (the program) into a true space of 'deliberation'"). And, of course, like the dramas themselves, the online users address "social issues."

One of those issues is gender and sexuality. Lacalle and her team discover that women contribute more frequently and more fully to social media on their favorite titles than do men (2013, 244). And the question of homosexuality, which we have already seen in *Como dice el dicho*, keeps coming up. For example, the topic of "homosexual initiation" is often tackled in TV drama (2013, 65). In Spain at least, gays are "frequently linked to the depiction of the sexual sphere" (2013, 120). But in the notoriously controversial high school series *Física o química* (Antena 3, 2008–11), each gay character comes to terms with his sexual identity in a different way (one is defiant, another timid, etc.).

It thus follows that stereotypes, the focus of previous studies, are by no means dominant. Moreover the theme of homosexuality is used both to problematize the whole area of sexuality and also to introduce in a disguised manner other topics such as abuse, prejudice, and the condemnation of behavior that goes beyond the norm (drugs, prostitution, criminality, etc.) (2013, 121). Betraying their producers' progressive stance, there is, writes Lacalle and her team, "an attempt at normalization" of homosexuality here, as it is shown merely as the "tip of an iceberg" that is both social and psychological.

Armed with this methodology, we can now go on to examine, textually and structurally, specimen episodes of *La rosa de Guadalupe* and *Como dice el dicho* that first aired within a month of each other and both focus on a theme that is also widespread in Spain: "homosexual initiation."

La rosa de Guadalupe: Specimen Episode

Episode 1004: "Amor distinto" ("A Different Love," first shown August 3, 2017; rerun February 1, 2018) (Illustration 6.1).

Esther le ayudará a su hijo Ernesto a afrontar las burlas y los prejuicios sociales por ser homosexual, juntos lucharán para que haya respeto a sus preferencias (lasestrellas.TV).

Esther will help her son to face ridicule and social prejudices for being homosexual, together they will fight for respect for his preferences (official Televisa synopsis)

Illustration 6.1 *La rosa de Gualalupe* (Televisa, 2008–present)

The first shot is a close-up of a middle-aged, middle-class woman with smooth chestnut hair, light skin, and eyes. A vase of tastefully selected flowers can be made out behind her. Straight to camera and smiling slightly, she says: "Yes I have a homosexual son. That's what this story is about." It is a story credited to longtime screenwriter Carlos Mercado-Orduña that in addition to its free-to-air audience has received two million views on YouTube.

The setting (as in a traditional telenovela) is one of those ample homes characteristic of the upper middle class. The first scene proper is of lunch with an extended family (the wary mother, silent father, three brothers, aunt, cousin, and grandmother), all shown at the table in a crowded group shot. Already there is tension between the mother and her sister. Ernesto, the male protagonist, is a cute slightly effeminate boy with adorable curly hair. He has helped his mother bake the homemade dessert, which his aunt suggests, bitchily, is shop bought. Ernesto's cousin makes a homophobic joke to the assembled family, which goes unremarked but makes Ernesto and his mother visibly uncomfortable. Later in the kitchen, the boy's aunt and grandmother talk darkly of her sister's "problem" with Ernesto. Overhearing, the mother reacts angrily, defending her son.

We cut to the schoolyard where, in an eyeline match, Ernesto and future boyfriend Gerry make silent amorous contact (the actors were just 14 and 15 at the time). In a low angle, the bullies, including the cousin we saw at the lunch, who make Ernesto's life hell, loom over the camera. The homophobe is at once told off by a teacher, who sets him an extra assignment as punishment. This cousin is not just a bad student, he is also a gossip who spreads rumors of Ernesto's "bad company": a friend who is "raro" or "rarito" ("strange," code for "queer"). In a rare exterior, Ernesto's macho brother and homophobic cousin commune on the soccer field, a no-go area for the femme boy.

Next Ernesto and Gerry work on their joint Spanish literature assignment together in Gerry's comfortable bedroom. Here editing is of the essence. Gerry says he wants to smash the cousin's face in for bullying them. The couple hug (fully clothed) and say, "I love you." There is then an ellipse as we cut to a romantic shot of the full moon outside. And suddenly the boys are seen getting dressed. Gerry hoarsely (sexily) ventures that they have had "such a great time."

There are many such linking shots or inserts in the episode (and the series), often of intense gold and violet sunrises or sunsets. As was traditional in movie melodrama, mise-en-scène speaks here implicitly of intense sensations that the plot (which focuses on romance rather than sexual activity) does not. The same goes for the camerawork, which enhances meaning and affect in the following sequence.

Now the two boys are alone in the classroom and their dialogue is shown in tight shot/reverse shot. The more vocal Gerry confesses to the more timid Ernesto: "When I'm with you I can't think about schoolwork." They move in to kiss, but the camera tilts up just before they do to show their teacher entering room. Apparently unsurprised, she insists: "I don't discriminate but this is not the place. Not because of me, but because your fellow students can be cruel." There is thus a complicity set up between the gay kids and the teacher, who has seen the kiss that we have not. The teacher says she won't tell Ernesto's parents, but suggests Ernesto does. She smiles and touches his face in tender close-up. But the course of true love is not, of course, smooth: Gerry soon breaks up with Ernesto because he (Ernesto) refuses to stand up to his bullying cousin at school. Now Ernesto is briefly shot from between the school stairs, a visual rhyme for prison bars.

The long delayed coming out scene is the climax to the first half of the episode (which is divided in two on YouTube). Mother and son retire to a lushly private garden, the kind of space to which few viewers of *La rosa de Guadalupe* could hope to have access. As the strings swell on the soundtrack, Ernesto tells her that he is gay, has no problem himself with it, but does not want to disappoint her. Showing a knowledge of current events, he also notes that now he can get married and have children, just not the way she might wish. Her response is poetic and didactic: "Now life has many different colors." She says she not only loves but respects and admires her son.

It is only fully 20 minutes in that we have the first religious reference. The mother enters her son's bedroom, watching over him as he sleeps. A blue framed portrait of the Virgin comes just into frame on the wall behind her.

Once more the dialogue (this time in voiceover) is explicit: "A mother's love is a different love, like the love you feel, son." Queer and maternal affect are thus equated. The mother (the undisputed female protagonist of the episode) is then granted a subjective or POV shot of the boy wrapped safely in a blanket. The camera pans left to the framed picture once more as she silently addresses the Virgin: "*Morenita*, you are a mother too. Give me the strength to fight for my son." The identification between the twin mothers of the equally threatened Christ and gay youth could hardly be clearer. And it is at this point that, as in every episode, the much-parodied white rose magically appears on the sideboard to the sound of a heavenly choir.

Soon mother and son consult a friendly bearded therapist, taking care to confirm to each other (and the viewer) that the visit is not because Ernesto is sick. Indeed in something of a refrain, it is repeated here that it is the other family members that have the problem, not the boy. The therapist confirms that Ernesto is "healthy" and "will be OK." However, an insert of a stormy sky suggests otherwise, in the immediate future at least.

The mother's announcement to her sister, Ernesto's aunt, does not go well: she says it is "terrible news" and Ernesto faces a lonely and unhappy life. Back at school the pugnacious Gerry finally fights the bully, Ernesto's cousin. At this dramatic high point, after 27 minutes, we cut to the series' regular credit sequence: in fast and slow motion, ordinary people (noticeably darker skinned and more mestizo-featured than today's cast) wearily tread the city streets, crosscut with those stormy skies. It is an image of the trials of everyday secular life far from the candy-colored sets of Televisa.

After the commercial break, all the boys are taken to see the principal. The latter repeats the teacher's line: discrimination will not be tolerated in her school. The cousin, now officially punished, vows vengeance and tells Ernesto's macho big brother all. The latter goes home and briefly strikes his brother. At this the angry mother tells him he alone has the problem. The conflict between good and evil (good gay and bad straight brothers) could hardly be clearer.

When the mother now calls a family meeting, the framing says it all. While the suddenly accepting businessman-father (hitherto clueless at what has been going on) and hitherto bad brother are shown to one side, the mother and son share the frame with the miraculous rose and a statuette of the Virgin. In a second much-parodied moment, which recurs in every episode, a heavenly breeze ruffles the pair's hair as their hands are clasped to their chests, eyes devotedly closed. The mother is now dressed in the Virgin's blue (previously she favored fuschia). The secularization of Catholic iconography is complete.

A final montage shows repaired social harmony: Ernesto implausibly triumphs on the soccer field and his boyfriend is invited to attend a convivial

6   Anthology Dramas: *La rosa de Guadalupe, Como dice el dicho*   87

family barbeque, a rhyme for the opening more tense and less accepting meal. Once more the mother speaks straight to camera. With some emphasis she cites Pope Francisco's then-recent question about gays: "Who am I to judge?" This is the only reference to a religious figure in the episode. No one ever attends mass or thinks to consult a cleric about the family "problem" in this episode or in any other that I have seen.

The secular pedagogy of the episode is thus insistent, as we can see from a narrative analysis. The mother's opening and closing statements serve, in Lacalle's terms, as an authoritative *actancial*. Indeed these fixed "roles" are so marked as consistently to sacrifice narrative tension. In terms of Lacalle's *aspectualidad*, given the mother's initial and very explicit understanding, the end of the episode is perfectly predictable from the start. And whenever drama threatens to flare up, an authority figure (an "informer" or "observer") at once takes a stand and protects the gay youth, a role taken successively by the teacher, the therapist, and the principal. There is almost no physical violence in the episode (a single blow and short fight) and little evidence shown of the bullying that is so critiqued.

What of sex? Homosexuality, even at this early age, is tentatively and discreetly sexualized in the very evident gap between the two shots when the boys first hug and then dress in the bedroom. Audiovisual discourse thus speaks louder than words, also through the use of vibrantly colored sets and costumes and dramatic musical prompts. The shooting style is equally loaded. We are given successive intimate close-ups of Ernesto and his amorous boyfriend, Ernesto and his kindly teacher, above all, Ernesto and his devoted mother. Conversely, family homophobes and school bullies are shown mainly in objective group shots. We have seen that it is only the mother who is granted an emotionally charged subjective perspective on her sleeping son as she herself addresses the Virgin in an also unique example of internal monologue.

In more narrative and less audiovisual terms, homosexuality serves, as Lacalle suggests once more, as a device to smuggle in other issues such as bullying, to show that perhaps this is just "the tip of the iceberg" (after all, the show will offer another case study and treat another social issue the next day). But the focus here is still on the immediacy of gay teen love (its tense and intense temporality) seductively cocooned in candy-colored comfort. Viewers might wonder how many homes are really so vibrant, even in the Mexico that has a great tradition of architectural appeal to color. But I would argue that here audiovisual stylization serves to enhance and dignify everyday life, rather than to distract or abstract from it. As we shall now see, the more modest narrative technique and audiovisual discourse of *Como dice el dicho* offer a slightly different take on the same theme.

Como dice el dicho: Specimen Episode

Season 6, episode 118: "Secreto entre dos lo sabe Dios, secreto entre tres descubierto es" ("A secret shared by two is known only to God; a secret known to three is open to all"; first shown September 27, 2017, rerun September 10, 2018) (Illustration 6.2).

Gerry sufre de acoso escolar y Randy se calla ante el abuso. Ambos tienen una relación sentimental secreta y, a pesar de los temores, poco a poco reconocerán y defenderán su derecho al amor (lasetrellas.tv).

Gerry is being bullied at school and Randy keeps quiet about it. They are having a secret relationship and, in spite of their fears, will slowly acknowledge and defend their right to love (official Televisa synopsis)

The opening scene is on the school stairs (once more), clearly a privileged site for encounters and conflicts. The protagonist, called Gerry (again), is having a conversation with his best (girl) friend, Mari. Two bullies drag him away. The camera rests on a third student (Randy), looking silently on. In ominous low angles, figures loom over the viewer. Now in the restroom (shown in showy high angles), the bullies slam Gerry against the door and steal his money as the silent Randy once more looks on. Rescued and defended by Mari, Gerry weeps. While the bullies go free, she is punished by the principal for being in the boys' restroom and Gerry is reprimanded for using make up (it is to hide his wound). Next Gerry is knocked down and kicked in the street by the same two bullies. Randy asks if he's OK. Now comes the first insert. Aerial shots of the city at night or by day establish an everyday urban context somewhat different to *La rosa de Guadalupe*'s more elemental sun, moon, and sky.

Illustration 6.2 *Como dice el dicho* (Televisa, 2011–present)

We cut to another lavish home where a husband in suit and tie dines with wife and daughter. An unusual centerpiece stretches the length of the extended table and a uniformed maid is glimpsed in the kitchen behind them, indexes of formal, moneyed domesticity. Gerry claims he isn't hungry and goes straight to his room. In awkward conversation we learn that the mother and sister have already guessed that Gerry is gay: the father who is clueless (again) says it's impossible. Weeping and wounded, Gerry is visited in his bedroom by his parents. His father says he should solve things "like a man"; the son replies, "You mean like a caveman." In overheard conversation, the mother plans to take Gerry to a therapist, as she doesn't want a "homosexual" son. The father rather uses the barely coded word "rarito."

In a unique split-screen shot Gerry is on the phone with Mari. Her solution is to "come out of the closet already." His father suggests Gerry join the soccer team (it's actually the daughter who wants to). Now the unsympathetic principal demands Gerry name his bullies. He refuses. In a rare exterior sequence, Randy takes Gerry to a secluded spot in school where Gerry verbally attacks him for doing nothing to help the day before. Randy invokes the proverb seen in Don Tomás' café to justify his silence, but professes his love. We also learn that Mari and Randy were formerly involved, or at least Mari thinks so.

Cut to the café. Here the young waitress (who is a regular in all episodes) serves as an improvised therapist. She knows about Gerry being bullied and says he can talk to her "about anything." Back at school Mari confronts the two bullies and defends Gerry, once more. However she also argues with Randy, who denies they were ever a couple ("I'm not for you") and tells her to stop harassing him ("You are the bully"). In the café the waitress advises Gerry to come out of the closet, but he is reluctant to "wave a rainbow flag wherever I go." She replies that it is his decision alone. But he has to get help with bullying, as violence tends to get worse.

A little later Gerry and his faithful sister ask Don Tomás for cakes to go (the skinny actors need not fear obesity). The sister asks for an explanation of the proverb on the wall and the camera cuts away to it, as it does in every episode. This shot is the more prosaic equivalent of the close-ups of the rose and the Virgin in *La rosa de Guadalupe*, with secular wisdom playing the same role here as Catholic (or post-Catholic) iconography in the fellow anthology drama.

At home the macho father buys a violent video game for his unwilling son. Gerry refuses to play (his sister once more shows interest). The son now (as in *La rosa de Guadalupe*) visits his mother in a lush garden. She asks for help in the garden as "the flowers are so colorful" (he refuses once more). Spurning stereotypical femininity, he also reacts angrily when his sister kindly invites him to play with her dolls.

Now comes the credit sequence, brighter and lighter than in *La rosa de Guadalupe*. It shows only the café's location and its familiar staff, a substitute family who tend a healthy juice bar for troubled guest stars, all set to a jolly brass-accompanied theme tune. Back home the little sister, another improvised therapist, acts out family ties using toys. Wise beyond her years, the sister says being gay "is the most normal thing in the world." Just like the different cakes they brought from the café, it's all a matter of taste.

In a unique long-tracking shot, the two boys walk in the schoolyard, one behind the other. Still they argue about secrecy: Randy can't take the chance of people thinking he's gay like Gerry. Now back in the café, Gerry's parents ask Don Tomás if he knows a psychiatrist who can solve their son's "problem." In dialogue identical to in *La rosa de Guadalupe*, he replies that it is they, not he, who are the problem. He warns them not to take their son to conversion therapy ("They are the worst people"). The parents just need to accept their son "with understanding, with love."

At school the bullies steal Gerry's phone and the muscular Randy finally fights and defeats them (the scene is more graphic and convincing than in *La rosa de Guadalupe*, although the actors here look older than their characters). In a telling contrast in the café, young waiter Pato tells the parents that it's now "abnormal" not to be gay but to refuse to accept gays. And if Pato's gay friends sadly suffer discrimination, so do the overweight and the dark skinned.

Now the boys are tearfully reconciled and tenderly kiss (the act that caused some press controversy is shown in several shots). But they are filmed by Mari on her phone (they are briefly shown from her POV). In the inevitable coming out scene at home, Gerry's mother (having learned better) is now delighted, although his father is horrified, still. After treacherous Mari sends the kissing video to the whole school, there comes a scene of genuine drama. The principal accuses Gerry of "indecency" in front of the class and demands he reveal the other boy's identity. Finally the straight-acting Randy identifies himself as Gerry's boyfriend. When the principal refuses to believe him, he says she is discriminating against him as he looks too masculine to be gay; and demands she expose rather the bully who made and sent the video. Mari is tearfully made to confess.

Now the principal, who now seems finally to have learned her lesson, insists Gerry make a complaint against the three bullies (the two boys and the girl) so this kind of abuse will never happen again at their school. And she reassures him that the offenders will not go to prison but rather to a correction facility for minors where they will receive "therapy" with their families. Mari, on the other hand, will be detained. In the last sequence, Gerry himself offers a somewhat awkward explanation of the legal process at the café before the whole cast.

As the jolly theme tune comes up on the soundtrack, Randy arrives with a red rose, a public gift of love. And the camera cuts back to the day's proverb as the cast recite it aloud: now, Don Tomás notes, there are no secrets left.

Where *La rosa de Guadalupe*'s episode was demonstrative and didactic, *Como dice el dicho*'s is more tensely dramatic. Indeed there is genuine ambivalence here. After all, Mari bravely defends Gerry from the bullies before, spurned by Randy, she makes and sends the kissing video, becoming a bully herself. And Randy spends most of the episode mutely witnessing his boyfriend's distress. Unlike *La rosa de Guadalupe*, once more there is no *actancial* here, no direct address to camera. And the institutional observers are deficient too. There is no kindly teacher or therapist to help Gerry. And the principal seems more concerned with the gay boys' misdemeanors than the straight bullies' crimes. It is telling that Gerry himself explains their legal position, thus enhancing his status as unique protagonist. In narrative terms, temporality and aspect are also relatively complex. The plot evokes an earlier period when Randy was with Mari not Gerry (or at least so she thought) and delays revelation of a perhaps lengthy past where Gerry and Randy, so discreet in school that even the viewer does not know that they are a couple, have kept their relationship secret. The episode's twists and turns are by no means predictable.

Likewise the audiovisual discourse is somewhat more varied than in *La rosa de Guadalupe*. High and low angles are more prominent. There is the showy split-screen sequence. And the only clear subjective shot belongs to bully Mari, the voyeur of the gay kiss, not protagonist Gerry. Here the intermittent topic of "homosexual initiation" opens up onto the dangers of social media and mobile telephony, a more frequent theme in both *unitarios*. Moreover where *La rosa de Guadalupe* was conservative on gender (the saintly mother has no other occupation than caring for her martyred son, like the Virgin before her), *Como dice el dicho* is more explicit on the critique of such roles. The smart little sister insists on her preference for the soccer and violent video games that her brother rejects. And if Gerry calls his father a "caveman," she calls him an "alpha male," acting out his attitude with a sarcastic fluffy toy.

The biggest difference with *La rosa de Guadalupe* is of course the permanent location and cast of characters in the titular café. Their familiarity to the audience lends them yet greater impeccably progressive authority than the institutional figures in *La rosa de Guadalupe*, as the café staff wisely advise and recommend. And this convivial social setting, to which all the characters have recourse, confirms not only the "positive messages" sought by *Como dice el dicho*'s producer, but also a collective consensus beyond the individual case of the day. The fact that it is an authentic location and not a studio set lends an extra reality effect to the day's moral.

Finally the proverb that gives the episode its title, which is repeated three times, is ambivalent. It warns of the dangers of sharing secrets, while the show itself praises truth telling to the whole world. Gerry and Randy, the show suggests, can be happy only when they are waving a rainbow flag, or at least holding a red rose as a very visible sign of openly acknowledged gay love. This is a kind of *extimidad*, or being private in public, that we will see also in the twin anthology shows' social network reach.

Anthology User Feedback

In spite of the supposed controversy over its same sex kiss, my episode of *Como dice el dicho* has left little echo on social media. This was not for lack of trying on the part of Televisa. The broadcaster, as is generally the case with the series, posted official short video interviews on YouTube with the main cast. Here the young actors struggle to reconcile the conflicting messages of their episode: keeping quiet for self protection and speaking out for self projection. It is a conflict that the episode itself does not resolve and, in typical TV style, will no doubt continue to be taken up in future episodes. The main result of these spin off videos was, ironically enough, digital stalking of one actor by one user in the form of repeated amorous posts, which, of course, went unanswered by their target (Cafe el Dicho 2017).

Rapidly and unofficially uploaded to specialist website Cinegayonline in 2017, the episode proved more polemical. When one fan wrote blandly enough that the central characters made a "cute couple," an angry respondent wrote a comprehensive takedown of the episode:

> TERRIBLE. What has it got to do with the film [sic] that "they make a cute couple"??? Your stupid comment is WORSE than the episode. It's produced by Televisa which is not known for its broadmindedness. It's more like a documentary on *bulling* [sic], but it would be better to cut it down to 2 or 3 Minutes, otherwise NO ONE would watch it. Full of CLICHES, CHILDISH situations, and characters WHO DON'T EXIST in Mexican society. There's no Real story; the performances are by beginners (obvious because of their age); and the Director is conspicuous by his absence. It seems like a "School Saga" which I suppose had good intentions but doesn't fulfill ANY of them. An evident example of WHAT SHOULD NOT BE DONE!!! (Raul Hector Rivas, no date)

In this unusually lengthy post, the user works through Lacalle's narrative and audiovisual elements (plot, character, acting, even direction), but makes only a passing reference to social issues (bullying) and permits himself no self-reflection or identification with the "childish" situations.

6 Anthology Dramas: *La rosa de Guadalupe, Como dice el dicho* 93

It is perhaps no surprise that the author identifies himself as a school teacher. But his post points inadvertently to the transnational reach of *Como dice el dicho*: even as he claims the show is not representative of Mexico, he identifies himself as being based in Argentina. And other users of Cinegayonline comment on this episode from Paraguay and Venezuela.

The fleeting format of the *unitario* is of course less likely than a continuing series or telenovela to engage audiences over time. There are, however, 40 extant tweets related to our episode of *La rosa de Guadalupe* at the time of writing, some 18 months after the episode first aired. All but one of these are either positive or neutral.

At first most are pragmatic: tweeters begin by sharing "likes" of a video uploaded on YouTube and give directions as to other unofficial urls where the whole episode can be seen. But they also make connections with other texts, especially a recent award-winning animated short on teen gay love called *In A Heartbeat*. @MeganaKatt writes that the two texts are "similar" (August 13, 2017); @Lennay1D asks "Did you see la rosa de guadalupe yesterday? … The characters are the same [as in the short]!" (August 4, 2017). Users post parallel pictures of the protagonists, one dark and one fair. Staying within the narrative field but offering subjective affect, @diaryofmane writes (in English): "I have to admit that the episode is beautiful, it's brilliant, it's love" (followed by two heart emoticons, January 30, 2018). Or again @gcfbusanboys writes that s/he is watching the episode and "DYING OF LOVE" (September 13, 2018).

Contrary to Lacalle's research on Spain, here users comment less on characters than on actors, or rather on one actor in particular. Curly-haired Joaquín Bondoni (who also has a singing career) soon graduated from *La rosa de Guadalupe* to primetime telenovela *Mi marido tiene más familia* ("My Husband Has Another Family," Televisa, 2018), where he played a gay character once more. So-called shippers (fans of a relationship) christened the teen couple in the novela "Aristemo" (after shortened versions of their names: Aristóteles and Cuauhtémoc) and looked back affectionately on Bondoni's previous role. @pskiensera writes that Bondoni was excellent in "Amor distinto" but not convincing in another episode of *La rosa de Guadalupe*, where he played a heterosexual role: "You're better in gay parts," he tells the actor (September 8, 2018). @Hylians_Lord even reminds the now famous Bondoni (who seems to have forgotten himself) that Ernesto in *La rosa de Guadalupe* was his first "homosexual" part, something the faithful fan well remembers (September 26, 2018).

Other users reveal their emotions in examples of what Lacalle calls *extimidad*, sharing private feelings in public and offering evidence of repeated viewings: "I'm crying like crazy:(Watch 'amor distinto' in 'la rosa de guadalupe' and you'll understand)" (@chiki_crew, December 21, 2017); or again "Yesterday I cried like a dummy [*gafa*] watching la rosa de guadalupe – amor distinto. I always cry when I watch it" (@Alanisse07, August 10, 2018). Elsewhere users venture at some length into social issues:

> There's an episode of "La rosa de Guadalupe" that's called "Amor distinto." Did you get it? So, they talk about accepting homosexuality, but they call it "Amor distinto"? No, *loca*, love is LOVE. It's not different to anything. Especially as it's not just love, it's sexual attraction, end of my rant. (@Ludmilxpineirx, November 26, 2107)

Here Twitter transforms the aesthetic object of the TV show into what Lacalle calls a "space of deliberation," in which the user explores the meaning of the episode and builds on it. Other tweeters also insist on the sexual component of gay love, elided by the series itself: one complains that "when Joaquín made [the episode] they didn't show the kiss" (@Mayra87937209, November 17, 2017). As I write, a new, playfully blasphemous tweet has appeared: "The camp guy [*fletito*] is soooo cute. *Morenita* lend me a hand and send me one of those" (@taequilazo, November 20, 2018).

But perhaps most interesting are two examples of extended "pragmatics." In the first, tweeters berate @PepeYTeo, Mexico's most famous gay bloggers, who had devoted a whole hour-long "reaction video" to verbally vilifying *La rosa de Guadalupe* as they watch choice melodramatic excerpts of the series (e.g. @Cyrus_Kev20, July 29, 2018). In the second, viewers link the episode to a new hashtag on Twitter and a collective action in the real world. Participating in #bluebondoni, fans tie blue ribbons around their wrists in order to show public support for the actor and his gay characters:

> Today is #bluebondoni and I couldn't keep from expressing my great affection for him and the story of how I "met" him. I saw him for the first time in the episode of **La rosa de Guadalupe** "**amor distinto**" and I loved the way he acted a character from the LGBTI community. (@GandaMallete, October 21, 2018)

The accompanying photograph shows a wrist wrapped in a blue band with the outline of a heart sketched around the thumb and index finger. The self-consciousness here about para-social relationships (the placing of "met" in quotes) joins with unusually accurate syntax and spelling to make the kind of developed and discursive commentary that Lacalle attributes to female users in Spain. And the user, no mindless dupe of Televisa, shows no difficulty in distinguishing between actor and character as she participates in a spontaneous political activity in defense of minority communities. We are far indeed from the morbid fascination, sensationalism, and disinformation of which critics commonly accuse *La rosa de Guadalupe*.

A Different Love

A recent interview with the producer and chief screenwriter of *La rosa de Guadalupe*, Miguel Ángel Herros and Carlos Mercado, attempts to answer the question of how the show can be so successful without casting big stars (Agencia Reforma 2018). Herros points to the "realist content" and the "research" process on real-life cases. Mercado cites the lack of censorship, which enabled episodes on controversial events such as New's Divine (a nightclub where the police were accused of killing clients). Both point also to the internet, which has given them access to new audiences and via hostile memes served to promote the show itself. They also state that *La rosa de Guadalupe* has "no type of relationship with the religious institution," a statement which is self-evident to those who have followed it over the years, but would come as news to the critics who, as Cueva, wrote have not actually turned on their TV to watch it yet regularly accuse it of Catholic conservatism.

As Lacalle noted, then, we should not stigmatize youth TV nor should we dignify it prematurely. In the episodes we analyzed how gender roles remain conservative (those protective mothers) even as sexual options are positively explored (those precocious gay sons). It is clear also that a generalized hostility to Televisa marks and mars the reception of its many and varied contents.

La rosa de Guadalupe is varied indeed. A copy of *TVyNovelas* chosen at random (August 10, 2018) has an article promoting a gritty episode on a topic cited by the student who warned viewers not to be educated by the show ("femicide") (no page) and evoked by the scandal of "Frida Sofía" (the missing child). In "Calcetitas rojas" ("Little Red Socks"), a young woman who has organized an informal group to clean up the trash in the countryside comes across the corpse of a badly beaten infant. She buries her, vowing that "not one more dead woman or girl will be tossed into a gulley." Then she comes across Florecita ("Little Flower"), a near feral child also the victim of battering…

The narrative, social setting, and even aesthetic (the muddy exteriors and grimy interiors) could hardly be further from "Amor distinto." Indeed *La rosa de Guadalupe* shifts radically in form and content from day to day, even as the format remains reassuringly the same. In the same issue Televisa's house magazine previews that week's episodes of *Como dice el dicho*. Premises are equally varied: in one, a corrupt policeman murders a teenage criminal and another gang member wonders whether to turn him in; in a second, a cynical youth uploads nude photos of his naïvely trusting girlfriend; and in a third, a biracial boy who has been deported from the USA experiences racism in Mexico, but is defended by his new teacher and classmate. In all cases, the series takes care to explain the legal as well as the ethical and emotional implications of the plots.

As Cueva notes, *unitarios* offer a successful business model for free-to-air TV in Mexico through a genre that is also popular transnationally in the USA and Latin America. The format might well be exported to countries where the original shows are not seen (Spain, say, has no equivalent of the genre). Anthology dramas thus offer the chance for a different and special kind of TV love to their faithful fans.

Also, and more rarely, they can provide a springboard for young actors and associated social movements, as in the example of #bluebondoni. Generally, however, and unlike the movie and primetime stars I have treated in other chapters, the multitude of guest stars on the daily shows rarely rise above the horizon of anonymity. And, to their casting directors' credit, these actors are often darker and homelier than those in more prestigious telenovelas (the casts in my episodes here are not fully representative).

These jobbing actors can thus plausibly claim to represent their audience, providing opportunities to engage in intense identification, emotion, and self-reflection. For example, the actor who plays waiter Pato in *Como dice el dicho* (the Afro-haired Benny Emmanuel) has uploaded self-made videos to YouTube in which he offers a tour of the real-life location, engages with fans watching the shoot on the street outside, and humorously chronicles his lengthy working day. His second video has received almost a million views (Emmanuel 2018). Emmanuel was also the star of a homoerotic short by Roberto Fiesco (*Trémulo* ["Tremulous"], 2015), a sign of the apparently unlikely connection between a television that is literally everyday and the unique aesthetic event that is art cinema.

On social media, anthology dramas are reviled in the abstract but beloved in the particular (comments on single episodes are much more positive than those on the supposed series as a whole). Elite critique is based not just on contempt for familiarity but also on hostility to feminization: this is TV made predominantly for and often by women (such as Genoveva Martínez, the proud producer of *Como dice el dicho*). The value of *unitarios* is that they point out the way for a television that continues to connect with the daily lives of mass audiences via, as Cueva puts it, stories that are "simple, everyday, similar to real life." They do so even as traditional telenovela declines and (as we see in Chaps. 5 and 7) new series on new platforms strive for innovation. Ironically enough, then, it is perhaps the most modest and old fashioned of formats, a story that is told in a single day, that has proved best able to engage with the new challenge of the internet in all its intensity and novelty.

References

Agencia Reforma. 2018. ¿A qué se debe el éxito de *La rosa de Guadalupe*, serie de Televisa y Univision? *La Opinión*, August 30. https://laopinion.com/2018/08/30/a-que-se-debe-el-exito-de-la-rosa-de-guadalupe-serie-de-televisa-y-univision/

Ayón, Cecilia, et al. 2016. Agarra el Momento/Seize the Moment: Developing Communication Activities for a Drug Prevention Intervention with and for Latino Families in the US Southwest. *Qualitative Social Work* 15 (2): 281–299.

Business Wire. 2018. Univision Network Is No. 1 Spanish-Language Network, Outperforming Telemundo with Double-Digit Audience Advantages Among Total Viewers. April 5.

Cafe el Dicho. 2017. Entrevista @memodorantes: Comments. *YouTube*. https://www.youtube.com/watch?v=my2WyzG5Dus

Cinegayonline. 2017. Secreto entre dos: comentarios. https://www.cinegayonline.org/p/secreto-entre-dos.html

Cueva, Álvaro. 2016. Aprendan de *La rosa de Guadalupe*. *Milenio*, July 20. http://www.milenio.com/opinion/alvaro-cueva/el-pozo-de-los-deseos-reprimidos/aprendan-de-la-rosa-de-guadalupe

———. 2017. *La rosa de Guadalupe*: reina de México y emperatriz de América. *Milenio*, January 17. http://www.milenio.com/opinion/alvaro-cueva/el-pozo-de-los-deseos-reprimidos/rosa-guadalupe-reina-mexico-emperatriz-america

El Diario La Prensa. 2017. Tuiteros compara caso de Frida Sofía con capítulo de *La rosa de Guadalupe*: las redes sociales estallaron en contra de la televisora mexicana. September 21.

El Universal. 2016a. *Como dice el dicho*, del diario. January 15.

———. 2016b. *Como dice el dicho* se consolida en el gusto del público. May 18.

———. 2017. *Como dice el dicho* busca dar mensajes positivos. January 24.

Emmanuel, Benny. 2018. Un día en El Dicho. *YouTube*. https://www.youtube.com/watch?v=SAdbVsUpZTw

Gómez Parga, Ana. 2014. *Qué no te eduque la Rosa de Guadalupe! A Textual Analysis of Gender and Stereotypes in Mexican Telenovelas*. MA Dissertation, University of Texas at El Paso.

La Opinión. 2017. Beso gay en telenovela de Televisa causa polémica: La serie toca temas sociales que viven los jóvenes de hoy en día. October 2.

Lacalle, Charo. 2013. *Jóvenes y ficción televisiva: Construcción de identidad y transmedialidad*. Barcelona: UOC Press.

Multichannel News. 2016. Stickiest Shows: Ranking Programs by Viewing Engagement. 37.22, June 13, p. 26.

Obitel. 2017. *Obitel 2016: Reinvención de géneros y formatos de la ficción televisiva*. http://obitel.net/wp-content/uploads/2016/09/obitel-espanhol-2016.pdf

Savard, Mary. 2014. *Parental Beliefs Regarding Defender Behavior When Children Witness Bullying Situations*. PhD Dissertation, Harvard University.

TVyNovelas. 2018. Detrás de *La rosa de Guadalupe*; Detrás de *Como dice el dicho*. August 10.

7

New Platforms, New Contents: Run, Coyote, Run

Fox and Friends

In recent years three artistically and commercially successful TV series have launched local content on global platforms in Mexico. As we saw in the previous chapter, *Capadocia* (2008–12) is a critically acclaimed women's prison drama made for HBO Latin America by Mexican indie producer Argos, which had long specialized in boundary-pushing and politically progressive content even on free-to-air networks. *Club de Cuervos* (2015–17), on which I have written at length elsewhere (Smith 2018, 57–88), is a soccer comedy for streaming giant Netflix, which pioneered social media address to Mexican TV audiences. Conceived as a sequel to a feature film and retaining that feature's Mexican director (Gary Alazraki) and star (Luis Gerardo Méndez, an actor with a distinctly intellectual profile), it was scripted nonetheless by an American team based in Los Angeles.

Finally *Run, Coyote, Run* (2017), the subject of this chapter, is a border-based dramedy whose showrunner Gustavo Loza is also a commercial movie director and yet whose star Harold Torres is (like Méndez) a stalwart of Mexican art cinema. Coproduced by FX, a Fox pay channel for quality-scripted content targeting young men, and Claro Video, which showed it on its over-the-top (OTT) app, *Run Coyote Run* began and ended its first season of just 13, one-hour episodes with the highest rating of any drama on Mexican TV, whether free-to-air or premium (todotvnews 2017). Analyzing the rapidly changing industrial mediascape that enables such novel productions in Mexico, this chapter will also suggest that this marquee series (like its predecessors) incorporates the global/local nexus into the fabric of its newly complex

© The Author(s) 2019
P. J. Smith, *Multiplatform Media in Mexico*,
https://doi.org/10.1007/978-3-030-17539-9_7

televisual text, as shown most transparently by the bilingual title of Fox's first Mexican project.

The most urgent problem raised by a phenomenon such as *Run, Coyote, Run* is whether the new platforms made available by changing technology facilitate new contents with new creative characteristics. In this chapter I propose to address this apparently simple question by employing a series of distinct matrices: academic theory, industrial practice, professional profiles, and, finally, textual readings of both the season and of two specimen episodes. As we shall see, the relation between technology and aesthetics is by no means self-evident.

Academic Theory

Let us begin with a survey of some of the diverse academic literature on new platforms and new contents, concentrating on Spanish-language territories. The negative position is taken up, as so often, by Enrique Bustamante in Spain. In his "Quality Contents in the New Audiovisual Structure" (2010), Bustamante restricts himself to the transition to Digital Terrestrial Television (DTT) and mentions no content titles. Bustamante acknowledges that "the link between … television structures and offered contents has been a close constant feature throughout the history of television." This is the case both in the US private model, where antitrust regulation long prohibited vertical integration, and in the very different European model for public television, in which, Bustamante writes, "the concept of the national role played by public television pedagogical, political, social, and cultural [sic] determined its programming for decades" (2010, 138). Bustamante's bleak vision concludes that "quality promises" were contradicted by a "growing poverty of contents" on national and local channels alike (2010, 149). Unsurprisingly, broadcasters themselves have a very different view of the possibilities of the multichannel platforms of DTT.

Elsewhere academics focus on pedagogy as a palliative for the alleged cultural or cognitive losses of audiences associated with digital media. Guillermo Orozco (Mexico's most distinguished scholar of TV reception), along with colleagues E. Navarro (based in Holland) and A. García-Matilla (from Spain), gives an account of "Educational Challenges in Times of Mass Self-Communication: A Dialogue Among Audiences" (2012). Taking for granted (unlike Bustamante) that viewers are now more active, they argue nonetheless that "significant differences are emerging between widespread consumption and connectivity, and the authentic, horizontal, and creative participation of audiences" (2012, 67). Their new course at Spain's University of Valladolid thus has the "aim of developing and reinforcing the skills required to achieve a global dialogue in the field of communication and education."

Elsewhere and simultaneously in Spain, Pedro Javier Gómez Martínez and Miguel Ángel Poveda Criado also offer a course on "Nuevos contenidos y nuevos métodos en narrativa audiovisual" (2013), which they describe as "un proyecto de innovación docente … orientado a conocer las necesidades formativas de personal cualificado que se dedica a las áreas de creación de contenidos en el ámbito de la ficción" ("A project in teaching innovation … intended to discover the training needs of staff qualified in creating fiction contents") (2013, 223). They identify two gaps in pedagogy that they seek to fill: one in the specificity of transmedia content and the other in "ethical and vital considerations" (2013, 231).

Orozco's "self-communication" and Gómez Martínez's "new methodology" find their counterpart in Mexico with the "media competence" of Abel A. Grijalva Verdugo and Rosario Olivia Izaguirre Fierro. In "Media Consumption Patterns and Communicative Competence of University Students" (2014), the authors define the latter as follows: "The concept of media competence arises in the last decade to describe audiovisual education levels of citizens, the interaction of individuals with complex media environments, and the effects of the screens and their influences on audiences" (2014, 23). The researchers conclude that "it is important to conceive university students not as a mass of individuals, but as a complex amalgam of subgroups that … play an important role within the limits in which individuals operate" (2014, 38). Audiences are thus neither atomized nor homogenized in their varied and mediated communicative competences.

While Grijalva Verdugo's survey shows a general bias among younger Mexicans in favor of internet and against broadcast television, a special journal issue edited by Milly Buonanno (perhaps the most respected European scholar of TV contents and author of the book *Television Anti-heroines* cited at length in the previous chapter) argues that the current situation is "(Not Yet) the End of Television." An empirical essay in this collection by Lothar Mikos treats "Digital Media Platforms and the Use of TV Content: Binge Watching and Video-On-Demand in Germany" (2016). Given the (perhaps surprising) fallibility of internet in this European territory, the analysis has some relevance for Latin American countries such as Mexico also. Mikos describes the industrial context as follows: "advancing digitalization and media convergence demands TV broadcasting companies adjust their content to various platforms and distribution channels [through] growing melding of classical-linear TV contents with online offerings" (2016, 154). While the

German subjects (like those in the USA) mainly watch TV drama series at Netflix or Amazon Prime, the essay seeks to relate "the audience practice to the new structures of the television market," thus "shedding light on the future of television."

Stressing the media competence of new viewers, Mikos concludes that "intensive watching of complex television series requires a high degree of emotional and cognitive participation on the part of the audiences" (2016, 160). And he ends by citing Raymond Williams, arguing that television will remain "what it always was: a technology and a cultural form" with users are "still trying to integrate the use of television series in their everyday lives and adapt it to their circumstances." It is a long way from Bustamante's neoliberal threat to public service, cultural diversity, and ideological pluralism.

Two further essays offer ambivalent takes on Mikos' account of distribution and Bustamante's attention to public policy, respectively. Thomas Guignard's "Digital Intermediaries and Cultural Industries: the Developing Influence of Distribution Platforms" (2014) provides a useful definition of our central term: "'platforms' [are] a new form of goods and services distribution [which] carry out the renewal of uses and related practices" (43) and aim to match production to consumption. Stressing both positive and negative dimensions, Guignard questions "the double dialectic in these sectors: in reconfiguration (integration/disintegration activities on the one hand and disintermediation/re-intermediation of the other hand)." We will see a concrete example of these technical processes later when Fox Networks Group Latin America sets itself up as a producer as well as a distributor of digital pay-TV (vertical integration), even as it also lends its new series to Claro Video's OTT app (re-intermediation).

Antonio Nicita and Maria Alessandra Rossi introduce an important new term in "Access to Audio-Visual Contents, Exclusivity and Anticommons in New Media Markets" (2009). Usefully the authors define "premium contents" here as "experience goods" with a "limited degree of substitutability with other contents from the consumers' perspective" (2009, 81). While they cite sporting events and blockbuster movies as typical of this sought-after genre, I will argue that an innovative drama or comedy series (such as *Run, Coyote, Run*) has come to count as "must have" contents also.

The key term here is "anticommons": "In the world of traditional media, the most pressing issue concerning virtual distribution networks was one of scarcity. Access of content owners to the delivery layer was constrained by the limited availability of distribution networks" (2009, 83). Now, however, "in the world of technological convergence and new media platforms, the distribution of bargaining power has shifted to some extent towards content right-holders." If, in the slogan of an earlier era, "content is king," then the proliferation of competing distribution windows for such content does not rob creators of their agency. As we shall see movie director Gustavo Loza (whose production company takes a credit with Fox for *Run, Coyote, Run*) claims to have "taken refuge" in television after being "disappointed" by Mexico's cinema establishment ("Decepciona" 2012).

I end this survey with two essays on digital practice and theory in Spanish-language territories from the *Handbook of Social Media Management* (Friedrichsen and Mühl-Benninghaus 2013). Firstly, Enrique Guerrero, Patricia Diego, and Alejandro Pardo examine the question of "Distributing Audiovisual Contents in the New Digital Scenario: Multiplatform Strategies of the Main Spanish TV Networks." Here again the scene is contradictory. In a territory that remains relatively unintegrated and intermediated, broadcasters should collaborate closer with creatives:

> The effort for developing cross-platform TV series requires a bigger understanding between networks and independent production companies. ... [S]creenwriters must widen the narrative universe of the story and the characters' backgrounds. ... [C]ast members must be more available for social networking. Despite recent advances in technology, creativity is still the cornerstone of the audiovisual industry. Thus, ongoing investment in format development is crucial... [as] in-house produced contents are dominant in new platforms. (2013, 369)

But networks are also reliant on viewers:

> Users ... have become more active, not only playing a part in programming contents, but also taking on a role in production and promotion campaigns via social networking sites. (2013, 390)

In the same volume Germán Arango-Forero and Sergio Roncallo-Dow offer a more theoretical account of "Social Media and the New Audiences as a New Challenge for Traditional and New Media Industries." They argue that:

> The new digital revolution has led to a new configuration on audiences consumption habits, content preferences and responses, even on emerging and developing media economies like the ones in Latin America where traditional windows for distribution and exhibition combine with new platforms on a hybrid and eclectic environment [to produce] a new audience culture. (2013, 635)

Arango-Forero and Roncallo-Dow rework some themes we have already seen: "technology beyond a simple evolution: convergence"; "interactivity as a new concept"; "produce and broadcast yourself"; and "the significance of the new audience: consumer autonomy" (2013, 636–40). But, more significantly, they appeal to fellow Colombian TV scholar Jesús Martín Barbero to suggest a theoretical move "from media centrism to the mediation process [or] relations between subjects that are mediated ... by media texts" (2013, 641). Finally, they conclude that "regardless of country, young Latin Americans are among social networking's most active users" (2013, 653). It is a significant warning that we can now go on to address in the industrial context of the trade press.

Industry Commentary

In January 2018, Fox Networks Group Latin American held an event at Miami's National Association of Television Program Executives that Mexican critic Álvaro Cueva called "unprecedented," adding: "[Fox] le mandó a toda la industria de la television mundial un spectacular mensaje de solidez, unidad, creatividad, y grandeza" ("Fox sent the entire industry of world-wide television a spectacular message of soundness, unity, creativity, and greatness"; Cueva 2018). Employing press conferences, parties, and project presentations, the platform launched its slate for the coming season: a political drama for Mexico's election year, directed and starring Gael García Bernal (*Aquí en la tierra* ["Here On Earth"]); the second season of *Sitiados* ("Besieged," an epic series on the Spanish conquest of Chile); and *Me chama de Bruna* ("Call Me Bruna," a Brazilian real-life drama on the country's best known sex worker). Central here is what Cueva calls the "prodigious" comic series "about the Wall" by Gustavo Loza, *Run, Coyote, Run*. Indeed in the group photo of the event, the two stars of the series (the Mexican Harold Torres and Dutch Eivaut Rischen) are physically front and center, holding the letters "F" and "O" in an oversized hashtag: "#SOMOSFOX."

If we look back over the coverage in *Variety* of Fox's incursions into Latin America, we can sketch the industrial context of the emergence of this exceptional title. The reports are written by John Hopewell, a veteran specialist in Spanish-language media who was once the author of a scholarly book on post-Franco cinema. Hopewell's authoritative work thus blurs the boundary between journalistic commentary and scholarly research.

On December 1, 2016, Hopewell published "10 Things We Learned About Latin America's New TV Scene at Ventana Sur," a report on an inaugural market in Buenos Aires, organized by Argentina's film institute, INCAA (Hopewell 2016). Hopewell's main theme is that: "Hollywood studios, behemoth broadcasters, [and] telecoms [are] pil[ing] into original series in Latin America." And the event reconfirms academic studies on the new power of content producers, even when facing up to behemoths. A Fox executive says that, after the "revolution" in platforms, "We're fighting to get to you," the "creative community." At this "historic moment," new platforms require content that is new in both genre and tone. While local giants like Televisa continue to produce many traditional telenovelas, foreign distributors favor short-run series of just 10–60 episodes. And, in Hopewell's phrase, "black is the new pink," as noirish thrillers replace romances in the "new TV market heartland" of Mexico, Brazil, and Colombia. The continent's indie production sector is, however, "very young" and unfunded. In this new, untried context, *Run, Coyote, Run* is cited as a "highlight," "a key new TV series in development."

Six months later, on June 26, 2017, Hopewell offers "Fifteen Takeaways from Conecta Fiction," the inaugural meeting on coproduction between Latin American and Europe – fiction (Hopewell 2017a). Now that American programming is relatively unpopular in Latin America, US studios, writes Hopewell, need a "way back into primetime and new SVOD [subscription video on demand] exposure via novel windowing." Fox Networks Group is here called a "pioneering studio producer in Latin America." While its strategy a decade back was "to produce for the whole region," now (says its SVP for development), "competition has obliged FNG to make higher risk, higher-quality product, with higher production values; [and] very significant cable TV penetration has allowed us to focus more on local markets." *Run, Coyote, Run* (described as a "rambunctious Gringo-Mexican buddy comedy, which comes in at immigration from a novel angle") is thus "targeting Mexico 100%." Yet in this transition in Latin America to "upscale pay-TV market-style fiction," odds remain low for indie producers: Fox Producciones Originales, its Spanish-language arm, received 1900 admissions for its call for applications. It chose to go forward with only two. The proliferation of windows thus leads to a huge majority of unmade projects, the very definition of an "anticommons."

On October 14, 2017, Hopewell continued his coverage with "Latin American TV Sees Burst of Activity" (Hopewell 2017b). Here we read that "galvanized by Netflix," "OTT [over the top] is blooming and SVOD will double." And while "Hollywood studios need to protect their established pay-TV operations and want part of Latin America's OTT cake," even conservative local media factories are "overhauling drama production." Mexico's heritage broadcaster TV Azteca is going in for "socially-relevant dramas," while Televisa has "opened up to foreign formats." Platform changes thus drive content changes, forcing companies to diversify: the key example here is once more Fox's *Run, Coyote, Run*, described as an "irreverent series."

Just three days later, Hopewell reported from Cannes' Mipcom ("the global market for entertainment content across all platforms") with an interview with the COO of Fox Networks Group Latin America on "Latin America's TV Drama Sea Change" (Hopewell 2017c). The executive here confirms the trends we have seen earlier: free-to-air series are shortening in response to audience demand ("People want to consume series faster"), but pay-TV formats are lengthening ("to engage with audiences longer"). Production values are higher, as are budgets. The production strategy is for local titles that can also be "pan-regional" ("part of the LatAm identity"), like *Sitiados*' version of the Conquest. Likewise Gael García's project is a "conscious effort to make a Latin American series which is premium," even as there is a battle for "premium talent" (directors, screenwriters) with experience in short-run series that remains rare in the region. Finally, for one Fox executive, *Run, Coyote, Run*, aired on FX Mexico, exemplifies these trends and connects with the new audience: its finale won 500% the primetime average on the channel and was the number one show on all channels in Mexico that night.

Having sketched the general industrial context of this "revolution," "burst of activity," or "sea change," we can now turn to examine the contradictory professional profiles of the rare talent that made Fox's premium content.

Professional Profiles: Gustavo Loza, Harold Torres, Luis Gerardo Méndez

Gustavo Loza is a writer-director-producer whose career (as charted in the press files held at Mexico City's Cineteca) embodies many of the tensions and contradictions in Mexico's audiovisual sector over some 15 years. His first fiction feature *Al otro lado* ("On the Other Side," 2004) was a worthy drama on the theme of immigration that already attracted the participation of prestigious Spanish star Carmen Maura. Adopting the middlebrow form of the network narrative (which we examined in a previous chapter) the film explores three cases of forced economic migration, based and shot in Mexico, Cuba, and Morocco, taking up the perspective of those left behind, including neglected children. *Al otro lado* thus pioneered the "trans-regional" content later sought by TV executives, focusing on an experience keenly felt both in

Mexico and beyond. Loza was supported in this ambition by international bodies such as UNICEF, which helped to promote his film (Calva 2005).

Yet the film and its successors received no nominations by the Mexican film academy for the national cinema awards, the Ariels. Loza was outspoken here and later in his contempt for the Mexican film establishment, claiming he would win an Oscar before he was awarded an Ariel (Aguilar 2012); and refusing to take part in the jury of Foprocine, the national quality film subsidy scheme which had refused to support his own projects (Hernández 2011). The polemic would continue through *La otra familia* ("The Other Family," 2011), based on another worthy and topical topic, in this case the adoption of a child neglected by his junkie mother by a caring middle-class gay couple (marriage equality had been approved by the local government of Mexico City on the day the shoot wrapped) (Huerta 2011). With *La otra familia* Loza was shut out of the Ariels once more and patronized by critics who accused him of exploiting "morbid curiosity" and seeking "fake polemics" and called attention to the telenovela credits of his photogenic cast (Aviña 2011). Loza again attacked the crony cinema establishment, claiming they relied on public subsidies to make films that were subsequently shown on just ten screens (Hernández 2011).

Parallel to this strand of issue-based drama, which anticipated the more edgy social content of pay-TV series in Mexico, Loza accumulated credits in comedy, to such an extent that he was crowned "king" of the genre (Orantes 2016). But even here, in an auteur touch, he continued his durable interest in child protagonists (after studying media studies at Mexico City's elite Iberoamericana University, he had taken courses in the direction of child actors). *Atlético San Pancho* ("Never Too Young to Dream," 2001) was a rare youth soccer comedy. *Paradas continuas* ("Stop and Go," 2009) was a farce based on the premise that two teenagers rent out their beaten-up minivan (identified by the Mexicanism "combi") for the peers to have illicit sex in. Even in this commission, Loza claims in interview that he introduced his own artistic contributions and references to Mexican film history (*Paradas continuas*' star Ramón Valdés was the grandchild of comedy legend Tin Tan) (Rodríguez Canales 2009). And the theme of intense male friendship would recur much later in *Run, Coyote, Run*.

Striking in this press coverage is the continuing hostility of critics, often TV motivated (the films are compared to a 90-minute sitcom), and Loza's defense of a commercial cinema that responds to changing audience demand (the same criterion will be invoked for the new TV series). And Loza continued his fusion of auteurist vision and commercial acumen with what became the biggest grossing Mexican film of all time, *¿Qué culpa tiene el niño?* ("Don't Blame the Kid," 2016). Here critics noted the plot's similarity with a classic title of Mexico's Golden Age, while still dismissing the film as "telenovela-like" (Aviña 2016). Yet the premise of the script, in which a rich professional woman falls pregnant after a drunken night with a younger working-class guy, addresses, albeit humorously, social issues which remain controversial such as abortion (recently legalized in Mexico City, once more) and persistent economic inequality.

In one aside, the dialogue of *¿Qué culpa tiene el niño?* even references the changes in the TV industry we have seen earlier. As Karla Souza (recently of US network drama *How to Get Away with Murder* [ABC, 2014–present]) lounges on the sofa, she insists to her working-class suitor that what she is watching on television is not a despised *novela* but a worthy *serie* ("series"). And, beyond his cinema credits, Loza had also built a parallel career in the new short-form genre favored by Mexican broadcasters that sought to renew their schedules, even as they clung to telenovela in prime time. *Los Héroes del Norte* ("Heroes of the North") was a regional musical comedy for Televisa that lasted for three seasons, was of 16–18 episodes, and starred Miguel Rodarte (2010–13); family sitcom *40 y 20* (named for the respective ages of an amorous father and son and graced, as we saw in chapter four, by *vedette* Wanda Seux) ran late night on Televisa also for just nine episodes in 2016; *Sincronía* ("Synchronicity," also 2016), treated in the last chapter of this book, used the greater freedom of Televisa's OTT platform Blim to produce a formally complex and socially charged network narrative, very different in tone to Loza's comic projects, whether on film or in television.

What is important here is that Loza had constructed an ideal profile for the new digital TV services. He had experience with the higher budgets and production values of feature film, which had now migrated to television. And his combination of edgy social issues (the "LatAm experience") and audience awareness (despised by the film establishment he criticized) was one sought by US corporations anxious to reconnect with local Mexican audiences by making ambitious but accessible fare. As he shot *Run, Coyote, Run* (one of the tiny number of pitched projects approved by the distributor), he was well placed to embody the "revolution" or "sea change" in Latin American TV series that was charted so minutely by John Hopewell in *Variety*.

Crucial here also was Loza's star, Harold Torres, whose professional profile deserves study. During the period that Loza was elaborating a pathway between art and commerce, Torres was acting, ironically enough, in the low-budget auteur films that Loza attacks. Indeed Torres admitted that his first films played in theaters for no longer than two weeks (Franco Reyes 2010). Torres has been long associated as an actor with *Run, Coyote, Run*'s key theme of emigration. He came to fame with *Norteado* ("Northless," Rigoberto Perezcano, 2009), in which he starred as a young migrant shyly romancing two Mexican women as he made fitful and unsuccessful attempts to cross the border. *Sin nombre* (Cary Fukunaga, 2009), where he played a supporting role, was another high-profile festival film on migration.

Torres' dark complexion and mestizo features problematize casting in commercial film and TV, where racist exclusion is still endemic. Indeed, to its credit, *Run, Coyote, Run* also cast, as Torres' sister-in-law and intermittent love interest, Maya Zapata, an actress who has publicly complained that dark-skinned women like herself ("prietas") are never given leading roles (Acuña and Limón 2018). Torres himself has even played indigenous characters. In the dramatized documentary *Hernán Cortés, un hombre entre Dios y el diablo* ("A Man Between God and the Devil" [2016], made for educational Canal Once), he depicted Moctezuma, complete with Nahua dialogue. In *La carga* ("The Burden," Alan Jonsson) the same year, he played a Tameme Indian who bore on his back a Spanish lady of the sixteenth century.

Such dignified historical roles were combined with boundary-pushing contemporary indie dramas, often prize-winning and on edgy themes. *Plan sexenial* ("Sexennial Plan," Santiago Cendejas, 2014) was a frankly bizarre urban dystopia, shot with gaudy-colored filters (2014). *Oso polar* ("Polar Bear," Marcelo Tobar, 2017) was the first mainstream Mexican feature shot on an iPhone (it won best film at the Morelia International Film Festival, Mexico's most respected event). And in publicity shots for short-run series *Crónica de castas* ("Chronicle of Castes," 2014), once more for minority Canal Once, where he played a humble taxi driver in love with a wealthy *criolla* woman, he even posed with the word "mestizo" written in scarlet letters on his forehead.

From his earliest interviews Torres stresses his professional ambitions, linked to a desire to transcend a working-class background and resist a racist society. Thus on being quizzed on the release of the breakthrough *Norteado* (for which he was nominated for a best actor Ariel award), he already avowed to a daily paper his desire to direct (Franco Reyes 2010). (To date, as we saw in the first chapter of this book, he has only produced one feature called *González* [2013], on the typically controversial topic of an evangelical churchman cum conman.) In one later lengthy interview with a news magazine, Torres stresses the cultural differences between him and his peers at the acting school where he claims to have been disadvantaged by his poor-quality public education; attacks celebrities who lend "only their signature" to political causes; and bemoans the social prejudice which remains interwoven with racial hatred in Mexico (Maillard 2015).

It is striking that Torres' Twitter feed (@HaroldTorres9), unlike those of other Mexican actors who prefer to promote their current projects, is composed almost entirely of Leftist political themes, such as the missing students of Ayotzinapa and the PRI government's project for an Internal Security Law. Indeed, unlike his costar, Torres did not post pictures on social media of the Miami event at which he so prominently helped hold the hashtag #SOMOSFOX, suggesting a certain unease with a commitment he was no doubt contractually obliged to appear at.

We might compare Torres' star profile with another actor of his generation who followed a different path to the same end, that of combining critical acclaim in indie cinema with mass popularity in a sitcom for a new platform. Luis Gerardo Méndez raises similar questions to Torres about cultural distinction and commercial connections, thus embodying broad changes in the Mexican audiovisual field, even as his persona (like that of all stars) remains unique.

Unlike Torres, Méndez's light skin and European features made it easier for him to score mainstream roles, in spite of his somewhat scrawny physique and angular face. But from the start of his career he alternated between mainstream and independent projects. Thus in the same year of 2008 he appeared as a semi-recurring character in both Eugenio Derbez's domestic sitcom *Vecinos* ("Neighbors," Televisa) and a low-budget independent film also with an apartment-share premise, Jesús Mario Lozano's *Más allá de mí* ("Beyond Myself"). Generally in television, however, he scored more prestigious titles and edgy roles in limited series. He had a starring turn in one episode of Televisa's gory real-life drama *Mujeres asesinas* ("Women Murderers," 2009) as the incestuous stepbrother to a murderer and a supporting role in the broadcaster's historical drama made for the bicentennial of Independence, *Gritos de muerte y libertad* ("Cries of Death and Freedom," 2010).

But where Torres specialized in working-class and ethnically marked characters, Méndez went for the sexually charged. He had a minor part in Gustavo Loza's gay-themed feature *La otra familia* (mentioned earlier in this chapter) and a larger one in the quality TV drama *XY* of Canal Once (2009–12), on the decline of the Mexican macho. Here Méndez's dramatic and nuanced story arc was of an openly gay man, less saintly than those in Loza, who has a lasting and plausibly depicted affair with a conservative, Catholic married man.

It was the very next year, however, that Méndez had his first great commercial success in the blockbuster film farce, *Nosotros los Nobles* ("The Noble Family," Gary Alazraki, 2013). Méndez's turn here as a *mirrey* or entitled kid who is reduced suddenly to poverty coincided with real-life internet memes on what was perceived as the new phenomenon of the idle, boorish rich (the female equivalents were christened "Ladies"). His commercial roles thus began to connect with the social and cinematic zeitgeist. Soon Méndez became an engaging regular in crowd-pleasing romantic comedies such as in *Cásese quien pueda* ("Marry If You Can," Marco Polo Costandse, 2014), where he played a shyly reluctant suitor of two sisters, played by Martha Higareda and her real-life sibling. Yet still Méndez remained a persistent presence in little seen and idiosyncratic independent films. In *Camino a Marte* ("Road to Mars," Humberto Hinojosa Oscariz, 2017), he played a disturbed drifter who claims to be an extraterrestrial.

Most relevant here, however, is Méndez's lengthy starring role in *Club de Cuervos* ("Crows Club," Netflix, 2015–17), first conceived by its showrunner Gary Alazraki as a sequel to the pair's film comedy *Nosotros los Nobles*. Like *Run, Coyote, Run, Coyote*, then, *Club de Cuervos* was the first Mexican-made title by a major US platform, in this case Netflix. And like *Run, Coyote, Run*, once more it was a multi-camera comedy with no laughter track that pushed the envelope of the genre in Mexico with location shooting and edgy topics. By comparison the studio-set *Vecinos* is at once obvious in its plotting and crude in its characterization.

Méndez's comedy persona as a shortsighted and selfish but likable and relatable klutz was thus leavened by his smart-acting chops in independent film and quality television series. And it made him, much more so than the more reserved Torres, inescapable in Mexican multimedia. In stubbly beard and black leather jacket, he was the ubiquitous spokesperson for a mobile phone company, Nextel. And, in a more challenging role, he alternated with Diego Luna in 2017 in the prestigious one-man theater play *Privacidad* ("Privacy") at Mexico City's hallowed Teatro Insurgentes.

It is striking that, like the much younger Polo Morín, Méndez survived a gay sex scandal, supported by colleagues (including Morín himself) who claimed to be outraged at the invasion of his privacy. Méndez was taped in real life setting up a threesome with his boyfriend and a young male stranger (León 2017), ironically enough even as he was performing in the play on the very theme of invasion of privacy. It was a situation similar to those his horny and clueless character had suffered in *Club de Cuervos* and could not be further from Harold Torres' more earnest image of social responsibility, even as Torres exploits his smoldering good looks.

If we look back, briefly, at Méndez's press profile, we see the unique configuration of his star image interacting with the same changes in the Mexican audiovisual field that also impacted Torres' career. In 2010 daily *Excelsior* ran an early interview already titled "Controversial" (Guerrero 2010). The strapline claimed that the actor liked "challenges" as when he had played a "homosexual." Méndez himself states here that he received an unusual tribute to his skills as an actor who sought above all to evoke "empathy" in his audience: respectable "married ladies" had approached him to say that they hoped his gay character on *XY* would find happiness with his partner. Méndez named nude scenes as another professional challenge he had had to confront.

In the same newspaper some three years later, Méndez claimed that he "never saw [him]self as a matinee idol [*galán*]" (Méndez 2013). Although he always thought his physique precluded pretty boy ("cara bonita") roles, it did give him other opportunities. Even as a teenager when he aimed to be an actor, he was told that he wasn't blond or hunky enough. Méndez presents himself rather as a professional, honing his craft at CasAzul, the acting school of independent TV producer Argos. There he was told that "pretty faces" lasted only a season, while real actors were forever. He thus focused on what made him unique and on his body as an "instrument" of his craft. That was a continuation, he says, of the personal struggle he waged with the skeptical high school friends so long ago. And it was, he continues, only after working for ten years that he was rewarded with a leading role (in *Nosotros los Nobles*).

This personal history of struggle links to a certain social concern, but different to that of Torres. The following year Méndez tells daily *El Universal* of his love for the "marvelous territory" inhabited by Mexicans who should "believe" in their country. The context, however, is that he is shooting publicity spots for tourism to the state of Michoacán, long troubled by drug-related violence. He has been asked to serve as the official "image," even though he has no personal connection to the state, beyond appearances at the Morelia International Film Festival (León 2014). There could be no clearer sign that he was now held to be an attractive and respected everyman to his fellow citizens who, he urged, should not "turn their back" on a failed state.

This kind of apparently public spirited promotional work, more ambiguous than Harold Torres' more direct political opinions, is combined here with a new claim to the creative freedom of production. Méndez was not only the undisputed star of *Club de Cuervos* when Karla Souza dropped out of the series but was also granted for the first time an associate producer credit (Contreras 2015). And he was laying claim to a newly active role in his career. As Netflix's series premiered, Méndez said he was "suffocated by success" and would henceforth spurn commercial film projects for more "dark, independent scripts" (Cabrera 2015). Yet he had recently been proclaimed the "King Midas" of comedy (Castillo 2014), a title he shared with his one-time director Gustavo Loza.

Luis Gerardo Méndez's star profile reveals, then, as in the case of Harold Torres, a unique physique and mentality marked by sexual and psychological factors in the first case and ethnic and class markers in the second. Such previously unattractive characteristics could now be linked for the first time to commercial success and traditional stardom (to leading roles as a "galán") via the new contents now offered by the new platforms. These were quality comedies that, unlike the cruder features made in the same genre for movie theaters, were welcomed by both elite critics and general audiences. Méndez and Torres are thus clear examples of Dyer's "structured polysemy" in which stars' personae take on different meanings for different demographics, even as their images interact unpredictably with technological change.

To return to Harold Torres, it would appear that the perennially serious cinephile actor was an unlikely candidate for Loza's raucous TV comedy. But Torres came usefully, as we have seen, with a lengthy backstory of working-class roles and a mestizo phenotype that contrasted with his costar (the pale and heavily accented American played by a Dutch actor). Equally importantly Torres brought with him to this new TV series for a new platform the cultural distinction associated with the cinema establishment from which Loza himself had been excluded. Perhaps, then, the true bromance was not between the characters (childhood friends called Gamaliel and Morris), but between a successful but disrespected director and a reputed but hitherto uncommercial actor. We can now go on to see how this alliance, at once artistic and industrial, played out in the first season of Fox's first Mexican series.

Run, Coyote, Run: The First Season

On the day that *Run, Coyote, Run* took its bow on Fox, Leftist daily *La Jornada* (a somewhat unlikely supporter) ran a piece on the new series, calling it a "comedy that tackles migration and human trafficking" (Run Coyote Run 2017) (Illustration 7.1). The anonymous journalist calls the series a "caustic reflection" on the border. The protagonists are Harold Torres' Mexican Gamaliel (who hails from the town in Sonora that is in both the series and real life improbably called Naco ["tacky," "trashy"]) and Eivaut Rischen's druggy slacker Morris (described somewhat optimistically as an "anti-Yankee who denies his origin and hates the capitalist system"). The two transnational buddies set up an agency specializing in "adventure tourism" as a cover for a people smuggling operation. Director Loza is aware that this is a "delicate theme for many Latin Americans" but claims that it is treated "from a sensitive place."

Illustration 7.1 Harold Torres (left) in *Run, Coyote, Run* (Fox Networks Group Latin America, 2017–present)

A representative of Fox Networks Group Latin America adds that the series is a "homage to … the search to cross all kinds of walls, whether real or imaginary" and praises the "contradictory but charming characters" that she hopes will make a "deep connection with our audiences."

On December 10, 2017, when his project had won Best Fiction Series at the Pantalla de Cristal awards, Gustavo Loza finessed this topic and treatment, describing himself as a "producer-director who wants to encounter the public" and as the "teller of stories that … portray… issues of vital importance to Mexico such as the border with the United States" ("Personaje de la semana" 2017). In keeping with the professional setting in which his remarks were made (industry journal *Revista Pantalla*), Loza also stressed his personal supervision of all aspects of production and postproduction (script, sound, cinematography, music), and underlined the significance of the bilingual name of the series for the show's cross-cultural premise: the repeated English word "run" "wraps up" or "encloses" ("envolver") the Spanish word (the show's dialogue actually uses the Mexican "pollero" ["chicken seller"] for people smuggler, rather than the more Anglo-friendly "coyote").

Press coverage, then, tracked the tricky tone of the piece: a short-run fictional comedy about a long-running real tragedy. And it appealed to Loza's unique profile as a socially concerned dramatist who also makes audience-friendly comedies. This aligned the "marquee" series (the most prominent of the year in its continent) with Fox's aim to make premium content for the new audience of pay-TV and apps. It is significant that Loza, who, as we saw, was consistently attacked by heritage film critics, can forge here in the context of new media platforms a plausible connection even with the strongly anti-Yankee and anti-capitalist readers of *La Jornada*.

7 New Platforms, New Contents: *Run, Coyote, Run*

Publicity material for the series, initially at least, seems more crude. Images, silkscreened with Warhol style day-glow colors, depict the two friends and their cronies apparently urinating against the Wall. The Trump-alluding tagline is bluntly bilingual once more: "Bad wall, good hombres." And each episode treats a separate social issue, of varied plausibility, through a new character who seeks to be smuggled across the border (a further tagline read "Pasa de todo," both "Anything goes" and "Everything goes over"). The pilot portrays through flashback the buddies' lifelong friendship, which is facilitated by a baseball thrown over the Wall. The second episode treats an unfortunate tiger whose stomach is stuffed with drugs (this too-familiar narco theme goes unstressed in the series as a whole); the third a fugitive Mexican politician (from the distant state of Veracruz, which is in real life notoriously corrupt); the seventh an elderly and ailing deportee from the USA, who no longer feels that Mexico is his home; the eighth an African dictator, also on the run from the police; and the ninth a mediocre Mexican boxer whose own manager is betting against him at the big match scheduled in Las Vegas.

A wide range of subthemes are thus added to the main trope of people smuggling, focusing especially on corruption. And the tone shifts radically between episodes that are only minimally serialized (only the last sequence is a bridge linking to the next installment). Much play is given to both solemn sentiment (the elderly deportee who, finally and with the friends' help, makes it back to his family in Arizona) and crazy comedy (the fugitive politician, who is cruelly hoodwinked and humiliated by the friends as he seeks in vain to cross the border).

Loza also quietly signals his auteurism through the casting of guest stars whose careers he had already nurtured. Cute heartthrob Ricardo Abarca, the naïve boxer, was the winning male lead in *¿Qué culpa tiene el niño?*, where he was, as here, frequently shirtless. Denia Agalianou, the novice actress playing a Slavic exotic dancer in episode 6, took a similar, albeit more tragic, role as an immigrant sex worker in *Sincronía*, Loza's grim experimental drama for Blim.

But the recurring nudity in the series (frequently female and occasionally male) signals a treatment of gender and, indeed, race that might prove problematic for some audiences. The boys tend to neglect their underwritten girlfriends for a continuing bilingual bromance that features lengthy expletive-ridden and beer-sodden dialogues in diners and on couches. And they are provided with a cowardly, grinning African sidekick whose depiction is worrisome. But elsewhere the series' humor is more caustic and politically charged where sex and nationality are concerned. For example, the corrupt mayor of Naco, who boasts a Hitler-style mustache, kills off his homely Mexican wife when advised that his political ambitions would be better served by a more photogenic consort (he chooses one of the scantily dressed Russian girls at his deceased spouse's wake). The reference is to the then-current first lady of Mexico, an ex-telenovela actress.

Beyond subject matter, and in keeping with the revolution or sea change in US-sponsored Latin American series (not to mention their increased budgets), *Run, Coyote, Run* is consistently expert in its aesthetic. Handsome landscape shots show the tiny figures and their beaten-up station wagon dwarfed by the immensity of the Sonora Desert's plains and mountains (Harold Torres' first starring vehicle *Norteado* had used a similar technique). Frequent aerial shots reveal the hated Wall (actually a fence) marching relentlessly through the arid landscape. The extensive use of authentic locations, including fly-blown Naco itself, with only interiors shot on sets in Mexico City, lends a potent reality effect to even the crudest plot points and distances this short-run series visually from the telenovelas still taped in Televisa's overlit studios. The locations in Las Vegas, where the impoverished principals get to stay in a casino hotel, are especially lush, brimming with forbidden pleasures unimaginable in humble Naco.

At a more basic and inescapable level, the on-screen contrast between dark-skinned Torres (who is, as previously mentioned, one of the tiny number of mestizo-featured actors to have made a successful career in Mexico) with the pale, blond Rischen makes an unspoken point about cohabitation in the border zone. Twin protagonists who happily (raucously) share Loza's very mobile frame, they mutely refute the supposed incompatibilities of two cultures, two nations. It is a visual contrast that is orally reinforced by the couple's code-switching dialogue.

Run, Coyote, Run aired on pay-channel Fox Mexico at 10 p.m. on Mondays (in other Latin American territories, perhaps even less tolerant than Mexico of profanity and nudity, it showed at midnight). But the series was also posted to Claro Video's app for a la carte viewing. And its leisurely plotting confirms the formal changes in series that were charted by academic commentators in an age of binge watching. There is little use of cliffhanger or recap (as mentioned earlier, there are minimal links between episodes). And the characters, even if they employ crude language that remains inadmissible on broadcast TV, boast enough psychological complexity to satisfy new, quality viewers. The first season's ratings success suggests it achieved the desired degree of emotional and cognitive participation on the part of such fee-paying audiences, as was hoped for by both its creator and his executive paymasters. If we look now at a couple of specimen episodes, we can see how urgent social issues and high production values combine to form a new national narrative for a TV platform that was newly investing in Mexico:

Specimen Episodes 1.3 La ley fuga ("Fugitive from the Law," first broadcast May 22, 2017); 1.9 Sin límite de tiempo ("No Time Limit," first broadcast July 3, 2017).

> A fleeing Mexican politician, – one of those rare cases – is wanted for a millionaire fraud in his state, so he wants to cross the border to the United States and disappear – Gama and Morris will make sure he never forgets his journey across the border.
> A Mexican boxer who's a contender to the world title, but who's flat broke; has two days to make it to Las Vegas where's he's scheduled to fight, otherwise he'll miss a chance of a lifetime. (Plot synopses from IMDb)

Two contrasting episodes, one toward the start of the season, one toward the end, dramatize the national and international conflicts implied in *Run, Coyote, Run*'s border theme. They also exemplify their director Loza's tricky mix of sociopolitical reference and comic relief and FX's quest for new content whose characters and narratives connect with the viewers for their new platform.

Episode 3 is set and shot almost entirely in Mexico (exteriors in the real-life Sonora township of Naco, convincing interiors on sets in Mexico City studios). The premise of a former governor from the state of Veracruz, accused of corruption and embezzlement and on the run from the law, is a quite specific reference to then-current Mexican politics. In real life Javier Duarte was arrested in Guatemala in April 2017, just one month before the episode aired. And the short, rotund actor cast as the fictional politician in the series bears a close resemblance to his original. When he comes calling at the friends' makeshift "adventure travel agency" (which boasts a dartboard with the face of Donald Trump), dressed in his shiny suit, the stage will be set for a cruel comedy of deception based on poetic justice.

Thus, after bargaining somewhat ineptly with their customer and assigning him squalid digs far from his accustomed luxury lodgings, Gamaliel and Morris promise the politician a "premium service," perhaps analogous to that Fox Networks Group Latin America offers to its moneyed audience. In this case it is a subterranean border crossing through a narco tunnel under the Wall. (The scary narco boss, who briefly kidnaps the politician, is played here, as in prize-winning art movie *Miss Bala* [Gerardo Naranjo, 2011], by the convincingly sinister Noé Hernández.) Once the ex-governor is safely underground, the friends keep him, increasingly desperate, confined there for some time.

The boys' habitual banter turns explicitly political in this episode. The American Morris claims that Mexican politicians are the most thieving ("rateros") of all; Gamaliel replies (in lines that could well be voiced by Harold Torres, the Leftist actor who plays him) that Mexico is a rich country and the political class should give back to the people the money they have stolen from them. This ideological argument is later embodied in a subplot. A further potential customer arrives at the agency, a young pregnant woman, underplayed with some dignity by an unknown actor. She says that she needs to cross over as she has been abandoned by the child's father and there is no work for her in her native village. In a pointed coincidence, she is also from Veracruz. The ex-governor, now released from the tunnel, is unabashed, telling her that "people are only poor because they don't want to work." But the boys force him to pay the expectant mother to stay in Mexico (thus literally giving back some of the money he has stolen from the people) and finally betray him to the US authorities as soon as they have taken him across the border.

This wish fulfillment of social justice and chivalric care for the unmarried mother are rather undercut by some gratuitous bare-breasted dancing in the club that is a frequent location in Naco and by the macho main characters' continuing neglect of their own female partners. But the explicit political references reveal that Fox's new series (blandly presented by the network as a "search to transcend walls, whether real or metaphorical") can embrace an explicit and direct critique of Mexico's then-ruling PRI party on the eve of an election year. And, ironically enough, that Mexican Leftist critique is made more effective by the high production values and prestigious guest stars permitted by a US media platform.

My second specimen episode takes place mainly on the other side of the border, with extensive location shooting in Las Vegas. "Sin límite de tiempo" ("No Time Limit," a reference to a boxing bout that continues until there is a final result) begins with a vertigo-inducing aerial shot of the endless inspections taking place at a border crossing point. It is a dizzying vantage point that will recur when the boys are lodged in their skyscraping resort hotel. Back on earth (and in everyday Naco) the episode begins with the manager and boxer (identified by the affectionate or dismissive diminutive "Bombardito") bargaining once more for a border crossing, this time to fight at the World Championship.

The cute but dumb Bombardito is played, as mentioned earlier, by Ricardo Abarca, whose career as a romantic hero had climaxed with his endearing role as a loyal working-class suitor in Loza's box office smash ¿Qué culpa tiene el niño? This means that, although the pay-TV audience's socioeconomic status is more likely to be aligned with Karla Souza's *fresa* (rich kid) character in the film, they are predisposed to be sympathetic to Abarca's underdog. His status here as sex object for female and gay male viewers is signaled not just by the shirtless fight scenes that are necessary to the plot but by a gratuitous sequence in which he strips naked in public to make the weight grade (the treacherous coach has been encouraging him to overeat and underexercise). And for once the boys' neglected girlfriends, initially left behind in Naco, get to join with their partners in the fun.

Here the corruption motif, which is arguably as pervasive in the series as the border crossing premise, is reinscribed within the entertainment industry (sport as spectacle) and the family (the double-dealing coach is the uncle of the boxer). And the fact that the coach is betting against his own charge suggests once more that (as in the case of the politician in the earlier episode) that it is perhaps not Americans but Mexicans who are their own worst enemies.

When the boys discover the coach's treachery, they have a long argument with him in the dressing room that is pointedly staged in front of a large Mexican flag. The flag even lingers in shot when the characters leave the frame. As in the earlier case of the Trump-faced dartboard, mise-en-scène is thus used to reinforce the national or nationalist theme. Morris' mangled use here of a Mexican idiom, "Hay alambres en tu pájaro," provides an auditory equivalent of this transnational commentary. Appropriately enough the original phrase is the equivalent of the English "walls have ears."

As in my earlier episode, this plot provides plentiful wish fulfillment for local viewers. The plucky Mexican, in an unequal fight with a lethal American known as "Killer," rallies nonetheless to defeat his opponent on points. It is a well-staged bout crosscut once more with aerial shots of the spectacular, but in this context forbidding and intimidating, skyscrapers of Las Vegas. While "La ley en fuga" reenacted a case of exemplary justice served on a corrupt politician within Mexico, "Sin límite de tiempo" celebrates a performance of Mexican prowess across the border, a performance in which cast and audience alike cheer on their attractive but disadvantaged stand-in. It is a dynamic explicitly acknowledged by creator Loza himself. In a report in *Milenio* on the shooting of the series' second season, he is quoted as saying that the public likes to get "revancha" even in fiction. It is a word that, appropriately enough, can be translated as both "revenge" and "rematch" or "return fight" (Ampudia 2018).

The title of this report by *Milenio*, which suggests the tricky tone of Loza's and Fox's premium content, is "Abordan con humor la cruda realidad de la frontera" ("They tackle the harsh reality of the border with humor"). It is a tense mix we have seen already in the director's professional profile as both earnest dramatist and accomplished comedian. And it would seem to coincide also with the US producer-distributor's aim for boundary-pushing but entertaining fiction in the industrial context of Latin America's "revolution" or "sea change" in series. But how, finally, can we relate the textual detail and audience reception of *Run, Coyote, Run* to the theoretical survey of new platforms with which I began this chapter?

Digital Territories

On February 9, 2018, Gustavo Loza tweeted (@gusloza) a photo of a section of the border wall customized with the colors of the Mexican flag and bearing a defiant slogan written in black on the central white section: "Bad Muro." His ironic caption, adorned with a heart emoticon, was "From MX with love" [@gusloza]. It was typical of his series' attempt to engage with actuality in a graphically stylized way.

A survey of the hashtag #runcoyoterun over the previous month, however, suggested that the new consumers for his series were not especially active. The overwhelming majority of tweets are from profiles on the production side: actors, including celebrity guest stars gracing the second season; the Spanish-language trade and general press; and the distributor Fox itself, across Latin American territories. There is some minor evidence, however, for the involvement of actors in social media (star Harold Torres offers a shout out to fans from the set @LaDarksVader February 2, 2018) and for viewer's extension of the series to real life: fan @DamSaRo posts a news video of US border agents destroying food and water left for migrants and comments that this wouldn't happen if they had crossed with the (fictional) Morris and Gama.

While the series' reception offers little sign of the authentic, horizontal, and creative participation of audiences, it does contradict Bustamante's account for Spain of the reduced cultural diversity and ideological pluralism after the transition to digital terrestrial television (which Mexico had also experienced). Indeed Maya Zapata, the actress who protested the treatment of mestiza actresses like herself by traditional Mexican TV, told trendy *Chilango* magazine that *Run, Coyote, Run* (described as "the most successful series in Latin America") was "reinventing" Mexican television, that the local audiences wants "new formats and stories", and that they deserve the same "quality television" that countries enjoy (Pacheco 2017). While Mexico has little tradition of public service TV like that of Europe, it did not reveal the growing poverty of contents allegedly experienced in Spain after the analogue blackout, in spite of the vertical integration of Fox and its rivals HBO and Netflix as joint producers and distributors. To the contrary, new formats and genres, previously unavailable, suddenly sprung up.

With its transnational premise and code-switching speech, *Run, Coyote, Run* echoes Orozco's proposal of a global dialogue in the field of communication and education. And, in spite of the crudity of much of its physical and verbal comedy, it clearly addresses Martínez's ethical and vital considerations for digital media, with episodes critiquing the corruption of the rich and promoting compassion for the poor. It could thus be read as both a cause and an effect of Grijalva's "media competence" in raising the audiovisual education levels of citizens. This is true both of *Run, Coyote, Run*'s treatment of themes little seen on free-to-air television and in its relatively challenging aesthetic, which strays far outside the reassuring limits of telenovela to which Mexican audiences were so accustomed.

As Mikos suggested, then, media convergence demanded that TV broadcasting companies adjust their content to various platforms (*Run, Coyote, Run*, we remember, was shown on Claro Video's app as well as Fox's pay-TV channel). Showrunner Loza did this by creating a relative narrative complexity and psychological ambiguity that produced an immersive experience integrated into everyday lives and adapted to viewers' circumstances. The cast takes the lead here once more: one actress uses the #RunCoyoteRun hashtag to chronicle an unrelated bowling outing with friends (@EmmaEscalante February 10, 2018). As Guignard wrote, Fox and Claro Video's new platform matches production to consumption, creating a new mass audience for what might once have been niche content.

Some 67% of Mexican households now have access to pay-TV (Orozco 2018, 24). Nicita and Rossin's fears of restricted access to premium audiovisual contents in Europe and "tragedies of the anticommons" thus seem little justified for the case of Mexico, even if creatives pitch many more projects than the new broadcasters are willing to develop. Moreover, broadening access for poorer audiences without reliable internet, *Run, Coyote, Run* was also available on the additional "window" of pirate DVD, although when I enquired about a copy from one *ambulante* (street seller) in Mexico City, he told me the series was "not commercial." If such "premium contents" are "experience goods," then that experience may well still be restricted by both social class and cultural capital, even for this raucous proletarian-set comedy.

Multiplatform-distributed, *Run, Coyote, Run* helped, as Guerrero suggested, to create a prestigious brand in a Mexico that was culturally nationalist and anti-American. Its fans are aware that *Run, Coyote, Run* plays alongside such challenging English-language FX titles as *The Assassination of Gianni Versace* (@oswaldozarate January 19, 2018). And Gustavo Loza bears comparison with *Versace*'s Ryan Murphy as a TV showrunner with auteurist credibility.

Finally, then, as Arango-Forero writes, technology goes beyond a simple evolution to help create a new audience mediated by new cultural texts. The gap between the traditional telenovela still stripped in primetime by Televisa and FX's innovative short-run series is wide indeed, in both form and content. Certainly the explicit political commentary of Loza's series (like its vulgar language and nudity) remains unimaginable on broadcast TV. Ironically, then, *Run, Coyote, Run*, made by the private broadcaster which is most reviled in the USA because of a hyper-partisan news channel that has no equivalent in Mexico, took on a national dimension, playing the pedagogical, political, social, and cultural roles that were attributed by Bustamante to public service television. Moreover, by staging a border drama, the series internalized that increasingly fluid movement between the local and the global which characterizes the current television fiction ecology in Mexico and beyond.

References

Acuña, Carlos, and Mariana Limón. 2018. Mosaico del racismo chilango. *Chilango*, February 6. http://www.chilango.com/ciudad/racismo-en-mexico-cdmx/7/. Accessed 28 July 2018.

Aguilar, Pamela. 2012. Loza asegura que primero llega el Oscar que el Ariel. *La Razón*, May 3. Entretenimientos: 2.

Ampudia, Libertad. 2018. Abordan con humor la cruda realidad de la frontera. *Milenio*, January 20: 36.

Arango-Forero, Germán, and Sergio Roncallo-Dow. 2013. Social Media and the New Audiences as a New Challenge for Traditional and New Media Industries. In *Handbook of Social Media Management*, ed. M. Friedrichsen and W. Mühl-Benninghaus, 635–655. Berlin: Springer.

Aviña, Rafael. 2011. Polémica light. *Reforma*, March 25. Primera Fila: 6.

———. 2016. Comedia telenovelera. *Reforma*, May 13. Primera Fila: 6.

Buonanno, Milly, ed. 2016. (Not Yet) the End of Television. Special Issue of *Media and Communication* 4 (3).

Bustamante, Enrique. 2010. Quality Contents in the New Audiovisual Structure. *Infoamérica* 3 (4): 137–154.

Cabrera, Mario. 2015. Sofocado por el éxito. *Reforma*, April 25. Sección Gente: 6.

Calva, Araceli. 2005. La UNICEF se pone de su 'lado'. *Milenio*, May 4: 2.

Castillo, Ana Luisa. 2014. Luis Gerardo Méndez: un rey Midas. *Excelsior*, March 13. Sección Teve: 52.

Contreras, Stephanny. 2015. Produce Méndez Club de Cuervos. *Reforma*, January 15. Sección Gente: 6.

Cueva, Álvaro. 2018. El evento de Fox. *Milenio*, January 18: 45.

"Decepciona." 2012. "Decepciona la Academia de cine a Gustavo Loza." *El Sol de México*, April 27. Espectáculos: 8–10.

Franco Reyes, Salvador. 2010. Suertudo en el cine. *Excelsior*, April 5. Función: 13.

Friedrichsen, Mike, and Wolfgang Mühl-Benninghaus. 2013. *Handbook of Social Media Management*. Berlin/Heidelberg: Springer.

Gómez Martínez, Pedro Javier, and Miguel Ángel Poveda Criado. 2013. Nuevos contenidos y nuevos métodos en narrativa audiovisual. *Estudios sobre el Mensaje Periodístico* 19: 223–232.

Grijalva Verdugo, Abel A., and Rosario Olivia Izaguirre Fierro. 2014. Media Consumption Patterns and Communicative Competence of University Students. *Global Media Journal* 7 (3): 23–39.

Guerrero, Jovann. 2010. Luis Gerardo Méndez: controvertido. *Excelsior*, April 15. Sección Teve: 14–15.

Guerrero, Enrique, Patricia Diego, and Alejandro Pardo. 2013. Distributing Audiovisual Contents in the New Digital Scenario: Multiplatform Strategies of the Main Spanish TV Networks. In *Handbook of Social Media Management*, ed. M. Friedrichsen and W. Mühl-Benninghaus, 349–373. Berlin: Springer.

Guignard, Thomas. 2014. Digital Intermediaries and Cultural Industries: The Developing Influence of Distribution Platforms. *Media Critiques* 1 (3): 43–53.

Hernández, Minerva. 2011. Rechaza Loza al Foprocine. *Reforma*, April 27: 2.

Hopewell, John. 2016. 10 Things We Learned About Latin America's New TV Scene at Ventana Sur. *Variety*, December 1. https://variety.com/2016/film/festivals/10-points-latin-america-new-fiction-tv-production-scene-1201931113/. Accessed 28 July 2018.

———. 2017a. Fifteen Takeaways from Conecta Fiction. *Variety*, June 26. http://variety.com/2017/tv/markets-festivals/15-takeaways-conecta-fiction-1202478193/. Accessed 28 July 2018.

———. 2017b. Latin American TV Sees Burst of Activity. *Variety*, October 14. http://variety.com/2017/tv/markets-festivals/latin-american-tv-sees-burst-of-activity-1202589864/. Accessed 28 July 2018.

———. 2017c. Latin America's TV Drama Sea Change. October 17. http://variety.com/2017/tv/global/mipcom-fox-edgar-spielmann-latin-america-tv-drama-sea-change-1202593075/

Huerta, César. 2011. Una historia sin prejuicios. *El Universal*, March 20: E1.

León, Ariel. 2014. No hay que darle la espalda a Michoacán: Gerardo Méndez. *El Universal*, June 15. Sección Espectáculos: 2.

———. 2017. Defienden en Twitter a Luis Gerardo Méndez. *El Universal*, October 3. http://www.eluniversal.com.mx/espectaculos/farandula/defienden-en-twitter-luis-gerardo-mendez. Accessed 2 Aug 2018.

Maillard, Tatiana. 2015 Harold Torres, Actor: 'Detesto sumarmea las causas sólo para salir en la foto'. *Emeequis*, July 6: 14–18.

Méndez, Nancy. 2013. Jamás me vi como galán. *Excelsior*, November 5. Sección Espectáculos: 8.

Mikos, Lothar. 2016. Digital Media Platforms and the Use of TV Content: Binge Watching and Video-on-Demand in Germany. *Media and Communication* 4 (3): 154–161.

Nicita, Antonio, and Maria Alessandra Rossi. 2009. Access to Audio-Visual Contents, Exclusivity and Anticommons in New Media Markets. *Communications and Strategies* 71 (3): 79–101.

Orantes, Fidel. 2016. La comedia tiene un rey. *Reforma*, December 29: 9.

Orozco, Javier. 2018. Tv de paga: competencia e inversion en crecimiento. *Milenio*, January 25: 24.

Orozco, Guillermo, E. Navarro, and A. García-Matilla. 2012. Educational Challenges in Times of Mass Self- Communication: A Dialogue among Audiences. *Comunicar* 38: 67–74.

Pacheco, Rodrigo. 2017. Entrevista con Maya Zapata sobre Run, Coyote, Run. *Time Out Mexico*, June 8. https://www.timeoutmexico.mx/ciudad-demexico/cine/entrevista-con-maya-zapata-sobre-run-coyote-run. Accessed 28 July 2018.

"Personaje de la semana." 2017. Personaje de la semana: Gustavo Loza ganador mejor director en Festival Pantalla de Cristal por serie Run Coyote Run. *Revista Pantalla*, December 10. http://www.revistapantalla.com/telenet/index.php?id_nota=19627. Accessed 28 July 2018.

Rodríguez Canales, Edith. 2009 'Paradas continuas,' en honor a Tin Tan. *El Sol de México*, October 20. Sección Escena: 1.

Run Coyote Run. 2017. *Run Coyote Run*, comedia que aborda la migración y el tráfico de personas. *La Jornada*, May 8. http://www.jornada.com.mx/2017/05/08/espectaculos/a14n2esp. Accessed 28 July 2018

Smith, Paul Julian. 2018. *Spanish and Latin American Television Drama: Genre and Format Translation*. London: School of Advanced Study University of London/ Institute of Modern Languages Research.

todotvnews. 2017. Estreno de Run Coyote Run coloca a FX como lo más visto. *Todotv*, May 19. http://www.todotvnews.com/news/Estreno-de-Run-Coyote-Run-coloca-a-FX-como-lo-ms-visto.html. Accessed 28 July 2018.

Part III

Transmedia

8

Two Media Crossovers: Cinema and Television for Day of the Dead; Live Theater Versions of TV Shows

Day of the Dead Media (2013)

It is a balmy 1 November, and according to tradition, dead children are returning to Mexico, to be followed by deceased adults. For Day of the Dead, Mexico City's main square, or Zócalo, boasts a 30-foot installation of skeletons based on the designs of renowned illustrator José Guadalupe Posada and a huge tent sheltering colorful "ofrendas" ("altars"). Government departments and public health projects, city boroughs and neighborhood schools, all vie to produce the best display, composed of marigold petals, sugar skulls, seasonal breads, and even beer bottles.

Though supernatural in origin, the celebration is clearly political: depictions of the Republic's president and the City's mayor, currently resident in that same square and precociously shrunken to skeletons, are prominent. Scurrilous "calaveras" (literally "skulls"), cheaply printed popular poems that are hawked by seasonally clad vendors, pillory public figures, consigning them to early death in life. Even much loved celebrities from the world of film play their part. One "ofrenda" features ghostly statues of stars of Mexican Golden Age cinema: comedian Cantinflas and beauty Dolores del Río grin grimly over the marigolds.

Keeping the calendar for the nation, a new Mexican horror movie has premiered this weekend. *Espectro* (which means both "spectrum" and "specter"), the third feature by Alfonso Pineda Ulloa, stars Spanish actress Paz Vega (previously from Saura's quintessentially Spanish *Carmen* [2003] and Almodóvar's *Hable con ella* ["Talk to Her," 2002]) as a Mexico City medium tormented in her haunted home. The English-language title "Demon Inside," more explicit than the Spanish, refers both to the protagonist's head and her flat. After being brutally raped in a garage, Vega's character Marta retreats to a rundown apartment in the ironically named and ramshackle "Victory Building." From the start she is troubled by visions. Ghostly nails scrape the parquet floor and blood overflows the vintage bathtub.

These current trials are crosscut with past traumas. As a child back in Spain, Marta kept hallucinating about a weeping woman, but could not see her face or that of the man who has abused her. More urgently the adult Marta's new neighbors are hardly ideal. She spies on the lesbian next door, whose orgasmic cries end only when she sinks a knife into her sex partners (or is this Marta's imagining?) And the guy loitering in a hoodie below her window may just be the sadistic rapist whose initial assault the medium was unable to foresee.

Espectro boasts enviable production values in its frequent special effects, a plot with several satisfying twists in the tail, and a brave performance from Vega as the woman in peril. But, beyond these genre staples, it raises unexpected historical and political questions. The Spanish female's rape by a Mexican male repeats and reverses the foundational fiction of Mexico, whereby Spaniards violated the indigenous women, engendering the mestizo inheritance of current national imagination. It is a trauma also referenced in an earlier and more successful Mexican horror film with a transnational cast *KM 31: Kilómetro 31* ("Kilometer 31," Rigoberto Castañeda, 2006).

This cross-cultural tension is highlighted by the play of contrasting accents among the cast. Vega keeps her native tones from the southern Spanish region of Andalusia, while her nemesis is played somewhat incongruously by Alfonso "Poncho" Herrera, still fondly remembered as the cute boy next door from northern Mexico's Monterrey in Televisa's teen telenovela *Rebelde* ("Rebel," 2004–6). And if the ancient battle between Europe and America is restaged, then so is the pervasive tension between past and present in a still modernizing Mexico. Marta may light candles and scrawl pentagrams in chalk, but she also sets up a sophisticated surveillance system, whose pixelated screens will prove equally unable to save her.

These transnational and transmedia currents are echoed in another, very different film playing in Mexico City that same weekend, Eugenio Derbez's dramedy *No se aceptan devoluciones* ("Instructions Not Included"). When Derbez's Acapulco playboy Valentín is suddenly presented with an adorable baby daughter, he is forced to take responsibility for another human being, a predicament better stated by the original Spanish title which translates as "no returns allowed." If *Espectro* stages a border crossing, psychic and geographic, between Mexico and Spain, *No se aceptan devoluciones* rewrites a transfer better known to English speakers, namely Mexican immigration to the

USA. Thus, searching for his new daughter's American mother, Derbez's homely, hangdog Valentín (more convincing as a doting father than an international Don Juan) lucks into a career as a Hollywood stuntman in spite of his comic timidity. In one significant sight gag, he is repeatedly slammed into a brick wall while dressed in full Aztec costume. Although American characters speak Spanish with varying levels of expertise and the blonde moppet of a daughter is fully bilingual, Valentín learns no English in spite of his extended stay in Los Angeles. Derbez's film (he directs as well as stars) thus speaks to and for a US Latino audience that remains fiercely attached to its heritage language.

While *Espectro* premiered for the Day of the Dead, *No se aceptan devoluciones*, although funded by Mexico's dominant broadcaster Televisa, catered to a different calendar. Released for Labor Day weekend in the USA before it was seen in Mexico, it took $10.4 million from just 347 theaters. *Entertainment Weekly* attributed this unexpected "box office sensation" (the biggest grossing Spanish-language feature ever) to three factors: Derbez's promotional appearances on Univision, the US network affiliated to Televisa; the US-first premiere, which forestalled piracy; and the family makeup of the Latino audience, the most frequent filmgoers of any American demographic (Smith 2013).

Back in Mexico, success abroad seems to have inspired pride rather than envy. But massive popularity was hardly unexpected given local audiences' loyalty to *No se aceptan devoluciones*' star. The latter has spent 25 years as a top-rated TV comedian, specializing in sketch comedy with beloved characters (including "El Diablito": "the little devil") but also appearing in telenovelas. Indeed the same Saturday that the adult dead were said to return to Mexico and Derbez's first feature was breaking records in movie theaters, the comedian's *XH-DERBEZ*, a show in the format of a mock network, played for a full three hours on Televisa. Moreover the clunky changes in *No se aceptan devoluciones*' tone that mystified US journals like *Variety* are explained by their origin in Mexican TV: smashing into the wall, Derbez invokes his sketch comedy; weeping over his ailing darling daughter, he echoes his soap serials.

While *No se aceptan devoluciones* reenacts the transnational and transmedia crossings of *Espectro*, it also repeats its problematic engagement with modernity. Derbez's infantilized character could hardly be more regressive, living as he does in a playhouse and dressing in matching pajamas with his daughter. But at one point the child's neglectful *gringa* mother returns with an unexpected partner. And, as in *Espectro* once more, here lesbianism signals social change. To its credit, *No se aceptan devoluciones* takes the female lover seriously (she is even played by Derbez's own real-life wife, a fact surely known to local audiences). Yet the film ends with a restoration of traditional familial order, albeit tragic and temporary: father, daughter, and biological mother return to the Acapulco surf for a lachrymose finale.

The doomed psychic infant of *Espectro* is thus the twin sister of the mortally sick moppet of *No se aceptan devoluciones*. But for true horror the Mexican viewer need look not to cinema but to the massively popular medium of television which, as we have seen already, serves as an essential support for big screen production. On this same Day of the Dead, TV Azteca, Televisa's rival, broadcast a double episode of its decade-long strand of stand-alone dramas, *Lo que callamos las mujeres* ("What We Women Keep Quiet," 2001–16). In the first, brutal narrative, an underage girl is kidnapped, transported across the US border, and forced into prostitution. Only when she is left for dead at the roadside is she rescued and returned to the grandmother who prayed to the Virgin for her release. In the second episode, another teen is raped by a boy who got her drunk and later gives birth to a baby damaged by fetal alcohol syndrome. Although plot and performance here are typically melodramatic, it is striking that it is not film but television, a medium so scorned by the elite in Mexico, as elsewhere, that directly addresses the urgent social issues that, lightly disguised, also underlie such folk festivities as the Day of the Dead and film genres as horror.

Live Theater Versions of TV Shows (2015)

Something is stirring in Mexican television. As a result of President Peña Nieto's telecommunications reform, there is for the first time a prospect of real competition for media dinosaur Televisa. Cadena Tres, a small channel known for such titles as lesbian- and feminist-themed telenovela *Las Aparicio* ("The Aparicio Women," 2010–11), and whose slogan is "La televisión más abierta que nunca" ("Television More Open than Ever"), has been awarded the franchise for one of three new national networks. It is to be called Imagen Televisión.

But the *ancien régime* is fighting back with convergence culture. This phrase has been synonymous with synergy between cinema, television, and internet since Henry Jenkins's 2006 book of that name. But in modern Mexico TV titles are now extending their brands into live theater performance. In 2015 I took in two such shows in provincial Mérida, Yucatán, and metropolitan Mexico City. What they suggest is that the future of television may lie in the past and that scholars might well look to the stage rather than the web for successful examples of intermediality.

My first example is a live version of Televisa's reality competition *Parodiando: Noche de trajes* ("Taking Off: Evening Dress"), which has aired since 2012 in a sought-after time slot on Sunday nights, when traditionally telenovelas are not shown. *Parodiando* is an unnecessarily complex contest in which amateur impersonators from around the nation first compete to be members of teams coached by celebrities before entering final rounds where the ultimate prize is to be "Mexico's best imitator." My theatrical spin-off was staged in a small but handsome historic theater in Mérida, the most culturally rich city of the south. And, prioritizing the provincial, the production was led by Josué Capetillo, a local boy made good who specializes in impersonating mature Mexican divas little known abroad, such as the matronly Lupita D'Alessio.

Called in its publicity precisely "As Seen on TV," the show also offered a chance for Mérida's drag queens to tread the boards of a legitimate theater for once, even if they sometimes forgot the unaccustomed family-friendly format with some off-color jokes (addressing one bottle-blonde audience member, a performer asked "if the carpet matched the drapes"). Interestingly, the formally dressed public responded equally well to US originals as to Mexican. A tribute to Michael Jackson proved especially popular.

More importantly, however, *Parodiando* offered a kind of archeology of Mexican popular culture as seen through its female singing stars. Capetillo himself, only begetter of the evening's entertainment in his hometown, offered no fewer than three impersonations of a veteran movie star, Angélica María, at different stages of her career: as a perky teenager doing the twist, a blushing bride attended by a pair of slim-hipped young grooms, and a feisty flight attendant wheeling her carry-on down the aisle as she sung a hymn to the freedoms of air travel, a sentiment no doubt deeply felt in geographically isolated Yucatán (I return to Angélica María in the second half of this chapter).

The show thus not only revealed a conservative audience's surprising tolerance for drag. It also confirmed their continuing affection for popular film and song of decades-long past, as channeled through a TV reality contest broadcast from the distant capital that was magically transported to a theater close at hand. Intermediality is here at once temporal and spatial, mixing up center and periphery, past and present, just as it does film, TV, and theater.

My second stage spin-off could not be more different. I saw *Mi corazón es tuyo* ("My Heart Is Yours," 2014–15), which had recently finished its run on Televisa's top-rated "Channel of the Stars," at the huge Centro Cultural I, tucked inside a shopping mall in central Mexico City. While fans could enjoy *Parodiando* for a handful of pesos, *Mi corazón*, a prize-winning musical telenovela with real (as opposed to impersonated) national stars would set back its legions of fans some $60 for the "VIP" section right in front of the stage, a hefty sum in a country where the minimum wage remains just $5 a day. And the show's residency in the capital marked just the midpoint of a months-long, lucrative tour around the far-flung cities of the Mexican states.

Mi corazón's premise is of a feisty nanny (somewhat implausibly, a pole dancer by night) who cares for the seven children of a disciplinarian widower. The Economist (2015), in a piece on booming Spanish-language TV in the USA (the show airs there on Univision), claimed the format came from classic musical *The Sound of Music* (Robert Wise, 1965). In fact it is closely and openly adapted from a Spanish original of the previous decade, which bore the more explanatory title *Ana y los siete* ("Ana and the Seven," RTVE, 2002–5), even keeping the name of the heroine. Inevitably, in both TV series (as in the musical), our warm-hearted heroine gets to wed the initially frosty hero, who (as in *The Sound of Music*) first flirts lengthily with an unsuitable villainess. And as in Mérida, the audience was the family one sought by Televisa, ranging from kids too small to sit still in their seats to seniors too frail to cope with the auditorium stairs.

The stage show thus gives valuable evidence for the reception of television fiction in Mexico, even as it exploits the special pleasures of live performance. While the original is relatively realist, the play was framed explicitly as a fairy tale, beginning as it did with the tiniest performer narrating the story from an oversize picture book. But the true magic was the physical presence of the actors. When the heroine (telenovela veteran Silvia Navarro) first came on stage, the little girl in the seat next to me exclaimed "Ana!" with genuine wonder. The TV playmate of countless weekday evenings was now in the same room with her in real life. Likewise when Ana's antagonist appeared, to loud boos, she was explicitly described as a "witch." The archetypal characters of telenovela here stood revealed as the elemental forces that they truly are.

For a slightly older demographic, the show capitalized on the teen idol in its large cast, played by a young actor fresh from Televisa's acting school, the blond and blue-eyed Polo Morín (I return to Morín in the second half of this chapter). When he lost his shirt onstage on the flimsiest of pretexts, to deafening screams from the crowd, the actress playing Ana turned directly to the audience, asking us to raise our hands if we wanted to touch him. Breaking the fourth wall in a way that is of course impossible on television, the show thus sought to connect in the most direct of fashions with its massive broadcast audience, here in the flesh. In yet more mercenary fashion, the cast also made themselves available, for a price, for selfies after the performance.

While the TV originals of both *Parodiando*, the all-too-familiar reality contest, and *Mi corazón*, the transnational telenovela, may seem global phenomena, the stage shows were thus thoroughly localized, testifying to the links between the Mexican capital and the states. One performer in Mérida's *Parodiando* warned the provincial audience to watch out for their wallets as she/he was from Mexico City. The villainess in *Mi corazón* threatened to send the show's kids to a "militarized boarding school in Iztapalapa," an impoverished borough of the capital that the wealthy brood are most unlikely to have set their fashionable feet in and with which many Latinos, watching the show in the USA, will surely be unfamiliar.

Yet, beyond the concrete realities of theater, both parent shows also exploit the less tangible attractions of social media to expert effect. Indeed *Mi corazón* won a prize from weekly magazine *TVyNovelas* for best use of the web by a telenovela. It was thus both best series *tout court* and best "multiplatform" fiction in its year (Notimérica 2015). In a less-planned internet outing, as we shall see later, twink Polo Morín suffered the leaking of a Cam4 jerk-off video by a technically savvy admirer. What is striking, however, is that this bad publicity, which might once have destroyed a career, failed to impact negatively his appearance in this squeaky-clean family entertainment, as he was stoutly defended by his producers and costars. Indeed one wonders how many of the screaming fans at the theater had been attracted by what their idol had revealed on the internet, rather than the torso that was so lengthily displayed on stage.

Soon, then, new TV market entrants may offer more open, original content than the shows I have examined here. Yet in the meantime, old dog Televisa, the incumbent for some 40 years, has learned a new intermedial trick to further monetize its traditionalist properties: going back to the future with live performance, the most ancient of dramatic media, even as it exploits a new digital spectatorship. We can now go on to examine the profiles of two of the stars cited above in my multimedia platforms.

Two Modes of Wholesomeness in Transmedia Stars: Angélica María and Polo Morín

Unlike most other stars I treat in this book, veteran Angélica María, born in 1944 and still described today as "la novia de México" ("Mexico's sweetheart"), has attracted academic as well as journalistic attention. In Olivia Cosentino's pioneering account of the media "trajectories" of female stars, Angélica María represents the "portal" of film, the medium in which she made the rare and perilous transition from child star to new teen idol in classic romances, comedies, and musicals of the 1960s (2018, 198).

Yet, as Cosentino acknowledges herself, Angélica María's career was already "multiplatform," engaging the later portals of television and music that are represented in her article by the younger, more sexualized figures of Verónica Castro and Gloria Trevi, respectively. And if Angélica María was born in the USA (her father was an American jazz musician), still her career was oriented primarily to Mexico, Latin America, and Spain (2018, 199). This reinforces Cosentino's new emphasis on stars who circulate domestically and are not dependent on crossover with North America and on Hollywood hegemony (2018, 198). Moreover, reading racially as "white" with her pale complexion and light brown or sometimes blond bouffant hair, she also eludes the ethnic othering favored by American scholars.

Cosentino places Angélica María within the context of star studies, asking such questions as how Dyer's concept of the "star image" ("constructed personages in media texts") can be extended to "the star's mass media trajectory and public perception as a whole" (2018, 196); and how monolithic "archetypes" can be replaced by Geraghty's "duality of image," which "emphasizes balance between the site of fictional performance and life outside." Working out from these theoretical perspectives to the historical arena, Cosentino also argues for an attention to female agency (and not to the men who supposedly made such women famous) and to the "constant fluctuation of mass media circuits" (which change radically over the decades) (2018, 196).

The consistent feature of Angélica María's star image is that she was always the good girl: "never overtly sexual, always safely alluring" (2018, 199). It is an image reinforced over half a century by photos of her misty-eyed and somewhat simpering smile. Yet we will see that her teen "rock and roll" movies were not always as "moralistic" as Cosentino claims (2018, 199); and that, off screen, Mexico's sweetheart was, briefly, touched by scandal. Conversely the question she raises is one that also applies to telenovela juvenile Polo Morín, a teen star for a new electronic era: how can the unspectacular quality of wholesomeness hold the attention of voracious audiences in changing times?

Uniquely in the case of Angélica María we have a book-length study of audiences' response to her star profile in the 1960s. Alva Lai Shin Castellón's *Recuerdos de juventud y rock and roll* (2016) interweaves sensitive close textual analysis of youth movies, almost invariably starring Angélica María, with the invaluable testimony of female audiences of the period in Mexico's second city of Guadalajara, whether in individual interview or collective focus group. Lai Shin even alternates film stills of, say, fictional movie weddings with moving snapshots of real-life nuptials.

After a theoretical introduction treating memory, cinema, and audience (2016, 13–54), Lai Shin covers the historical material of film scheduling and exhibition in the Jalisco capital and the "ritual" of cinema going (2016, 55–82). But most important for Angélica María's star image is Lai Shin's thematic account of female "fantasy" ("ensueño") on screen, which is divided into the four areas of love, courtship, transgression, and matrimony (2016, 121–66).

These themes are closely linked to specific titles by Angélica María, which prove surprisingly varied. Thus in *Vivir de sueños* ("Living Off Dreams," Rafael Baledón, 1963), which matches Angélica María with her consummate chaste movie suitor, the delicate-featured Enrique Guzmán, the young couple fall in love at first sight on a railway platform and subsequently fantasize about each other over the course of a train journey to Veracruz. Until the very last scene their only communication is through musical dream sequences. Lai Shin praises Angélica María's "subtle energy" as the young romantic dreamer here in this rare plot that makes quite explicit the role of the other as a fantasy "receptacle of desires and expectations" (2016, 129–30).

Courtship is represented by *Me quiero casar* ("I Want to Get Married," Julián Soler, 1966), in which, in a nod to her real-life birthplace, Angélica María plays an American visitor, enraptured by the romance of Mexico. In spite of her illusions, she is nonetheless perfectly able to repel the advances of an overly eager, and mildly rebellious, Mexican suitor, even as they sit perilously alone in a sports car admiring a distant view of the city by night (2016, 134). Angélica María's status here as foreigner (as before as a dreamer) once more allows her certain "concessions and adventures" unavailable to her Mexican sisters (2016, 135).

Angélica María is characteristically absent, however, from Lai Shin's account of "transgressions," but returns for the section on "marriage." In the significantly titled *Romeo contra Julieta* ("Romeo Versus Juliet," Julián Soler, 1968), Angélica María plays a stuck-up rich girl engaged to a mama's boy of a fiancé of her own class. After a solitary journey (once more), this time to Cuernavaca, she ends up spending a drunken New Year's Eve with the mechanic who has offered to repair her car, played by her other regular partner the husky Alberto Vázquez. Obliged by her uptight family to marry this proletarian in the (erroneous) belief that she is no longer a virgin, Angélica María's character would seem to embody the traditionalist views to which Lai Shin's real-life informants also subscribed: snapshots of the latters' smiling white weddings are juxtaposed with a still of Angélica María's less happy cinematic event in this film (2016, 156, 158) (Illustration 8.1).

Yet the young star remains a voice for modernity and freedom even here. When her original fiancé says he wants to protect her from gossip, she attacks his "machismo," using the same word that the actress will use herself many

Illustration 8.1 Promotional material for *Romeo contra Julieta*, starring Angélica María (Julián Soler, 1968)

years later. And she declares that she refuses to be a submissive wife locked up in the marital home and running to fat at age 30 (2016, 155). Angélica María thus embodies Cosentino's "duality of image," at once reinforcing and rebelling against stereotypes which were yet more rigid in life outside fictional performance: Lai Shin's informants confirm that, just as Angélica María's character has no alternative but marriage, 1960s' brides were supposed to be physically "enterita" ("nice and intact"), even as they secretly longed for sexual experimentation (2016, 157).

The extensive press files on Angélica María also testify to this curious combination of rigidity and flexibility. Thus the very earliest press clipping in the Cineteca Nacional has the young star engaging in an unlikely, but no doubt heartwarming, charity event: performing as a clown in a benefit for retired circus folk ("Angélica María y López Ochoa" 1971). An undated press release from the same period has her stating that she will not "betray her image" with nude scenes (Boletín de prensa n.d.). Here she stresses not just her virginal integrity but her self-conscious crafting of an image since she was a child in many media (song, telenovelas, cinema) and her unswerving determination since that time ("nothing and no one will make me change my mind").

In the following decade, she is said to "wear once more the crown of Mexico's sweetheart" and, even after a temporary absence from television, tops the lists of popular stars via her singing career ("Angélica María vuelve a lucir la corona como 'La Novia de México'" 1986). It is a title that the press continues to celebrate in an extended three-part interview when the star reaches the 25th anniversary of her immaculate career (Hernández 1987a). In the second installment of this interview, the star tells readers defensively that "rock and rollers [such as herself some twenty years before] are not to be blamed for drug addiction" (she says that her adventures on tour were squeaky clean) (Hernández 1987b).

Yet in the third installment of the interview, a dissonant note appears. Like her character two decades earlier, she attacks "Mexican machismo," which she claims holds back the development of women's talents (Hernández 1987c). Here her career narrative is very different to the one endlessly repeated before. Angélica María now presents her life as destined for "disaster" in an environment "hostile" to women like herself: the daughter of a divorcee and a child actress since the age of three. Later still, she says, the Mexican people could not bear to see their "sweetheart" married, especially to another divorcé, from whom she too would soon separate. Scandalous at the time, her marital misadventures made many "turn their backs on her." The only consolation was her daughter, who shared the name Angélica with her mother and herself.

As the anniversaries roll on ("Mexico's sweetheart at 60"), the narrative turns yet darker: Angélica María, we are told, "suffers in solitude," and has spent so long without a man that she has "even been called a lesbian," a rumor she is quite happy to repeat (Zúñiga 2007). The star now claims she was long "controlled" by her stage mother, that her courtship with costars like Enrique Guzmán was repressively chaste (in the Mexican idiom just "manitas sudadas" or "sweaty palms"), that her unfaithful, chauvinistic husband was a "disappointment", and that her daughter suffered greatly from her parents' divorce.

Yet, as Cosentino remarks, the star sailed through such scandals. Indeed her enduring solitude seems to have endeared her to faithful fans of the aging national sweetheart. Recent years bring a succession of celebrations: a tribute at the Guanajuato International Film Festival ("Nací para actuar" 2014); a 70th birthday marked by a rerun of the telenovela in which she starred with her daughter ("Angélica María cumplirá años" 2014); and even the unveiling of a star on Hollywood Boulevard, accompanied by her daughter once more and grandchildren ("Angélica María devela estrella en el Paseo de la Fama" 2016). An unlikely feminist when confined to the starched petticoats of the 1960s, Angélica María, who jettisoned from the start her father's surname of Hartman, finally constructed against all the odds an all-female lineage: three generations of women named Angélica.

Alva Lai Shin Castellón begins her study of "female fantasy" by citing an essay from a fond fan of Angélica María. It is novelist Luis Zapata, still best known for his novel of graphic gay hookups *El vampiro de la colonia Roma* (1979; English translation: *Adonis García: A Picaresque Novel*). Zapata recounts in 1998 how as a lonely provincial 11-year-old he carried out a written correspondence with the star, assuring her of his devotion. He claims that she replied "punctually and patiently" to his missives, even sending greetings to his parents and "abuelitos" (Lai Shin Castellón 2016, 121). Testifying to her "amiability and freshness," Zapata also ascribes to Angélica María an intimate intuition: that boys like him felt terribly alone and her letters offered "priceless company" (2016, 122).

Angélica María might seem an unlikely object of devotion for drag queens, who are not known for their love of wholesomeness. Yet we saw earlier in this chapter that she was a favorite in the theatrical touring version of Televisa's reality impersonation competition *Parodiando*, where she featured in three separate stages of her lengthy multiplatform career. Moreover, Zapata's testimony reveals how an apparently insipid figure could be constructed in memory as a treasured icon for gay men.

We can now go on to ask whether wholesomeness can survive the newly brutal era of social media, most especially in the case of telenovela juvenile Polo Morín, whose first name is a somewhat childish diminutive of his original "Leopoldo." As described earlier in this chapter, I had the pleasure of witnessing Morín's close connection with his youthful, mainly female audience at a theater version of his best known television success. Where Angélica María took decades to attempt a feminist twist on Mexico's virginal sweetheart, Morín has been obliged in recent years to put a queer spin on his image as a bland, blond and blue-eyed TV heartthrob. And like his more illustrious female predecessor, he has suffered apparently unscathed through personal scandals at odds with the conventional Mexican morality of his time.

Angélica María transitioned from cinema via pop music to television. And much of her corpus has an afterlife on the internet. For example, the youth movies mentioned earlier play at full, if grainy, length on YouTube. Although he began with one off roles on the anthology dramas treated in a previous chapter (featuring in *La rosa de Guadalupe* in 2010 and 2011 and *Como dice el dicho* in 2013), Polo Morín, a more recent youth star, became well known for his juvenile roles in traditional telenovelas broadcast in the afternoon on Televisa's so-called Channel of the Stars. Indeed he won the "Kids' Choice Mexico" award for favorite actor in 2015. But he has also successfully transitioned, this time into social media, with at the time of writing 380K followers on Twitter @Polo_Morin and (more importantly perhaps) 1.4 million under the same handle on Instagram.

Like Angélica María his career is focused on Mexico and thus challenges North American hegemony in star-making (it is telling that he has no photo on IMDb). And, like Angélica María again, he is a test case for the way in which monolithic archetypes can merge with a duality of image, which emphasizes no longer a balance between the site of fictional performance and life outside, but a discordant disequilibrium between them.

Yu and Austin's book offers some initial pointers to celebrity in the age of social media. As they write in their introduction:

> For particular types of stardom … fans can play a more decisive role than the industry and media…. With the proliferation of electronic communication channels … the amount of star discourse and more direct interaction between stars and fans has been significantly increased. The new media … have vastly extended the public sphere and generated new forms of fan discourse and activities. As a result, the boundary between the private life and the public image of a star has been further broken down, and fans have assumed more power in star construction. The dispersal of authorship in star discourse … is continuing and deepening. (2017, 10–11)

I will suggest that the telenovela juvenile, a traditional but somewhat marginalized role, lays itself open to active and decisive participation by fans. And Morín experienced, no less than twice, a dramatic breaching of the boundary between private and public, which both offered fans greater power and dispersed authorship of his persona.

Ironically Morín, the squeaky-clean juvenile heir to Angélica María's virginal girlfriend, has much in common with art-core porn star James Deen, beyond their shared slim physique and handsome face. According to Clarissa Smith and Sarah Taylor-Hartman, also in Yu and Austin's volume, Deen's social media presence, even from the supposed margins of pornography, "taps into new cultures of intimacy with and through star fandom" and "offers a version of masculinity which avoids the most stereotypically macho elements." Finally "his youth, boy-next-door good looks, and social media accessibility all offer a particular articulation of the desirable male with is not premised on adulation from afar" (2017, 275). In Morín's case, the closeness of telenovela, with its daily date with faithful fans, is supplemented by the more jagged immediacy of Twitter and Instagram, whose flow is so much easier to disrupt.

Yet Morín's modest star image seems fixed, even archetypal, from the start. Arguably, the daily shows treated in Chap. 6 of this book, even more so than telenovelas, are in Mexico this decade's equivalents of the teen movies of the 1960s, giving rise to a tsunami of youthful stars and offering their viewers life lessons as didactic as those in Angélica María's rom-coms but now in very different circumstances.

Morín's first starring credit in 2011 is as protagonist in "Cuidar el amor" ("Taking Care of Love"), episode 3 of Season 4 of *La rosa de Guadalupe*, the series treated at length in Chap. 6. Already he is Mexico's (male) sweetheart: morally perfect but menaced by unwholesomeness all too close to home. As suggested by the title, Morín's Osvaldo is a precocious caretaker in an upper-middle-class family. The episode begins with a montage showing his sweet dedication to his schoolmate girlfriend, with flowers and gifts marking their monthly anniversaries. Surprisingly, perhaps, the couple have already made love, the first time for both. And Osvaldo promises always to be faithful to his blissful partner.

Slim, smiling, and blondly handsome, Morín offers (like James Deen) a version of masculinity which avoids the most stereotypically macho elements without disavowing sexual potency. Those macho elements, however, are attributed with a vengeance to his brother and father. When the former tells the latter that his sibling has finally scored with a girl, the father takes Osvaldo to a pole- and table dancing club (the same location so scorned by Mexico's old school *vedettes*) and later to the secret bachelor apartment where he regularly entertains sex workers without using protection.

Osvaldo nobly rejects his father's offer of paid intimacy with a hired companion. And he later scolds his brother for violating his "privacy" by telling the father that he (Osvaldo) has slept with his steady girlfriend (this defense of privacy will soon be made by Morín himself in real life). More dramatically, Osvaldo begins to hint to his mother that she should ask his father to wear a condom when they are intimate. When one of the father's many female lovers tests positive for HIV, Osvaldo faithfully accompanies each parent in turn to the clinic, where they receive negative results. Finally the brother and father are cured of their machismo and the family are happily reunited under the sign not only of the Virgin Mother but also of the immaculate fictional son.

Morín's limited acting abilities here go well with his archetypal character, whose compassionate caretaking is more traditionally coded as feminine than masculine. Yet his blond virtue, subtly suffused by a sensuality that is shown to be healthy, is ever threatened by a pervasive harmful sexuality that is to be found not just in the table dance club but in the heart of the home itself. Yet by faithfully wooing his girlfriend and bravely defending his mother, he endears himself to the female fan, whatever her age, as he does to the Virgin, who, as in every episode of the series, graces the family residence with her miraculous rose and breeze.

Morín's greatest success remains *Mi corazón es tuyo* ("My Heart Is Yours," 2014–15), the telenovela whose stage version I saw in Mexico City. This series holds a lasting place in audience's memories as shown not only by its (unusually extended) first run of 177 episodes but by its rare rerun on weekday afternoons at the time of writing (2018) (Illustration 8.2).

Here Morín's character is, initially at least, not just virtuous, but prissy. Trussed up in suit and bowtie, wearing round spectacles and with his usually vigorous hair now severely slicked back, he seems now prematurely, albeit piquantly, aged. Nando (nickname: "Nerd-ando") is contrasted with his more sensual sister (played by Paulina Goto, a teen star in her own right), his younger brothers (which include photogenic identical twins), and, of course, the pole-dancing nanny Ana who will finally win the heart of a father as repressed as his eldest son. The series ends with a "fairytale" white wedding.

Illustration 8.2 Polo Morín in *Mi corazón es tuyo* (Televisa, 2014–15)

But it takes care to specify that Ana (skilled telenovela and theater veteran Silvia Navarro) hails from the notoriously dangerous working-class city of Ecatepec in Mexico State. Indeed she is battered by biblical floods and fires in the first episode.

Here once more Morín's Scandinavian phenotype, rare indeed in Mexico, stands in for a high-class position that is equally rarified and could not be further from Ecatepec (the location for exteriors of the family's mansion is Huixquilucán, a wealthy town just outside the western borders of Mexico City). The telenovela's huge brightly lit set, necessary to contain the large ensemble cast, is overwhelming in its luxury and scale, even by telenovela standards. Yet, interestingly, the juvenile's romantic plotline (which is of course subordinated to that of the telenovela's main adult couple) will be an on-off affair with a Goth girl, whose black hair and ample eyeliner are accessorized with a nose ring. Once more, then, blond virtue and virginity are juxtaposed with a darker sensuality that offers a different, perhaps fatal kind of attraction. It was the kind of casting that, 50 years earlier, also juxtaposed Angélica María's spoiled rich girl with Alberto Vázquez's working-class motor mechanic.

Yet Morín's character Nando is from the start shown to be something of an outsider himself. In the first week's episodes, he declines to take part in his siblings' practical jokes on successive nannies, preferring to keep his nose in a book. Bullied at school and inexperienced with girls, he is reduced to passing off the nanny as his date to a dance, a strategy that predictably does not work out well. As he shyly admits to Ana, his fellow boys think he is "raro" ("strange," or perhaps "queer").

It was during the first run of *Mi corazón* that Morín suffered his first internet scandal: the release of a masturbation videotape. As mentioned earlier, the young star was defended by the powerful executive producer of the show, Juan Osorio, who argued that young people make mistakes when they "trust someone they are in love with." Osorio's own younger son played one of Morín's siblings (and would later play gay himself) (Amézquita Pino 2014). Morín, after a discreet pause, emerged to appeal for privacy, once more, but also invoked resistance to bullying, a goal newly prominent in Mexico and one which parents could hardly fail to join the young star in supporting. His real-life predicament thus aligned with that of his character at the time, the attractively vulnerable Nando.

The original source of the video went unmentioned in the coverage but is significant. Cam4 is a platform where anonymous exhibitionists can display themselves on webcam in real time to the general internet audience. It also permits private performances, often by professionals who request "tokens" from their eager audience. It is thus not so far from being a digital form of the analogue sex work so vigorously critiqued by Morín's episode of *La rosa de Guadalupe*. While it is unclear for whom Morín was performing at the time he was surreptitiously recorded (his eyes are fixed on his computer screen), the short three-minute video, still hosted now on porn aggregator sites such as XVideos (where it has over 400K views), violently collapses the space between public and private (XVideos n.d.).

The setting is a somewhat-austere interior, with a bare white wall and a dark door bisecting the frame. A single small picture (of flowers?) hangs behind Morín, whose spiky hair, cheeky face, and slim torso are initially all that is visible. As he masturbates out of frame, the setup is similar to Warhol's (equally blond) *Blow Job* (1964). Finally at the end Morín moves closer to the camera. His erect penis comes into shot and he briefly ejaculates over his smooth stomach.

The minimalist mise-en-scène and camerawork contrast, of course, with the overloaded telenovela aesthetic from which he is so familiar. Beyond this, we are reminded perhaps of James Deen, whose relative youth, boy-next-door good looks, and social media accessibility offer an erotic articulation of the desirable male which is not premised on adulation from afar. The everyday proximity of television is in the case of Morín overwritten by the closeness of the internet, which makes the exceptionally private suddenly available to all.

Moreover the prohibited sexuality conventionally attributed to other characters in Morín's television works, and with which his blameless figures are contrasted, here comes back to suffuse the image of the star himself, an image already suffused by a certain solitary queerness. Of course what remains invisible in the video is the original privileged addressee of Morín's performance, at whom he gazes and to whom he smiles.

While this experience might have made Morín more cautious in his use of social media, he later faced a further breach in his intimacy. When his Facebook account was hacked, still snapshots of the star with another handsome male Televisa juvenile, Lambda García, were released. They show the couple standing proudly together on vacation in exotic locations (Barcelona, Venice) and, fully clothed, kissing at home on Morín's birthday (E-Consulta 2016).

After an interval, once more Morín posted a sorrowful video on Facebook Live, lamenting again the violation of his privacy but stating that he was "happy" to love and be loved (he did not mention his presumed lover) and claiming he had never hidden anything from "you" his audience. The mise-en-scène is eerily similar to the original sex tape, with Morín now wearing a white T-shirt and a basketball cap, riding high on his unruly hair, but posed in front of a plain gray wall and shot in a single take (La Mana MX 2016). The video received a quarter of a million views.

Where Angélica María had to reconcile the duality of sweetheart and divorcee, Polo Morín needed to synthesize the twin apparently irreconcilable positions of immaculate straight sweetheart (his TV star image) and sexually active gay lover (his leaked internet role). And all this from a position of relative weakness: the telenovela juvenile who is always subordinate, financially and narratively, to the lead. Morín soon appeared on Televisa's morning show *Hoy*, where the familiar presenters joined him in denouncing bullying and the violation of privacy and signally failed to ask about his private life and supposed partner.

Let us look how Morín, to his great credit, has negotiated this conundrum on his social media over the period of summer 2018. His Twitter account is full of self-help bromides which arrive with metronomic regularity: "smile and don't get bitter over anything or anybody, that's the attitude" (@Polo_Morin, September 2, 2018); "Whenever you say 'I can't' you lose the chance to show yourself what you can do" (August 31, 2018); "Mistakes have three steps: accept them, overcome them, and never make them again" (August 23, 2018). Such clichés may, however, take on a more heartfelt sense in his particular context, given fans' knowledge of Morín's public tribulations.

Elsewhere those fans are addressed directly in fragments of an electronic amorous discourse, using the special resources of Spanish personal pronouns and verbs: "THANKS to all the public for following *My Heart is Yours* ['tuyo' in the singular] once again … My heart is for ever YOURS ['suyo' in the plural]" (August 24, 2018). Or again over a photo of Morín looking out from a cliff: "I confess to you [plural] that I have a terrible fear of heights, but slowly I've been forced to find beauty in everything that requires effort from me" (August 22, 2018). Or simply, over a shirtless and tousle-haired early-morning selfie: "Have [singular] a lovely day" (August 16, 2018). We are thus invoked alternately in the singular, as uniquely interested individuals, and in the plural, as a collective united by our shared love. And we are privileged to follow the star both as he lives his ordinary day (gym, work, sleep) and as he makes his extraordinary travels (frequent visits to New York and California at a time when some less privileged, and no doubt darker-skinned, Mexicans were being refused entry by US immigration).

But Instagram is more Morín's medium, especially as the comments are arrayed directly beside each carefully curated picture, rather than trailing behind as they do on Twitter. Here we can identify the locations of Morín's travels. For example, the panoramic viewpoint is in Antoquía, Colombia (@polo_morin, August 22, 2018). Commenters, male and female identified, in Spanish, English, and Portuguese, praise Morín's beauty and dress sense and invite him to enjoy all the "high points" of Colombia.

Another post is less flattering, more threatening: "You're there and Lamda [*sic*] is cheating on you in Cancún with @mauriciogarcia [a rival young actor]." Social media accessibility thus raises the possibility of fans (or indeed enemies) promoting alternative narratives: here that Morín's rumored lover is faithless. This is a clear and ambivalent example of the newly active constitution of star profile whose agency is now tensely and unpredictably shared between star and audience.

It is striking that over the years of social media production (an unknown Morín was an early adopter of Twitter in 2009), his once-slim physique becomes increasingly muscular. This process is presented once more as part of discourse of self-help and motivation, with the star in selfies blearily pumping iron at the early-morning gym or earnestly exercising at the beach. But, once more, it is not difficult to see this musculature as another kind of defense mechanism, toughening the once-fragile body to a more masculine definition, but without compromising the star's characteristic juvenile vulnerability.

Unlike these selfies, which offer the promise of unique communion with the star who links into the camera as if seeking us out, two-shots enshrine his treasured relationships and blur the division between public and private, fictional and real. Thus Morín frequently pictures himself embracing his TV sister, actress Paulina Goto, and very rarely shows himself alone with rumored lover Lambda García. Teasingly, however, he sometimes offers gay (and gay-friendly) fans food for thought: he poses smiling by a sign that reads in English and Spanish "Normal is boring" (July 8, 2018); and in a three-shot with Goto and García the trio wear white T-shirts with the "equals" sign, denoting marriage equality, a goal yet to be achieved at a Federal level in Mexico (June 24, 2018).

Morín's presentation of self as erotic object is also ambivalent, playful. A plurality of the shots are of Morín posing in his bathing suit at the beach, albeit often in a smiling or self-mocking mode. One particular picture was said by the Mexican press to have "broken the internet" (Barrios 2017). In a tease once more, Morín first posted, deleted, and then reposted a frankly sensual picture of himself naked in bed, seen from behind (July 28, 2018). Along with the reposted image he provides a textual commentary of self-motivation once more, claiming that although he was originally shocked by negative reactions to the photo, he later decided that no one should be "repressed" by other people's judgments. Rather we must live "free and happy" (these words in uppercase). Morín was here rewarded with 188K likes.

What is striking, then, is that Morín repeats and reverses the two episodes of unwilling revelation which sought to shame him, claiming them as his own. And exposing himself both physically and mentally, he offers himself as a vulnerable object for fans to cathect more strongly with than they could with the more perfect (and more macho) mode of celebrity traditional in Mexico. While some commenters joke here about anal sex ("he's hurting after being fucked by Lambda"), most enter into Morín's game, professing their love for the naked actor or praising his self-confidence in ignoring the people who have got "the wrong idea" about him. And yet still this newly erotic photo interacts with and overwrites Morín's original virginal TV star image: one commentator writes the single word "Nanditoooo!!"

Kids' Choice

In his unusually dark episode of *Como dice el dicho* ("Al mal paso" ["A Bad Step"], Season 3, Episode 4), Polo Morín plays a high school attempted rapist and triple murderer. Appropriate for Day of the Dead or Halloween, although it was not shown at that time, most of the action takes place in a cemetery. The star himself informed his fans on Twitter that they should watch him playing a "bad and crazy person" (January 22, 2013). It would seem that wholesomeness, then, is not incompatible with excursions into unpleasantness. And even Angélica María's spoiled rich-kid roles are not always sympathetic.

Yet both actors managed the rare and perilous transition from youth star to young adult idol on multiplatform media that circulated domestically with great intensity. Their enduring star image (or constructed personage in media texts) thus coincided with their mass media trajectory and public perception as a whole. And their positive archetypes were rarely inflected on screen by a duality of image. It is true that the balance between the site of fictional performance and life outside proved temporarily problematic for both as they negotiated divorce and gay sex tapes, respectively. But within the constant fluctuation of mass media circuits, they remained the good girl and boy: rarely overtly sexual, always safely alluring. And Morín's TV dramas are nearly as moralistic as Angélica María's film musicals, focusing on the traditional themes of love, courtship, transgression, and matrimony, once more.

The question of scandal, however, raises significant problems of audience response when fans feel their stars' status as receptacle of desires and expectations may be compromised. Both actors benefited from concessions here. Angélica María was forgiven her divorce and, enduringly single, built a new image based on her loving relationship with her namesake daughter. Polo Morín was pardoned his sex tape and supposed boyfriend by fans who, in social media commentary, repeat his insistence of the right to privacy and vigorously defend him from homophobic bullying. Both stars, then, can be seen as voices for modernity and freedom in very different eras.

The 1960s' brides were supposed to be virginal. The same would seem to be true of gay juveniles: Polo claims to love and be loved but does not acknowledge the physical dimension of that love, even as he displays his increasingly muscular body at the gym and on the beach. Indeed, in spite of headlines saying he came out of the closet, Morín has never confirmed that he is gay. Social media responses, however, many of which come from male-identified posters, suggest that, like Angélica María for the provincial Luis Zapata, Morín can still serve as priceless company for isolated young gays, who, led or fed daily by their smiling idol, tap into new cultures of intimacy with and through star fandom. On Twitter the tousled star regularly wishes his followers a good morning and good night from his apparently solitary bed. Even if Morín's social media feeds are curated by a third party, still they walk a fragile and evidently successful line between private and public.

Morín's eminence on Instagram belies his secondary status on television, where he is a mere juvenile (compare the veterans pigeonholed as "first actors" in the same telenovelas). This suggests that fans can and do play a more decisive role than the industry and media than before, especially when the boundary between the private life and the public image of a star has been broken down. While fans have clearly assumed more power in star construction, Mexico's sweetheart of the 1960s and Kids' Choice of the millennium serve similar, valuable functions in their respective multimedia eras, testifying as they do to social changes in the figures of the independent woman and the young gay man that they have come to embody.

References

Amézquita Pino, Carolina. 2014. Juan Osorio defiende al actor Polo Morín luego de que este publicara fotos de su intimidad. *People en Español*, July 8. https://peopleenespanol.com/article/juan-osorio-defiende-al-actor-polo-morin-luego-de-que-este-publicara-fotos-de-su-intimidad/. Accessed 9 Sept 2018.
"Angélica María cumplirá años". 2014. *La Prensa*, September 27. Sección Espectáculos, p. 31.
"Angélica María devela estrella en el Paseo de la Fama". 2016. *La Jornada*, May 26. Sección Espectáculos, p. 8a.

"Angélica María vuelve a lucir la corona como 'La Novia de México'". 1986. *El Nacional*, February 21, p. 8.

"Angélica María y López Ochoa actuaron de payasos en el circo". 1971. *Esto*, January 17, p. 11.

Barrios, Carlos. 2017. Polo Morín rompe el Internet con desnudo sobre su cama. *Debate*, December 30. https://www.debate.com.mx/show/Polo-Morin-rompe-el-Internet-con-desnudo-sobre-su-cama-20171230-0067.html. Accessed 9 Sept 2018.

Boletín de prensa. n.d. Dice Angélica María quien filma 'Yo amo, tú amas, nosotros amamos'.

Cosentino, Olivia. 2018. Starring Mexico: Female Stardom, Age, and Mass Media Trajectories in the 20th Century. In *The Routledge Companion to Gender, Sex, and Latin American Culture*, ed. Frederick Luis Aldama, 196–203. New York: Routledge.

E-Consulta. 2016. Los saca del closet: Hacker revela noviazgo de Polo Morín y Lambda García. December 8. http://www.e-consulta.com/nota/2016-12-08/espectaculos/los-saca-del-closet-hacker-revela-noviazgo-de-polo-morin-y-lambda. Accessed 9 Sept 2018.

Hernández, Hugo. 1987a. Y 25 años después… Angélica María sigue siendo la Novia de México. *Sol de México*, April 22. Sección Espectáculos, no page.

———. 1987b. Angélica María sostiene: Los Rocanroleros no son culpables de drogadicción. *Sol de México*, April 23. Sección Espectáculos, no page.

———. 1987c. Angélica María opina: El machismo mexicano frena el desarrollo del talento femenino. *Sol de México*, April 24. Seccion Espectáculos, no page.

Jenkins, Henry. 2006. *Convergence Culture: Where Old and New Media Collide*. New York: New York University Press.

La Mana MX. 2016. Polo Morín sale del closet – Facebook Live. December 7. https://www.youtube.com/watch?v=XnMGOI4Lgg8. Accessed 9 Sept 2018.

Lai Shin Castellón, Alva. 2016. *Recuerdos de juventud y rock and roll: rescate y difusión de la memoria fílmica femenina en Guadalajara durante la década de los sesenta*. Guadalajara: Paraíso Perdido.

"Nací para actuar". 2014. *Ovaciones*, July 26. Sección Reflector, p. 5.

Notimérica. 2015. Premios TVyNovelas 2015: *Mi corazón es tuyo* es la gran triunfadora. *Notimérica*, March 9. http://www.notimerica.com/cultura/noticia-premios-tvynovelas-2015-corazon-tuyo-gran-triunfadora-20150309122116.html. Accessed 29 July 2018.

Smith, Grady. 2013. How Spanish-Language Comedy *Instructions Not Included* Became a Box-Office Sensation. *Entertainment Weekly*, September 4. http://ew.com/article/2013/09/04/instructions-not-included-box-office/. Accessed 29 July 2018.

Smith, Clarissa, and Sarah Taylor-Hartman. 2017. 'I Want James Deen to Deen Me With His Deen': The Multi-Layered Stardom of James Deen. In *Revisiting Star Studies: Cultures, Themes, and Methods*, ed. Yu Sabrina Qiong and Guy Austin, 261–278. Edinburgh: Edinburgh University Press.

The Economist. 2015. Hearts and Minds: Fifty-Seven Million Latinos Are a Mighty Market for the Media. *The Economist*, March 12. https://www.economist.com/special-report/2015/03/12/hearts-and-minds. Accessed 29 July 2018.

XVideos. n.d. Polo Morin: 3 min. https://www.xvideos.com/video11609491/polo_morin. Accessed 9 Sept 2018.

Yu, Sabrina Qiong and Guy Austin, eds. (2017). *Revisiting Star Studies: Cultures, Themes, and Methods*. Edinburgh: Edinburgh University Press.

Zúñiga, J.F. 2007. Angélica María sufre en la soledad. *El Universal*, August 6. Sección Espectáculos, p. 4.

9

Earthquake Media

The Earthquake: 2017

On the morning of September 19, 2017, there was an earthquake drill in Mexico City. Later that afternoon, as my hotel room rocked like a ship on the high seas, there was no doubt that this was the real thing. After three seemingly endless minutes of tremors, I turned on the TV. Of the two heritage networks, Televisa was still showing an old telenovela; Azteca, its rival, had already switched to nonstop quake coverage. The networks would improvise competing slogans: the first's was the rousing "¡Fuerza México!"; the second's a perhaps overoptimistic "México de pie." Mexico, sadly, was not on its feet. Twitter was soon full of surreal cell phone videos: shiny new skyscrapers rocking along the grand avenue of Reforma; the placid touristic canals of Xochimilco whipped into a frenzy by seismic activity.

While the Historic Center, where I was staying, was little affected, two fashionable neighborhoods further south favored by film folk were rocked. Roma and Condesa, where beaux arts mansions mingle with minimalist apartment buildings, are reputedly the homes of hipsters and movie stars (Roma was where Alfonso Cuarón had recently shot his new feature, named for the colonia (*Roma* would go on to win Best Film at Venice in 2018); Condesa was the location for *Amores Perros*' car crash, back in 2000). Along Roma's central boulevard of Álvaro Obregón, lined with neo-classical statues and well-pruned topiary, a large building collapsed, thus becoming, along with a devastated school, the Colegio Rébsamen, one of the recurring, heartbreaking images of postquake coverage.

It is the street where Cuarón once more shot the film that started Mexico's still-burgeoning rom-com cycle (*Solo con tu pareja* ["Only With Your Partner"], 1991) and which now hosts the Mexico City offices of the Morelia International Film Festival, perhaps Mexico's most important. While the launch of this year's edition of the festival was delayed, the offices were unharmed. Less lucky was the home in Condesa of Fernanda Solórzano, senior film critic of respected *Letras Libres* magazine. She posted pictures on Twitter of her apartment's wrecked interior. The books and DVDs were familiar to cinephiles as, tidily placed on shelves, they had served as a background to Solórzano's self-shot video reviews. Now they were scattered all over the floor.

September is the "patriotic month" in Mexico and the nation had just celebrated its Independence Day. In an ironic mise-en-scène reminiscent of a cheap disaster movie, tinsel decorations in the national colors of red, green, and white were now juxtaposed with flags at half-mast or, worse still, piles of smoking rubble. Amidst this chaos, the tragedy posed a thorny scheduling problem to TV broadcasters. The network morning shows, *Hoy* ("Today") and *Venga la alegría* (a now-incongruous "Bring On the Happiness"), first pivoted from their accustomed celebrity guests to seismologists, priests, or trauma therapists. Soon they found a more amenable angle: the many stars who joined masses of Mexicans (especially the young) as volunteers at disaster sites.

In the days that followed, celebrities themselves improvised charity schemes they could promote on the web and television. Eugenio Derbez, who is (as we saw in Chap. 8) the king of local comedy on Mexican film and TV and whose bilingual feature *How to Be A Latin Lover* (Ken Marino, 2017) crossed over to US theaters, promoted the hashtag #LoveArmyMexico. Global stars García Bernal and Diego Luna (still fondly remembered as the teenage protagonists of *Y tu mamá también* [Alfonso Cuarón, 2002] and more recently founders of the successful Ambulante documentary festival) sought out donations both at home and abroad, where Luna appeared on US late-night talk shows (Luna and García Bernal 2017). In one month they attracted almost 1500 backers and raised over $1 million on web platform Omaze for their charity "Levantemos México" ("Let's Lift Up Mexico"). (I return to Bernal and Luna's star profiles at the end of this chapter.)

Mexico's twin TV gossip magazines also flew the flag, devoting whole issues to the rescue effort and praising a newfound sense of solidarity. *TVyNovelas* (2017) went with Televisa's patriotic "Fuerza México"; *TVNotas* (2017) with a defiant "Esto sí es México" ("*This* is Mexico") over multiple shots of anonymous rescue workers with just a small number of celebrity cutouts in the foreground. Most moving was a simply worded poster pasted over cracked city walls. It read, with self-deprecating modesty and tempered optimism: "De mayor quiero ser mexicano" ("When I grow up I want to be a Mexican").

Such unity of purpose was deeply affecting, especially in a country which is in normal times (like so many others) bitterly divided along partisan political lines. But more ambivalent memes quickly made themselves felt. The raised fist seen everywhere was a sign not (or not only) of brave defiance but of the call for silence made by rescuers listening out for still-hidden victims. At the collapsed school that was sadly ubiquitous on television screens, there were rumors of a trapped child, the unusually named "Frida Sofía." When the case was revealed as a hoax, there was much soul-searching among media folk, including TV critic Álvaro Cueva, who kept up a daily commentary on the coverage in newspaper *Milenio* (Cueva 2017). Televisa was accused of turning an all-too-real tragedy into mere telenovela. By coincidence, a rescue Labrador was also named "Frida." Said to have saved some 50 people, she became a media celebrity. Wearing a distinctive visor to protect her eyes from dust, she was silkscreened onto Warhol-style prints to be sold in the street to benefit quake charities.

A new organization also took up the image of a rescue dog as its profile picture on Twitter. "Cinescombros" ("RubbleCinema") organized screenings of independent films, including programs for children, in the tents where newly homeless people were obliged to spend the night. A volunteer dressed as Batman also visited the shelters to entertain the smaller victims. Meanwhile many cinemas, including the huge complex of the Cineteca or national film theater (equivalent to Lincoln Center in New York or the British Film Institute in London), ceased all programming and transformed themselves overnight into donation centers, accepting and distributing food, clothing, and medicine to quake victims. Conversely there was new concern for the survival of fragile picture palaces, which had previously been closed to the public and now risked collapse. The famed Churubusco Studios, Mexico City's equivalent of Hollywood's back lots, was also hard hit.

Two relatively new art houses had contrasting experiences. The Casa del Cine ("Cinema House") is housed in an atmospheric period building in the Historic Center and had been screening titles from Mexico's annual French film festival. Almost two weeks after the tragedy, it remained closed, awaiting inspection by engineers who had to evaluate the safety of thousands of such buildings before they could be reoccupied (the Casa del Cine did indeed reopen months later). Cine Tonalá on the other hand is a trendy theater in the now damaged *colonia* of Roma, which has won a name for itself by combining indie film with gourmet food and live events. Just days after the tragedy, it was already hosting a stand-up comedy night for *chilangos* (Mexico City residents), who were much in need of light relief.

In a city where the dead now numbered in the hundreds (thousands had been killed in the 1985 quake that also occurred on a 19th September), perhaps a little pity can be spared still for the films and TV series that had the misfortune to premiere in the week of the tragedy. Art house Cine Tonalá was showing the inspiring documentary *Made in Bangkok* (Flavio Florencio, 2015), on a Mexican transgender soprano who travels to Thailand for surgery. When the commercial chains reopened, their main local release was romantic comedy *Me gusta pero me asusta* ("I Like Him But He Scares Me," Beto Gómez, 2017) in which an unfashionably dressed youth from the narco-ridden north of Mexico courts with sweet persistence a silly, snobby girl from the capital.

Both titles had taken years to achieve their precious theatrical release. And the timing of that release was of course fortuitous. However when I saw *Me gusta*, charming but trivial, in a sparsely populated Cinemex theater that had just reopened in the Center, it came now with added pathos. The apartment the heroine shares with the twin sidekicks of an Argentine girl and the inevitable gay best friend is located in a Condesa street that is explicitly named as "Amsterdam." This is an idyllic park-fringed circuit which would become notorious as one of the hardest hit in the whole megalopolis. It was difficult not to think of the real-life dust-covered victims on TV when watching this candy-colored farce in the cinema.

Maybe it was just the subdued mood or the damp and chilly weather, but when normal programing restarted on TV the new novelas seemed strangely dark for a genre that was once the preserve of true romance. Televisa's *Caer en tentación* ("Yielding to Temptation") was a downbeat and claustrophobic chamber piece on twin adulterous couples with the former star of fluffy *Mi corazón es tuyo* (Silvia Navarro) now more sexual and more emotional. Azteca's *Las Malcriadas* (both "Rude Girls" and "Bad Maids") boasted no fewer than five female protagonists, each exemplifying a painful social issue, from domestic abuse to forced sex work.

Having previously avoided the damaged areas while rescue work was continuing, on my last day in Mexico City I took a walk through Roma and Condesa, whose biggest problems had once been dog-owner etiquette and restaurant noise. The densely built streets were now punctuated by cavities, where buildings had been shattered. The jewel-like parks, previously familiar as picturesque movie locations, now housed great white tents, refuges for victims who had not found shelter with friends or family or who hesitated to leave their possessions unguarded in ruinous homes.

It has to be said that poorer boroughs of Mexico City that suffered similar losses, such as Iztapalapa in the east and Xochimilco in the south, received somewhat less media coverage. And a quake just weeks earlier had devastated the already-impoverished southern states of Oaxaca and Chiapas. In the capital, however, the media response (from cinemas, via TV, to social media) had already revealed a great city determined to get back on its feet as soon as it could. This would be a painful process that, if the 1985 earthquake is any guide, would take not months but years. It would be time enough for film and television to work through a national trauma for Mexicans who have already proved themselves to be newly active and engaged, both as spectators and as citizens.

The Commemoration: 2018

Twelve months later in 2018, two exhibitions in Mexico City commemorated September 19, the all-too-memorable day of double earthquakes. "19S: El día que nos encontramos" ("9.19: The Day We Found Each Other") was held in the open air on the grand avenue of Reforma, a boulevard based on the model of Paris' Champs Elysées, in the section that stretches from the Angel of Independence monument to the traffic circle or Glorieta of the Palm. Produced by Pinhole and Cuartoscuro ("DarkRoom," a photo agency), the exhibit was made up of 40 large format black-and-white photographs mounted on black metal frames, which were themselves placed in concertina formation on the sidewalk. The images were positioned alongside the lengthy lines of passengers waiting for the new double-story Metrobus service along Reforma, thus ensuring a mass audience.

Presented explicitly as a "homage" to the rescuers of 2017, the exhibition was focused, in the tradition (as we shall see) of Carlos Monsiváis' and Elena Poniatowska's writings on the earlier earthquake, not so much on official disaster workers as on the representatives of civil society. Some pictures also ventured beyond ever-centralizing Mexico City, showing the devastation in provincial capitals Puebla and Oaxaca. Two formats predominated. On the one hand, there were wide shots showing groups of volunteers, often with fists raised. On the other, close-ups focused on faces or body parts, such as anonymous arms shoveling rubble. There were no too-troubling scenes of explicit death or mutilation.

The Metrobus line, by which the exhibition stood, is one of the recent innovations in infrastructure in Mexico City. This new route along Reforma (which is not served by underground railway) speeds from Chapultepec park, via the traffic circles devoted in turn to Diana the Huntress, the emblematic Angel, an implausibly tall palm tree, the indigenous leader Cuaúhtemoc, and the European adventurer Columbus and beyond. This, then, is a very loaded location for an exhibition on the disaster, steeped as it is in the monumental depiction of national history. What is more, the much loved Angel monument fell and shattered in an earlier earthquake in 1957 and swayed dangerously in 2017. An exhibit with aspirations to aesthetic excellence was thus also integrated into the everyday space and time of *chilangos*, whether still traumatized or now indifferent, addressing the citizens who staffed the high-rise office blocks and hotels along the avenue.

A second exhibit was more substantial, albeit cloistered inside the walls of a specialist museum that, unlike the first, separated it from the traffic and tumult of daily life. "Sismos 1985/2017" ("Earthquakes 1985/2017") was housed in the Museo de Memoria y Tolerancia ("Museum of Memory and Tolerance"), opposite the "Hemiclico" in the Alameda, the spotlessly white semicircular marble monument that is dedicated to Mexico's most beloved and respected president, Benito Juárez. The exhibit's poster was of an anonymous raised fist surrounded by a force field of concentric red circles. And its opening statement was taken from Monsiváis in 1985, when he claimed that "civil society exists even amongst those unfamiliar with the term." A brief historical prelude showed the Aztec or Mexica glyph of *tlalollin*, derived from the twin signs denoting, respectively, "earth" and "movement" (today Ollin is the name appropriately chosen by a local motion picture visual effects company).

In the 1985 section, lined with devastating black-and -white photographs, the most prominent ruin depicted is of the Hotel Regis, which stood just down the road from the museum site. Here a wall sign echoes Monsiváis: Elena Poniatowska writes that "the government wasn't there; the poorest Mexicans were." This section is devoted to what is called the broader "legacy" of the first earthquake, an "urban movement" illustrated by the photo of a child holding a sign demanding "decent housing for the people" ("vivienda popular digna").

Next we move on to a small video room of documentary footage, entered through feigned jagged broken walls mimicking real-life ruins. Texts on those walls offer differing perspectives. Rescuer Ramón Ortiz is quoted as saying that Mexicans after the quake were "living a new time [*época*], a kind of new internal time [*tiempo*]" that went beyond external, material demands, however crucial the latter were at that moment. Nearby journalist Ignacio Padilla speaks rather of the eternally "adolescent Mexico of the 80s," while Emilio Carballido of daily *El Universal*, claims that young people (identified by the distinctively Mexican term "chavos") were indeed well up to the demands of the disaster.

The mood in the section on 2017 is somewhat different, marked by large-scale photographs that are now in more immediate color. The section on the collapsed Colegio Rébsamen pays tribute to a martyred teacher, who stayed with the small charges who also perished. A text on the wall urges the visitor to move "From memory to grief, from grief to action." Most interesting perhaps is the section in this room contrasting media in 1985 and in 2017. Here the exhibit points to a radical change: from the dubious government control of information in the first earthquake (belied only by trusted exceptions, such as Televisa's Jacobo Zabludovsky) to "first hand" news via smartphones that empowered "a new society, transformed and informed" in the second. (In fact in the aftermath of the impact there was no cell phone or internet service.) Beyond image and text, precious objects are also enshrined in a glass case: an "emergency backpack" is made to hold invaluable, everyday items such as an old-fashioned transistor radio, a flashlight, and cat food.

While the exhibit claims that the leitmotif of 1985 was "Incompetence" and that of 2017 "Corruption," a moving section called "Denunciation" features only large color headshots of weary, wary *topos* ("moles" or volunteer rescue workers), male and female. And throughout the museum space we hear an echoing soundscape of shouts, sirens, and crashes. Most effectively, a darkened alcove is dedicated to the rescuers once more. It contains no visuals, only recordings of anonymous cries, rumbles, and shovels. There is an attempt here, then, to recreate in the gallery space the bodily, multisensorial experience of the quakes and their aftermath, without, however, inspiring a paralyzing fear that would disable the necessary resistance to incompetence and corruption.

Also unshowy, but effective, is the section on "Reconstruction," which features video footage of members of the NGO #LoveArmyMexico rebuilding shattered homes with none of the film star supporters who were so prominent at the time of the disaster now visible. Reference to this activist agency leads on to an attempt to introduce a collective political context for these singular tragedies: phenomena, we are told, are natural, but disasters are human. In such disasters around the world, we are informed, four women die for every man, because poverty is feminized; and the elderly are also disproportionately affected by disasters. Meanwhile back in Mexico, although fatalities was less in the second quake (in 1985, 9000 are thought to have died; in 2017 just 300), buildings still collapsed because of corruption, most especially in the poor outer boroughs of Xochimilco, Iztapalapa, and Tláhuac. A video display shows a still-devastated apartment building in Tlalpan, another working-class area.

Illustration 9.1 *El día de la unión* (Kuno Becker, 2018)

A jagged black crack snakes along the wooden floor of exhibit. Like the recorded cries, it is graphically expressive, but not exploitative. Although the first exhibition benefited from its central setting on the city's major avenue, the second also served as a stimulus to thought and action, especially perhaps for the groups of schoolchildren crowding the gallery when I visited. And beyond the specific traumatic event (or events), the venue of "Sismos" places Mexican disasters in a broader historical, political, and ethical context: the Museum of Memory and Tolerance contains a permanent display devoted to the Holocaust (Illustration 9.1).

The same week that these two exhibits opened, a rare feature film on the 1985 earthquake premiered in commercial theaters throughout Mexico. *El día de la unión* ("The Day of Union," originally titled more prosaically *El día del terremoto* ["The Day of the Earthquake"]) was written, directed, and produced, by Kuno Becker, a telenovela graduate who had also appeared as national hero Ignacio Zaragoza, the mild-mannered general who won the Battle of Puebla against the French intervention (*Cinco de mayo, la batalla* [Rafael Lara, 2013]).

While a previous minimalist title on the same subject, named austerely for the time the quake hit (*7.19* [Jorge Michel Grau, 2016]), had focused grimly on two men trapped in rubble, *El día de la unión* stresses, beyond physical agony, the social bonds and even hope supposedly created by disaster. There is, however, a problem of retrospection here. The many years of preparation and production, doggedly carried out by Becker, were interrupted by the second quake. According to the auteur, the theatrical release was delayed for a year and was now timed for a bow on the double anniversary (Barranco 2018). In spite of such lengthy labor devoted to the film, press reception proved negative. One journalist asked whether audiences really want to revisit a trauma that now seemed so recent (it was a dilemma no doubt also faced by exhibitors) (Moscatel 2018). Another review found the film's plot clichéd and its critique of corruption in a subplot unconvincing (Salinas 2018).

El día de la unión follows disaster movie conventions by first setting up the everyday life of its characters, focusing here on the tensions in a broken family. The overworked journalist played by Becker himself picks up his adorable son from the wife from whom he is separated. He drives the child to his office instead of school, as he had promised the mother, and the boy is subsequently trapped in an underground parking lot. Meanwhile a taxi driver, still mourning his deceased wife, takes a pretty young female fare to her destination nearby: the Regis Hotel, where soon she will meet her death. Finally, a corrupt businessman schemes to bury incriminating evidence stored in the same building. After the quake the now heroic father will rescue his son in an underground odyssey, finally sacrificing himself so that his son may live. The modest taxi driver will, initially unwillingly, become a leader of the newly named *topos* or "moles," the spontaneous rescue teams, making a rousing speech on the glories of Mexico atop the smoking ruins. And the corrupt businessman will be taken away by the authorities to the jeers of the local heroes gathered in the ruined streets.

Beyond this conventional plot, accomplished digital effects show us the devastation in the wake of the quake to visceral effect. Meanwhile the physical sets for the subsequent main action were constructed on the back lots of Churubusco, the same studios that would be hit by the second tremor. And fictional recreation is supplemented by grainy documentary footage, integrated into the feature film by the presence of journalist-characters sent to document the tragedy (an actor standing in for real-life Zabludovsky is also shown from behind as we hear the respected newsreader's actual voice). While some critics attacked the limited scale of the film, restricted as it is for the main part to a single city block, the spatial limitation here coincides to some extent with Mexican media coverage of the events. The latter also tends to focus on single sites that metonymically take the place of a whole that resists representation, the main ones being the aforementioned Hotel Regis in 1985 and the Colegio Rébsamen in 2017.

There is also some attempt in Becker's film to expand beyond the unique event to engage with broader social issues, as in the exhibit at the Museum of Memory. One *topo* who stands bravely against the tractor which seeks to demolish a building where victims might still be saved is a feisty young woman. And the film's corruption subplot alludes to the economic dimension of a natural phenomenon that became, all too soon, a human disaster.

But, no doubt fearing unwelcome controversy around such a charged event, the film's ideology remains conservative. It is symptomatic that the poster shows the father, mother, and son as they do not appear in the film itself, holding hands as they stand among the ruins. And this threatened patriarchal family is restored not just once but twice: first, by the sacrifice of the erring father, who is finally rehabilitated in the eyes of his newly devoted wife; second, by the taxi driver's adoption of a baby he saves from the ruins, which substitutes for the child he did not have with his own dead spouse.

Familial reconstruction merges definitively with patriotic rehabilitation in the final scenes of *El día de la unión*. Decades after the quake the taxi driver, now dressed in the orange uniform of the *topo*, proudly attends the anniversary ceremony at the monument in the small garden by the Alameda park that was created on the site of the fallen Regis Hotel. By his side stands his adopted son, the now adult child formerly rescued from the ruins, who has in turn become a rescuer himself. The two men briefly fear that citizens have forgotten the tragedy that has effected them so deeply, until at the last minute the crowds flood in. Their raised fists imitate the monument itself, which consists of three disembodied hands laid over each other, clenched around the pole on which a Mexican flag flies. The music swells and the camera rises high above the city to show the recently restored park (the oldest in Latin America) now lined by large and shiny new buildings (the Hilton Hotel, the Museum of Memory) with the picturesque Palace of Fine Arts and lofty Latin American Tower (monuments that survived both quakes) in the near distance. The sequence suggests a filmic day of union, indeed: of past and present, of city and citizen.

This final shot is an image of a metropolis reconstructed and a citizenry remade somewhat at odds with the experience of the second earthquake, which, as we saw earlier, emphasized a continuing vulnerability. The second earthquake is of course unshown in a film which was nearly completed before that disaster took place. But it is surely inescapable to viewers. And it is striking that the feature film's appeal to unabashed sentimentality and unashamed nationalism was more soberly avoided by the exhibits described earlier.

I saw *El día de la unión* in the week of its release and on the day before the earthquake anniversary in the Cinemex Reforma, one of the first multiplexes to be constructed in the city. The sparse audience was diverse, including some senior viewers who no doubt remembered the historical event recreated somewhat problematically on screen. Other audience members saw fit to bring children, who one hopes were not too traumatized by the lengthy and disturbing travails of the trapped boy in the film. What I had initially failed to realize is that we were watching the film in the theater physically closest to the site of the events it so laboriously recreated. The Cinemex Reforma is on the edge of the Alameda and just a hundred yards from the twin sites of the fallen hotel and the risen monument that took its place in a renamed Plaza de la Solidaridad ("Solidarity Square"). It was an area central also to the commemorations that took place the same week.

On September 16, 2018, the massive military parade celebrating Mexican Independence Day that traditionally makes it way from the Zócalo past the Alameda and down Reforma featured a new star guest. Frida the rescue dog came out of retirement and posed stolidly complete with iconic goggles on the back of a truck, receiving the crowd's delighted ovation. The extensive participation of service women was also noticeable and unusual.

Three days earlier, a different, more eerie demonstration had taken place along the same route. Students marched in silence, recreating a mute protest by the youth movement 50 years earlier in 1968 that would culminate tragically in the massacre by the military at Tlatelolco. Today's students were also protesting the violence against their number carried out in recent days by criminal gangs on the campus of the UNAM, Mexico City's largest and most emblematic university. It would seem, then, that in Mexico, as elsewhere, the ideals of unity and solidarity are difficult to reconcile with a violent past and a problematic and conflictive present, outside of movie theaters at least.

On September 19, 2018, at exactly the time of the second quake, a renewed drill or "simulacro" was held. In the city center, traffic stopped and office workers filed out to line up in orderly fashion in their allotted places outside. Orange-clad *topos* displayed their rescue skills by rappelling from the top of the large Scientology building that also now overlooks the Alameda. The monument by the park was freshly decorated with wreaths of flowers, all in white. Helicopters hovered overhead. The laudable practical mission of earthquake awareness was combined somewhat uneasily with the day's other essential aim: commemorating the victims whose lives had been lost in spite of the efforts of the brave civil defense operatives whose representatives were on display that day.

Television was once more in something of a bind also. Televisa's morning show *Hoy* did not now focus on the charitable activities of stars but rather on the ordinary people of its audience. Coincidentally it was a strategy also favored this time by the gossip magazines, *TVNotas* and *TVyNovelas*, which focused in the week of the anniversary on inspiring and endearing stories of photogenic victims, now generally recovered, fleeting media stars of the original earthquake coverage. On September 20, 2018, *Hoy*'s cameras visited one woman still confined to grim temporary accommodation after her building had collapsed 12 months earlier. Brought to the studio, she was given a makeover by specialists in hair, cosmetics, and fashion, seemingly cloned from the recently revived US *Queer Eye* reality show (Bravo, 2003–7; Netflix 2018). Finally she was displayed to the regular hosts who declared themselves delighted by her transformation.

On the same morning, *Hoy*'s "Camioncito" or "Little Bus," a regular feature, was sent out into the Historic Center to capture vox pop interviews. Citizens in the grand square of the Zócalo or more humble but traditional markets were encouraged to shout out last year's slogan "México de pie," but this time followed by an enthusiastic "Hoy" or "Today," thus promoting the name of the program as well as the urgency of national reconstruction.

A third segment, this time not earthquake related, highlighted the limits of television's compensatory make-believe. Melancholy matrons who had been deprived (by illness or poverty) from enjoying the *quinceañera* of their dreams were brought to the studio once more to take part in professional choreography set to the music of their time or choice: from the Backstreet Boys to salsa standards. *Hoy*'s regular hosts, their celebrity status burnished by the proximity of everyday people, got to choose the winner. Like the notorious US reality show *avant la lettre*, *Queen for a Day* (NBC, 1956–60; ABC, 1960–4), Televisa thus gave its viewers the briefest taste of media fame before sending them back to their postearthquake lives, humdrum or tragic as the case may be.

Meanwhile the charity "Levantemos México," the subsidiary of Gael García Bernal and Diego Luna's film festival Ambulante, sent out a sober email to donors documenting in admirable detail the reconstruction schemes to which it had contributed, one year after the disaster (hola@ambulante.org, September 19, 2018). Collaborating with many local organizations from Oaxaca to Xochimilco, it had distributed 33 million pesos via the two schemes called "Community Leadership" and "New Social Actors." This precision and concision are remarkable when contrasted with the much promoted schemes of some celebrities: popular young YouTuber and would-be actor Juanpa Zurita, a figurehead of #LoveArmy a year before, was pilloried by the press for his misleading and ineffectual effort, which signally failed to produce decent housing for the people (*TVNotas* 2018).

What is striking is that Ambulante's original and very effective charity now makes no mention of the publicity-shy stars who had promoted it so vigorously a year before. We can now go on, finally, to see how the lengthy press profiles of the most celebrated actors involved in fund-raising (at least, the most celebrated outside of their home country) anticipated their media intervention in earthquake reconstruction. Theirs is a story of how political solidarity can indeed be combined, albeit precariously, with commercial success and private intimacy.

Diego Luna and Gael García Bernal: Solidarity and Autonomy

On August 14, 2018, gossip magazine *TVNotas* ran a double-page picture spread on Diego Luna (unpaginated), playfully telling his career by numbers. Thus he had sung once in a film (the animated *The Book of Life*), had taken part in two pop videos (for the Puerto Rican Calle 13 and the American Katy Perry), had had three long-term girlfriends, acted in five telenovelas, begun work at the age of six, had his first sex scene at the age of 11, left home at 16, and made 18 films abroad and 22 in Spanish. The article, in a magazine normally focused on telenovela celebrities, thus reveals that Luna's star profile still intersects to some extent with a mass Mexican audience even as it plays out transnationally: the main picture used by *TVNotas* is of Luna's character in *Rogue One: A Star Wars Story* (Gareth Edwards, 2016).

If we turn to Luna's press clippings in the Cineteca files, we can trace how this rare profile emerged, parallel to but distinct from that of his friend Gael García Bernal. This local press was not of course accessible to Luna's future foreign fans or potential employers in Hollywood. Some of the general themes that emerge here relate back to those thrown up by the specific circumstances of the earthquake presented above. Beyond social solidarity, these include the status of television, the role of adolescence, and a celebrity thrown into relief by an appeal to the proximity of everyday people.

The very first clipping in the Cineteca's files, published when Luna was still known for his telenovelas, is headlined prophetically "Diego Luna, A Life Connected to Cinema" (Peguero 1998). A year later, an interview illustrated by a grungy photo of the young star (floppy hair, baggy shirt and pants) confirms that he is "fascinated by the big screen" (Mendoza de Lira 1999). Or again we are told in the same year "Diego Luna combines acting on TV with his true passion: cinema" (de la Cruz Polanco 1999). The young Luna admits here that his role as the bratty son in Azteca's *La vida en el espejo* (Argos, 1999), who learns responsibility when confronted by unwanted fatherhood, is challenging, but he still disavows the television that has made him famous. This telenovela, he asserts, is "completely different to the rest," offering the actor as it does a chance to show a situation he claims is "common among young people today, whatever their social or political position."

This rejection of everyday television (and of its stars who are the fodder of daily gossip shows and weekly magazines) is combined, however, with a display of modesty and qualified national allegiance. Often compared physically to Leonardo Di Caprio at this time, Luna repeatedly rejects the association, adding that it is not his dream to go to Hollywood (Sánchez Dávila 2000; Mendoza de Lira 2000). Luna also says here that he is not concerned at being typecast as a "youth" ("chavito," the same Mexican word used to describe the teenage heroes of the earthquake). Rather he welcomes the fact that, where once young Mexicans struggled to find work in their home country's cinema, now they are made more welcome. Luna's youthful ordinariness, then, his apparent closeness to his audience at this time, is clearly a great part of his appeal. And when he is pictured alongside a more conventionally good-looking member of his young cohort of actors (one who was not to enjoy Luna's international success), his greasy hair and crooked teeth (later corrected) stand out by comparison (Anonymous 2000).

This avowed ordinariness came under pressure after Luna's first great critical and commercial success, *Y tu mamá también*. The press and festivals insisted on treating Luna and García Bernal together (indeed, the pair were awarded jointly best actor prizes at Venice and Valdivia) (Anonymous 2001). It was only now, when safely legitimized by international cultural institutions, that Luna felt able to comment on his craft and on the "serious game" of acting (Anonymous 2002a). In this interview, he is now described in an oxymoron as an "old kid," one who, despite his success, holds fast to the shuffling walk and battered backpack typical of teenage boy (Maristain 2002).

Luna begins now to also discuss the state of Mexico and its cinema. When asked what it means to be Mexican, he says he rejects nationalistic flag-waving but also laments the lack of "solidarity" among his country's movie people, all too eager to trample each other (p. 33). Continuing his critique of the industry, he also claims that a successful Mexican film enriches only the exhibitors, "those who risk the least and care the least about cinema." As opposed to merely screening films, making movies in Mexico is to "get into the boat with your buddies [*compas*] and getting it done come what may" (Olivares 2003). Creative solidarity is thus held to trump commercial self-interest.

Soon this industry commentary takes an openly political turn. Claiming that "in this country, culture is not valued," Luna now attacks the PAN government of Vicente Fox for its lack of interest in Mexican art, which deserves to be promoted at "an international level" (Mata 2003). In the next decade, Luna will go on to call into question specific laws by another PAN government; to protest against US President Trump in Berlin by the remains of a symbolic wall; to argue for "peace and unity;" and repeatedly to demand "an end to corruption" (Castañedo 2016).

Luna's nonpartisan initiative (Spanish "convocatoria") "El día después" in which he was joined by fellow film luminaries Gael García Bernal, Alejandro González Iñárritu, and Alfonso Cuarón, posed the question "What will citizens do" on "the day after" the presidential elections of 2018 "whoever wins" (Vértiz de la Fuente 2018). This very visible political activism is combined somewhat easily with Luna's promotion of luxury brands, such as Swiss watches, and his casting in the *Star Wars* saga. But his role in the latter is presented in anti-American style in the local press as "A Mexican against the Empire" (Anon. 2016a). And Luna describes himself modestly once more as "the luckiest Mexican in the galaxy," arguing for the social relevance of the *Rogue One* that "talks about racial and cultural diversity" (Ayuso 2016).

The connections between Luna's star profile, based on a generalized sense of unity and solidarity, and the specific opportunity offered him and others by earthquake media are thus evident. Luna rejects the much criticized medium of television as mere telenovela, even as he participates in that medium and that genre. He presents himself from the start as the representative of a civil society that is integrated into the everyday space and time of *chilangos* (unlike Gael García Bernal, he was born in Mexico City and speaks fondly of his native Coyoacán). Most especially, his status as a new kind of adolescent (even as he ages), shuffling with practiced stylish shabbiness across the world's red carpets, appeals implicitly to the Mexican youths of the 1980s and beyond, when the so-called *chavos* stepped up at times of national emergency.

Luna's main mode in the press is the one we have seen in the media response to the earthquake, that of denunciation: successively he denounces everyday television, the film industry, government cultural policy, and finally government *tout court* as the supposed embodiment of corruption. Here he places his limited and individual experience within a collective political context, without however proclaiming allegiance to a particular political party (see the nonpartisan "El día después"). This broader historical, political, and ethical context seeks to engage the social bonds that are more charged at times of disaster and are repeatedly invoked by Luna as his career progresses and expands. It might seem that the ideals of unity and solidarity are difficult to reconcile with Luna's status as a Mexican "ambassador" for global luxury brands and to the Hollywood empire. But Luna's celebrity status, like that of the TV hosts he avoids, is underwritten by the continuing proximity he professes to everyday people and by an studied aura of ordinariness aided by the fact that he is not movie star handsome. Diego Luna, the Mexican press dutifully tells us, is "the same as ever" (Gutiérrez 2003).

If Luna's close and continuing friendship with Gael García Bernal is a fundamental part of his star image, Luna seems to have been in a subordinate position to his *cuate* (the Mexican word for "buddy" that both repeatedly employ). Indeed the press had written that, in, say, taking on roles based on historical figures, "Diego Luna follows in the footsteps of Gael García Bernal"

(Anon. 2002b). It is perhaps no surprise, then, that García Bernal's profile is consistently more confrontational and defiant than that of his friend.

Even before his breakthrough with *Amores perros*, García Bernal is cited as saying that "actors are not respected in Mexico" and that, no longer willing to work in the telenovelas that he had taken on only for money, he was obliged to take his chances in Britain (Hernández Villegas 2000). The press stressed his "luck": a successful telenovela as a child, a prize-winning feature at Cannes as a teenager, and, all grown up, "nude scenes" in a film then in postproduction (*Y tu mamá también*) (Silva 2000). Unlike Luna, García Bernal's image is thus from the start "unstoppable and international," based on a professional training that took place not just in London but also in Buenos Aires (González 2001). Yet, on receiving the Ariel for best actor, García Bernal claimed cannily that the Mexican prize was "the one that mattered most" and even that he "would give his life for [Mexico's] cinema" (de León 2001a).

This avowed cultural nationalism leads on to a political commitment more early and explicit than that of Luna. Calling on culture to "exorcise Mexico's demons," he praises the Zapatista leader Comandante Marcos ("a fundamental figure") and claims Mexico must remain neutral in the USA's war against Bin Laden (de León 2001b) (these opinions do not prevent from becoming around the same time the face of Levis jeans in a campaign seen only in the USA). Next he takes on religion, arguing that "the Catholic church has not adapted to the passing of time" and "Mexicans want [the Church] to stop repressing them" (Anon. 2002c). The press rewards these statements on the "controversial" *El crimen del padre Amaro* with appropriately blasphemous headlines: "The Divine Look" (García Bernal's penetrating eyes are a fetish for many critics) (Fernández-Santos 2002); or again "Gael's Confessions" (Anon. 2002d).

Elsewhere his career is described as "promising and polemical," a case of "stolen innocence" (a reference once more to his then-current film role as a sexually charged young priest) (Castillo and Franco 2002). Here former colleagues strike notes of caution. Pedro Damián, a famed telenovela producer who first cast García Bernal in *El abuelo y yo* ("Grandad and Me," Televisa, 1992), says he could never have imagined that the "happy, hardworking" child he once worked with would later enjoy such success. One costar warns that if he keeps choosing controversial roles, "people will desert him."

García Bernal clearly paid little heed to such warnings. Typical later headlines read "Gael García Bernal Reflects on Politics through Film" and (when he appeared as a Chilean policeman hunting down the Marxist poet) "Neruda Provided Many Weapons through his Words" (Salgado 2017). Even as his friend Diego Luna was starring in *Star Wars*, García Bernal was quoted as saying "Hollywood is no longer the greatest" and was acclaimed by the Mexican press as "a man with values" (Waintal 2017). One of those values was the defense of local cinema: García Bernal told *La Jornada* on receiving a prize in San Sebastián (which, as we saw in the first chapter of this book, promotes its festival as a bridge between Spain and Latin America), "We need policies to promote Latin American cinema" (Anon 2016b).

Ignacio Sánchez Prado (2013) has read García Bernal's career as an example of "neoliberal" stardom. He notes how, after his early trio of Mexico-based box office hits (*Amores perros*, *Y tu mamá bien*, and *El crimen del padre Amaro*), García Bernal was cut off from associations with his home territory by international roles that had him play Spanish, Argentine, or Chilean rather than Mexican. Yet, in spite of this international access, García Bernal failed to make a successful career in US indie film. Sánchez Prado contrasts García Bernal's star persona with that of Salma Hayek, who (despite her Lebanese heritage) embodied a physical type that was welcomed by US audiences as "typically Mexican." By conforming to bodily stereotype, Hayek thus achieved a more lasting professional life north of the border. We have seen from my account of his local press profile that García Bernal struggled, more so perhaps than his friend Luna, to reconcile political activism and cultural distinction with commercial success, at home as well as abroad.

Dolores Tierney (2018) gives a slightly different account of García Bernal's star persona in her close reading of his performance in one transnational role, as the young Che Guevara in *The Motorcycle Diaries* (Walter Salles, 2004). Tierney argues that the "key factors" in García Bernal's stardom are not just "the connection to political and cultural activism" I have mentioned above, but also his "sex appeal" which "reflects a more classical version of Latin stardom: the sensual *Latin lover*" (297). Rejecting "expressive-realist assumptions in which 'good acting' is 'true to life' and at the same time expressive of the actor's 'organic self'" (297), Tierney argues rather (drawing on Richard Dyer) that García Bernal's performance here should be read as "a set of culturally and historic specific codes" in which the twin aspects of his stardom combine with his director's commitment to realism and their film's mise-en-scène (298). Significantly in the close analyses of sequences that follow, Tierney traces this discursive (rather than psychological) mode of performance style even in semi-improvised scenes in which the modern star as "ravishing revolutionary" encounters ordinary Latin Americans (nonprofessional actors) on his cinematic and political journey through the continent (299). It is a charged and ambivalent confrontation with the everyday that we have also seen in Diego Luna's media persona and one which prepared them for their joint role as charismatic, but down-to-earth, disaster activists.

Finally, however, the two friends' careers are also explained by Pierre Bourdieu's account of the paradoxical "rules of art," which the French sociologist elaborated for the nineteenth century but which remain pervasive in our own time and can be briefly sketched here. According to John R. W. Speller's account of "autonomy" in *Bourdieu and Literature*, there are three phases in the historical process by which art came to set its own rules (n.d.). The first is "a critical moment when a faction of writers turned their back on the buying and reading public and began a competition according to their own rules and standards" (para. 2); the second "the opposition between art and money, one of the field's fundamental 'mental structures' or 'structuring principles'"; and the third "Zola's intervention in the Dreyfus affair, the point at which writers broke out of their self-imposed isolationism and brought the field to … its highest point of autonomy." What is new here is "the position or post of the 'pure' autonomous writer and the associated dispositions of disinterest (indifference to the verdicts of the market), moral neutrality (not immorality), and political independence (… an independent 'political' authority)" (para. 9).

If, then, "writers sacrificed economic profit, they received a different form of 'symbolic' capital, which offered its own rewards and gratifications" (para. 13). Moreover the committed autonomous artist "did not convert into a politician … Nor did he try to compete with his political masters at their own game … [Zola] intervened in the political sphere *as an intellectual*, in the name of the values and principles in operation in his own field" (para. 18).

The stardom of the two *compas* or *cuates*, whose global reach far exceeds that of the other actors treated in this book, follows Bourdieu's prescription for artistic autonomy, cultural capital, and political commitment. By disavowing early on their participation in telenovela, the twin stars first turn their back on the mass TV public, asserting their own rules and standards (e.g. a concern for "situations common to young people" that trumps commercial mass media). The opposition between broadcast TV and feature film maps on to the structuring principle between money and art (both actors assert they only take money from television because it allows them to dedicate themselves to their purer and more perilous cinematic vocation, compared by Luna to a communal boat trip). Sacrificing a degree of economic profit, they then receive Bourdieu's corresponding symbolic reward of cultural capital. This can in turn be reconverted into political intervention. Crucially, however, that intervention is as artists and not as politicians. This is why Luna's postelection "Convocatoria" (official call or notification) must be nonpartisan and why the humanitarian goal of earthquake reconstruction, one that transcends party politics, fits so well with the couple's artistic trajectory.

Finally, according to Speller, "it is by affirming their right to transgress the most sacred values of the state – those of patriotism for example …, that intellectuals can assert their independence to the highest degree" (para. 19). As we have seen, both stars are eager to distance themselves from Mexican flag-waving. Indeed the segments they directed for *Revolución* (2010), a portmanteau film made to commemorate the centenary of the Mexican Revolution, are characteristically iconoclastic. And in line with Bourdieu's flexible habitus (in which social positions and cultural dispositions are free-floating, even as they are perceived as natural), both stars can return to television late in their careers. This is because (as we have seen throughout this book) traditional outlets have been usurped by newly prestigious streaming services: Luna will appear in a series for Netflix and García Bernal for Amazon Prime.

On November 4, 2018, a now-gray-haired García Bernal (no longer the cheeky *chavito*) posed on Instagram grinning at a masked Zapatista leader in Chiapas. Below an image that was soon to become a meme (García Bernal himself mentioned his likeness to "Pepe Grillo," the Spanish-language version of Jiminy Cricket), the star spoke very generally of a "place to share utopias" and of "a conversation that makes us buddies [*compas*]." While Speller warns us that on the internet "the boundary between the artist and the general public is becoming once more indistinct" (para. 27), here García Bernal's appeal to male comradeship on social media, in this case with a radical Leftist, confirms his and Luna's tricky strategy of negotiating art, commerce, and politics via the key term of friendship. It is the most disinterested (most autonomous) of relations and was the most suited to the admirable goal of earthquake reconstruction.

References

Anonymous. 2000. ¿Sabía Usted? Diego Luna, Osvaldo Benavides. *El Universal*, October 10. Sección Espectáculos, p. 2.

———. 2001. Diego y Gael: otra vez los mejores. *Esto*, October 7. Sección B, p. 20.

———. 2002a. La actuación, juego serio. *Excelsior*, April 2. Sección Espectáculos, p. 1.

———. 2002b. Diego Luna le sigue el paso a Gael García. *Crónica*, November 10, no page.

———. 2002c. Les mexicanos quieren que dejen de reprimirlos. *México Hoy*, August 15. Sección B, p. 7.

———. 2002d. Las confesiones de Gael. *Reforma*, August 11. Sección Magazzine, p. 10.

———. 2016a. Un mexicano vs. el imperio. *24 Horas*, December 14. Sección Vida +, p. 19.

———. 2016b. Urgen políticas para promover el cine iberoamericano: Gael García. *La Jornada*, September 18. Sección Espectáculos, p. 6a.

Ayuso, Rocío. 2016. Diego Luna, actor: 'Soy el mexicano más afortunado de toda la galaxia.' *El País*, December 13. Sección Cultura, p. 29.

Barranco, Daniela. 2018. *El día de la unión*, un homenaje cinematográfico a las víctimas de los 19S. *Chilango*, September 19. https://www.chilango.com/cine-y-tv/pelicula-el-dia-de-la-union/

Castañedo, Iván. 2016. Diego Luna denuncia corrupción mexicana. *Milenio*, September 28. Sección Hey!, p. 42.

Castillo, Alberto, and Salvador Franco. 2002. ¿Inocencia robada? *El Universal*, August 14. Sección Espectáculos, pp. 1–2.

Cueva, Álvaro. 2017. El sismo y los medios. *Milenio*, September 9. http://www.milenio.com/opinion/alvaro-cueva/el-pozo-de-los-deseos-reprimidos/el-sismo-y-los-medios. Accessed 29 July 2018.

de la Cruz Polanco, Fabián. 1999. Diego Luna compagina su actuación en TV con su verdadera pasión: el cine. *El Universal*, November 5, p. 6.

de León, Angélica. 2001a. Daría la vida por el cine nacional. *Reforma*, November 4. Sección Gente, p. 25.

———. 2001b. Da Gael García clave para la cultura: llama a exorcizar demonios de México. *Reforma*, November 24. Sección Cultura, pp. 2–3.

Fernández-Santos, Elsa. 2002. Gael García Bernal, la mirada divina. *El País: Revista de Agosto*, August 15, p. 19.

González, Enrique. 2001. Gael García: es imparable e internacional. *Reforma*, May 1. Sección Gente, p. 1.

Gutiérrez, Vicente. 2003. Diego Luna, el mismo de siempre. *El Economista*, October 15. Sección La Plaza, p. 8.

Hernández Villegas, Ernesto. 2000. Falta respeto para los actores en México. *El Universal*, June 17, no page.

Luna, Diego, and Gael García Bernal. 2017. Join Diego Luna and Gael García Bernal in Supporting Mexico. *Omaze*. https://donate.omaze.com/mexico. Accessed 29 July 2018.

Maristain, Mónica. 2002. Un chico viejo. *El Universal*, April 28. Sección Día 7, pp. 29–33.

Mata, Gabriela. 2003. En este país no se cuida la cultura. *Milenio*, October 1. Sección Hey!, p. 6.

Mendoza de Lira, Alejandro. 1999. Diego Luna, del brazo de la diosa fortuna. *El Universal*, July 19. Sección Espectáculos, p. 6.

———. 2000. No me siento el DiCaprio mexicano. *El Universal*, February 10. Sección Espectáculos, p. 7.

Moscatel, Susana. 2018. ¿Quieren ver la película del terremoto? *Milenio*, September 14. http://www.milenio.com/opinion/susana-moscatel/estado-fallido/quieren-ver-la-peliculadel-terremoto

Olivares, Juan José. 2003. En México una cinta exitosa sólo enriquece a los exhibidores: Luna. *La Jornada*, August 26. Sección Espectáculos, p. 8.

Peguero, Raquel. 1998. Diego Luna, una vida conectada al cine. *La Jornada*, April 20. Sección Espectáculos, p. 27.

Salgado, Ivett. 2017. Neruda dio muchas armas con sus palabras. *Milenio*, March 10, no page.

Salinas, Mabel. 2018. El día de la unión: crítica. *Cine Premiere*, September 14. https://www.cinepremiere.com.mx/el-dia-de-la-union-critica.html

Sánchez Dávila, Carmen. 2000. Niega Diego Luna ser el 'Di Caprio' mexicano. *El Heraldo*, February 10. Sección Espectáculos, p. 3.

Sánchez Prado, Ignacio. 2013. The Neoliberal Stars: Salma Hayek and Gael García Bernal and the Post-Mexican Film Icon. In *Latin American Icons: Fame Across Borders*, ed. Diana C. Niebylski and Patrick O'Connor, 147–156. Nashville: Vanderbilt University Press.

Silva, María. 2000. ¡Qué perra suerte! *Reforma*, June 18. Sección Magazzine, pp. 13–15.

Speller, John R.W. n.d. *Bourdieu and Literature*. Open Book Publishers. https://books.openedition.org/obp/482?lang=en

Tierney, Dolores. 2018. Gael García Bernal in *The Motorcycle Diaries*. In *Close Up: Great Cinematic Performances II*, ed. Murray Pomerance and Kyle Stevens, 296–305. Edinburgh: Edinburgh University Press.

TVNotas. 2017. Special issue: "¡Esto sí es México! 19/S ¡Un soldado en cada hijo te dio!" October 10.

———. 2018. Por esta razón Juanpa Zurita no ha entregado todas las casas a los damnificados. *TVNotas*, September 20. http://www.tvnotas.com.mx/noticias-espectaculos-mexico/por-esta-razon-juanpa-zurita-no-ha-entregado-todas-las-casas-los

TVyNovelas. 2017. Special issue: "¡Fuerza, México!" September 25.

Vértiz de la Fuente, Columba. 2018. El día después, convocatoria de Diego Luna. *Proceso*, June 24, no page.

Waintal, Fabio W. 2017. Hombre con valores. *Excelsior*, January 22. Sección Función, pp. 8–11.

10

Essay Film, Network Narrative, Streaming Series: *Vive por mí, Sincronía*

Thinking the Essay Film

This final chapter begins with an account of a new approach to the essay film from Laura Rascaroli's *How the Essay Film Thinks* (2017). It goes on to compare that account with a genre in fiction feature film and television series, the network narrative. It then analyzes a failed feature film *Vive por mí* ("Live for Me," Chema de la Peña, 2016) and the more successful *Sincronía* ("Synchronicity," 2017), a long-form fiction drama from Televisa's streaming platform Blim in light of these two paradigms. In conclusion it treats the very different, but strangely similar, star profiles of two women actors in my two audiovisual texts, released in Mexico in the same year: Martha Higareda and María Rojo. I suggest that their extratextual roles as entrepreneur and politician, respectively, inflect their fictional characters. I also argue, finally, for a new mode of temporality in the case of the series, whose episodes, most unusually, are intended to be viewed in any order and from multiple points of view.

Vive sin mí, directed by a little-known Spaniard with a track record in documentary, is a standard example of the network narrative in feature film, unchanged since at least González Iñárritu's founding feature in Mexico *Amores perros* (2000). *Sincronía*, on the other hand, acclaimed as "revolutionary," is a novelty, exhibiting a very visible formal experimentation, characterized by disjunction, juxtaposition, and insterstitiality previously unknown on free-to-air television. But it is also both an auteur project, the creation of a showrunner (Gustavo Loza) who is (as we saw in Chap. 7) a successful feature and TV series director, and a sociopolitical intervention, voicing as it does an uncompromising critique of corruption in the national institutions of political parties, policing, and the church. Beyond this unique case study, then, I argue for an extension of the conception of the "essay film" to embrace long-form fiction narrative streaming over the top (OTT).

It is striking that, according to Rascaroli, the film that provoked the first article comparing a film to an essay (by Jacques Rivette in 1954) was a fiction feature, Rossellini's *Viaggio in Italia* ("Journey to Italy," 1954), which was said to exhibit "freedom, inquisitiveness, and spontaneity … the true language of modern art" (2017, 2). Or again that Bazin writing on Chris Marker (1958) should say that the latter shows "nothing we have ever seen before in films with a documentary bias" (2017, 2). And if the essay film is held to be a "cinema of the word," exemplified by its frequent use of voiceover, its "hybridity" and "freedom" also attest to its "moment," defined as "its historical import and relevance" (2017, 2).

In her historical survey of accounts of the new genre, then, Rascaroli alternates between textual, political, and even technological frames. Thus for Hans Richter in the 1940s, the essay film exhibited "transgression and crossover of generic boundaries, inventiveness and freedom from conventions and expressive constraints, complexity and reflexivity," a lightness embodied by Astruc's "caméra-stylo" of 1948 (2017, 3). But for the global promoters of essayistic practice in the 1960s, such as Solanas and Getino with their Third Cinema (1969), the essay film was a "revolutionary, anticolonialist, anticapitalist film-making practice" (2017, 4) or in the words of Noel Burch (1981) the "most relevant [genre] to contemporary needs" (2017, 4). This "emphasis on the modernity of the form and its contemporary relevance … at once personal and intellectual" is for Rascaroli "utopian … linked to the pre-condition of almost futuristic technological development." She goes on to extend this vision (as I will myself) to "digital technology [with its] new channels of distribution and consumption" (2017, 4). This is perhaps the culmination of what Truffaut had called the portable and flexible "film of tomorrow," whose form is "politically inflected [by the] 1960s desire for increased participation, democracy, and self-expression… [the] dissident analysis of actualities" (2017, 5).

Such temporality is complex, however. If the essay film is contemporary, it is also against its time, according to Adorno both transgressive of the orthodoxy of form and manifesting "anachronism, untimeliness" (2017, 5). Moreover the genre slows time down. Boulous Walker writes in 2011:

> By refusing too hurriedly to seize the world, to understand it by containing, to speak definitively, to summarise, or assimilate it, the essay offers us a future

philosophy – one that holds out the hope for a slow engagement with the complexity and ambiguity of the world. (Cited by Rascaroli 2017, 6)

Part of that complexity is Rascaroli's "Method of 'Between'" (2017, 6). In Adorno's works, once more this method is characterized by "disjunction and differentiation... the object's scattered parts... discontinuity and juxtaposition" (2017, 7). In Deleuze's textual account, the in-between is the signifying power of interstitiality: "between two actions, between affections, between perceptions, between two visual images, between two sound images, between the sound and the visual" (2017, 9). In Homi Babha's more sociopolitical vision, the interstice is rather "the social articulation of difference, from the minority perspective, ... a complex, on-going negotiation that seeks to authorize cultural hybridities that emerge in moments of historical transformation" (2017, 14). Perhaps the most enigmatic of Rascaroli's examples of the in-between is the "lacuna-image," which is neither full presence nor absolute absence (2017, 13).

Finally, then, for Rascaroli, beyond attempts to define the essay film (typically as "subjectivity, reflexivity, hybridism, dialogism, voiceover commentary, mix of fiction and nonfiction, and autobiographical elements" [2017, 15]), the genre implies a new subjectivity and a new audience: "multiple or split narrators, embrac[ing a] contingent viewpoint [and] address[ing] a real, embodied spectator, who is invited to enter into a dialogue" (2017, 16). Moreover Rascaroli's embrace of multimedia in her corpus (of films both feature-length or short, sound or silent, composed of archive and original footage, exhibited as installations, on celluloid or on video) grants us license to extend her theoretical account, as she does not to the texts and practices of TV and internet fiction.

Thinking the Network Narrative

Paul Kerr's "*Babel*'s Network Narrative: Packaging a Globalized Art Cinema," an essay from 2010, offers (like Rascaroli) a historical account of the development of a genre parallel to that of the essay film and an analysis that is at once and alternately textual, sociopolitical, and technological. And it does so (unlike Rascaroli) by close analysis of the practice of a Mexican movie director. Kerr's interest is mainly in this last industrial dimension, or rather in the interaction between text and context, base and superstructure. He writes that "the current prevalence in international art cinema of the network narrative, exemplified here by *Babel* [Alejandro González Iñárritu, 2006], can be explained through analysis of the mode and social relations of production characterizing the global film and media companies involved in making such films" (2010, 37); or he announces again that "I want to look at a contemporary film form, the network narrative, as a kind of superstructural process or cultural practice …, and to try to unpick the impact on that choice of form of the film's industrial base" (2010, 38).

Kerr draws on David Bordwell (who coined the term "network narrative" in his essay "Mutual Friends and Chronologies of Chance" in 2008) to identify what he calls "a common norm of storytelling in contemporary cinema… tales of interlocking lives and converging fates" (2010, 38). Bordwell, writes Kerr: "offers several metaphysical, zeitgeist-based ideas as explanatory models, including a culture of disconnectedness – or, conversely, increasing connectedness – the Internet, connectivity, networking, chaos theory and so on" (2010, 39). It is a combination of formal disjunction and juxtaposition and contemporary reference and relevance ("actuality") which we have seen in the essay film. But unlike Rascaroli's or Bordwell's theoretical frameworks, Kerr seeks a material explanation linking narrative and production processes: while the films "often dramatize the unseen connections between apparently disparate, dispersed peoples and situations," the talent "packaged" together in films like *Babel* can themselves be seen as circulating objects: commodified, casualized laborers or, for those names above the title, "brands", such as Iñárritu, who was of course a pioneer of the genre with *Amores perros* in 2000 (2010, 39).

We have seen that the essay film values the in-between. The network narrative would seem to privilege to the contrary connection. But crucially, according to Kerr, those connections are random. Citing Bordwell once more Kerr writes: "The most common chance-based convergence, as conventional as a Main Street shootout in a Western, is the traffic accident" (2010, 43). Indeed Bordwell had defined art cinema (even before its new network narrative variant) as "defin[ing] itself explicitly against the classical narrative mode and especially against the cause-effect linkage of events" (2010, 41).

This new causality and temporality is combined with three factors: realism, authorial expressivity, and ambiguity (41). Thus, on the one hand, the realism of art cinema "shows us real locations … and real problems (contemporary "alienation," "lack of communication" etc.)," especially sexuality ("the aesthetics and commerce of the art cinema often depends upon eroticism") (2010, 42). But on the other, it "play[s] with time and space as well as formal stylistic experiment" (2010, 41). In Latin America, moreover, writes Kerr, "an indigenous realist movement, somewhat comparable to Italian neorealism, becomes more conscious of the conventions involved in realism, and develops more abstract experiments in form" (2010, 42). The self-conscious reflexivity of the network narrative only intensifies this unstable combination of sociopolitical address (alienation, lack of communication) and formal complexity and fragility (anachronism, fragmentation) that is for Kerr a mirror of the films' plots and production process, with their restlessly circulating subjects and objects.

Now, after *Babel*, Iñárritu, sensing perhaps the exhaustion of the subgenre, moved away from network narratives: *Biutiful* (2010), *Birdman* (2014), and *The Revenant* (2015) focus on single, troubled figures. Yet the network narrative remains current, in Mexico as elsewhere: multi-thread fiction feature *Vive por mí* ("Live for Me"), directed by Spaniard Chema de la Peña and focusing on the Iñárritu-like themes of traffic accidents and organ donation, was released in Mexico City in 2017, the same year as streaming series *Sincronía*. And if the subgenre exemplifies critical conflicts between art and industry and between the local and the global, it also confronts the twin media of cinema and television: Kerr, who was a pioneer scholar of quality TV, cites (via Bordwell once more) "the influence on cinema's assimilation of network narrative of the ensemble seriality of TV drama series like *Hill Street Blues* (1981–1987)" (2010, 41). We can now go on to see how the network narrative's existing but disavowed connection with television extends and mutates when a series is made for a new streaming platform and how that emergent medium allows it to align with the textual, social, and technological claims of the essay film. But first I offer an account of *Vive por mí*, as a film version of the dominant genre of network narrative.

Vive por mí: A Text Book Network Narrative

> Una noche tres personas reciben la misma esperada llamada; tras el fallecimiento de una persona en un accidente de tráfico, tienen la oportunidad de obtener el ansiado trasplante de riñón que necesitan.

> One night three people receive the same phone call they have hoped for; after the death of someone in a traffic accident, they have the chance of receiving the longed for kidney transplant they need (Illustration 10.1)

Vive por mí's synopsis, reproduced here from the back of its DVD, makes explicit the film's allegiance to the network narrative both formally and thematically: the script's ternary structure and the plot devices of intense connection and disconnection between random inhabitants of the city (car crash and organ transplant) are highly reminiscent of González Iñárritu's early trilogy (of *Amores perros* and *21 Grams*, respectively). Moreover Tiaré Escanda, who plays Valentina, one of the three hopeful donor recipients, is known for *El*

Illustration 10.1   Martha Higareda in *Vive por mí* (Chema de la Peña, 2016)

callejón de los milagros ("Midaq Alley," Jorge Fons, 1995), perhaps Mexico's first example of the multi-strand genre.

In the opening shot, the hand-held camera follows a stubbornly unglamorous Marta Higareda as Ana (no makeup, hair pulled severely back, curvy body camouflaged by an unflattering hoody) as she retrieves her alcoholic mother (Mariluz, played by Colombian actress Margarita Rosa de Francisco) from a sordid bar. The credits play over a night-driving shot that will prove typical of the film that follows. The actors are lit by sickly greens and blues and the city outside the car reduced to out-of-focus street and vehicle lights glowing to the sound of the droning soundtrack. This is the very image of urban alienation as interpersonal noncommunication (even or especially within members of the same family). But it is also highly reminiscent of the aesthetic, both visual and aural, of *Amores perros* once more, even as it lacks Iñárritu's vibrant dynamism.

We cut to a modest city center restaurant (named for the provincial city of Pachuca), where Escanda's Valentina is mopping the floor. And then to a cinder block evangelical church in the urban outskirts (the roads are unpaved) where a white-bearded patriarch is addressing his flock. His appearance is very similar to that of El Chivo, the homeless hit man in Iñárritu's first film. Next we are returned to the wealthy milieu, where Higareda's Ana, clad in the uncharacteristic red gown her mother has forced on her, downs ill-advised drinks at the wedding of her more glamorous sister. At the 20-minute mark, the first act finishes as the three main characters (rich girl, modest waitress, proletarian pastor), summoned by phone, first come together at the alienating, fluorescent-lit hospital ward where only one will receive the kidney for which they are competing.

Director Chema de la Peña thus consistently cuts for contrast: between social classes (high, medium, and low) and the urban locations with which they are associated (lavish gardened mansion, anonymous street in the popular historic center, impoverished exurb). The editing thus mimics the ideological bias of the network narrative: the random and violent juxtaposition of mise-en-scène and montage that speaks, supposedly, of a fragmented and disconnected community. Director de la Peña even reproduces Iñárritu's polemic against television in *Amores perros*, the alleged bad machine of modern society: on a family TV we glimpse a scene of Azteca's *Lo que callamos las mujeres* ("What We Women Don't Say," 2001–present), a melodramatic anthology drama in which, coincidentally, María Rojo, star of *Sincronía*, made a guest appearance.

Yet *Vive por mí* addresses less evidently than *Sincronía* the urgent social issues of the country or city in which it is made. As mentioned earlier, the director is Spanish. And his main theme of the crisis in organ transplants normally receives relatively little media attention in Mexico. Moreover, the topic of class conflict is hardly original, having being a constant theme of telenovela since the genre began. Here the coincidence of common kidney disease will bring together wealthy Ana and modest Valentina, while an implausible erotic connection will unite Ana's aging blonde mother with the pastor's handsome young dark-skinned son Gavilán, played by Tenoch Huerta, the best-known actor in the cast after the top-billed Martha Higareda.

As in Iñárritu, once more, these apparently social issues of class and race give way to abstract moral, metaphysical, and even theological questions. Ana is initially punished for her drinking bout by being refused a transplant. The waitress suggests she trust in God for relief, as does the pastor to a parishioner whose small child is sick (when he dies, the priest is troubled by guilt). Gavilán fights his own brother inside the modest church, their struggle the very image of that of Cain and Abel. And if at one point Ana's disappointed mother calls her lover a "fucking Indian" ("indio de mierda"), the role of their relationship within the plot is rather to embody that primal eroticism which is also a necessary component of the network narrative. In spite of the precision of reference to Mexico City streets as Ana cruises the city for traffic accidents (at one point, the radio even mentions Juan Escutia, the small street in the *colonia* of Condesa, where *Amores perros*' famous crash was shot), the real-life megalopolis is aesthetically abstracted into a blur of pulsing colored lights.

It is, however, the final act of *Vive por mí* that is the most reminiscent of *Amores perros*. Ambulance-chasing Ana and Valentina transport a bloody body in the back of their car in a high-speed race to the hospital just as Iñárritu's two teenagers did for their injured dog. Tenoch Huerta's Gavilán (a very telenovela-type name) dies in a car crash precipitated once more by his own faithful canine. And his organ is received by Ana, who thus profits from the tragedy of her mother's adulterous lover. It is a highly unlikely plot- and people-connecting coincidence similar to those that structure *21 Grams* (which of course also focuses on organ donation) and *Babel*.

Vive por mí thus repeats the erotic, social, and structural conventions of the network narrative, but in a way that shows it is now nearly exhausted (the film was not a success in theaters in either Spain or Mexico). But it cannot reproduce the most treasured resource of the genre, the authorial voice, as its signature style is so closely identified with a Mexican master and not the Spanish neophyte who directed it via one of the typically transnational production deals tracked by Paul Kerr.

But in one crucial way, de la Peña's film coincides unexpectedly with one aspect of our related genre of the essay film cited by Rascaroli: direct address to the spectator. Of course the film's very title is an imperative in the second-person singular. But after *Vive por mí*'s modestly hopeful conclusion to the fictional narrative (Ana is reunited posttransplant with her now-sober mother) there comes an unexpected sequence of on-screen titles with documentary intent. We are informed that 20,000 people in Mexico are awaiting organ transplants, yet only 5600 received them in the past year. And, belying the specific narrative of the film, but confirming its general premise of social alienation, 80% of donations come from family and not deceased strangers. We the audience are asked directly what we want to become of our organs. And the audience is finally interpellated through the intimate form of the verb once more: "Tú decides" ("You decide"). It is exactly the same formula that will be used by Blim's streaming series *Sincronía*.

Sincronía: Essayistic and Network Narrated

With *Sincronía*, ensemble seriality returns to TV after its detour into art cinema, bringing with it the cultural distinction still claimed by the latter medium. In the only critical account of the series of which I am aware, Álvaro Cueva, Mexico's most prominent TV critic whom I have cited with some frequency in this book, claimed in *Milenio* on March 1, 2017, that *Sincronía* makes a "revolutionary" contribution to global television; that its online distribution lets viewers come to their own conclusions; and that, distancing itself from what he calls "light" Televisa, the series treats "our most delicate social conflicts through an exquisite cinematic language and an excellent cast."

The promotion of the series, through its posters and trailer, also suggests both the scattered parts, the discontinuity, and juxtaposition of the essay film and the multiple perspectives of the network narrative. The three posters for *Sincronía*, prominent in Mexico City in March 2017, show composite portraits of the four characters in each plot, collaged together in a way that heightens the fragmentation and in-betweenness of the resulting image. The series' trailer, meanwhile, contains shots of direct address to camera by individual characters (unseen in the series itself and more typical of the documentary mode) in which they challenge viewers to "choose how to see reality" even as they remind them that they "know nothing" (TeVeAdictos 2017).

A fragmentary aesthetics thus combines with a skeptical epistemology in the service of interactivity with the audience: taking advantage of the simultaneity of the streaming service, viewers are advised to choose their own order of viewing episodes, a radical break with the seriality preserved by Blim's foreign rivals such as Netflix.

The series itself is thus divided into three "blocks," each boasting four points of view on a single story with evident sociopolitical interest. The first plot is of the kidnapping of a wealthy, entitled young man (identified with the Mexican internet meme *mirrey*) as seen in turn by his father, a corrupt businessman, his put-upon chauffeur, the father's young girlfriend, who asks for ransom money from a friendly *narco*, and the victim himself. The second plot is on human trafficking. It is seen from the perspectives of the unwilling Greek escort herself, another corrupt businessman (briefly featured in the first "block"), a brave investigative journalist, and the steely Madame played by distinguished veteran María Rojo (other actors in the series are familiar from art cinema and the quality TV fiction of public channel Canal Once). The final plot treats a pedophile priest in a Catholic school, with the story shown from the perspectives of the wary janitor, the child's devout mother, the priest himself, and a fellow student (the *mirrey* of the first block also features here). While this complex structure stresses the synchronicity of the title, the series' credit sequence, signaling its distance from Televisa's traditional telenovela, shows none of these 12 characters. Evocatively focusing on cogs, whose linked operation suggests the intricate connections of the network narrative, the sequence also shows the breaking of a thread, suggesting the cognitive and expressive disruptions familiar from the essay film.

The series' form thus mimics the characteristics of Kerr's (and Bordwell's) network narrative: realism, authorial expressivity and ambiguity. It focuses on real locations (glamorous Acapulco, gritty Mexico City, picturesque San Miguel de Allende, respectively) and real issues (often sexual or erotic) that, although hardly unique to Mexico, hold a special purchase in that nation. Although, as we saw in Chap. 7, series runner Gustavo Loza is best known for romantic comedies (*¿Qué culpa tiene el niño?* is one of the biggest grossing Mexican films of all time), he takes a writing credit for all 12 episodes and a directing credit for 8, and presented the series to the press. And the ambiguity of this authorial expression focuses on social division as much as on textual perspectivism: the chauffeur, who arranges the kidnapping in one episode, is humiliated by his boss, father of the victim, in another; the immigrant, stripped of her papers and clothes, is progressively powerless before the traffickers, who force her into prostitution; the janitor, who at first seems complicit with the pedophile priests' cover-up, is in fact, as we learn, desperate for money for his sick son's operation.

These shifting points of view sometimes encourage us to take up ambivalent or problematic perspectives: in one episode, María Rojo's Madame weeps bitter and apparently sincere tears on the death of the prostitute she has groomed and abused elsewhere; in another the pedophile priest asks plaintively why he is not permitted to have a "partner." And the eroticization of the escort and schoolboy remains troubling, even when the sexualizing mode is attributed to the viewpoints of their respective abusers. While key sequences are repeated verbatim in each episode, they thus take on different meanings in different contexts. And in spite of its name, the series' temporality is not synchronous, with episodes beginning and ending at different points (and in different places) in relation to their common diegesis.

As Kerr and Bordwell wrote of the network narrative, realism here gives way to more abstract experiments in form. The authentic locations (palatial beach homes, squalid urban hovels, the hallowed Ópera Bar in the Historic Center) are shown not in documentary *vérité*-style but with showy low and high angles that call attention to camera positioning. And the stylized dramatic scenes segue into repeated dreamy aerial shots which punctuate them, implying an omniscient point of view (urban, maritime, ecclesiastical) belied by the fragmentary disjunction of plot points. The lightened technology of the drone that can now spin vertiginously around sites such as Mexico City's fragile Angel monument is reminiscent of the camera-pen in its expressivity. And of course the liberties of digital distribution mean that episodes of around 40-minute length are freed from the rigid constrictions of the broadcast programming grid for both producers and consumers.

There is little doubt, then, that *Sincronía*, the first series made for its streaming platform by still dominant free-to-air channel Televisa, aspires to the status of national narrative, even as its themes (kidnapping, the sex trade, pedophilia) have global relevance. Indeed the prepublicity cited a "real, contemporary Mexico," implicitly contrasted with the more fantastic and less actual visions of everyday telenovela. It is with heavy irony that the businessman addresses the corrupt political candidate in block one: "You're the kind of Mexican we need."

Yet, beyond totalizing ideological perspectives, this diegetic space is as in the film essay, in-between: both textually and socially. As mentioned earlier, class conflict is unreconciled (the businessman never finds out about the resentment of his maltreated chauffeur). And corruption is ubiquitous (the policewoman investigating the schoolboy's death is submissive to the priests in one episode but in another asks for a bribe). While this skepticism to institutions coincides with Leftist views of contemporary Mexican politics, unlike in the 1960s, the heyday of the politically committed essay film, resistance is now shown to be impossible. Contradictory points of view remain unresolved; and the insistent repetition of scenes renders visual evidence unreliable, differently interpreted.

And while the three plots move briskly within single episodes, over the course of the series the narrative, obsessively replaying key moments, is slowed down. As in the essay film once more, what proves important is the interstice (the space between perspectives, between episodes). Indeed each "block" boasts lacunae, vital unseen moments that are neither wholly present nor absent: the *mirrey's* girlfriend is humiliated by a sex tape unshown in the series, which she compares to his kidnapping; the sex worker's suicide is precipitated by a beating by a politician-client behind closed doors; and the schoolboy's abuse is represented only by a recording on his cell phone and a security video of the couple retreating into a shadowy room. While such absences testify to Babha's social articulation of difference, they also suggest Boulous Walker's slow engagement with the complexity and ambiguity of a world that resists assimilation.

Although it may still seem a leap from the essay film to the streaming series (albeit via the network narrative), *Sincronía*, embracing the possibilities of a new medium, would seem to embody Rascaroli's perspectivist description: multiple or split narrators, embracing a contingent viewpoint and addressing a real, embodied spectator, who is invited to enter into a dialogue. As the series' tagline put it so explicitly: "You choose how to see reality." Finally, then, the link between the three genres is not the audiovisual texts themselves but rather a newly active audience that can embrace both a sociopolitical commentary and a formal complexity that remain bracingly, disturbingly, unresolved.

Two Working Women Actors: Martha Higareda and María Rojo

Central to the appeal of *Vive por mí* and *Sincronía* are two actresses of different generations who would appear to be polar opposites, but whose careers trace parallel arcs: a dramatic veteran and politician (María Rojo) and a comic ingénue (Martha Higareda). Both, however, engage with stardom as workers and entrepreneurs. How do they fare here in the context of network narratives that necessarily prize the ensemble over the individual? I argue that their strategy is to highlight that sense of in-betweenness and ambivalence that we saw in the essay film.

Little known outside Mexico (although she has most recently appeared in Netflix's sci-fi dystopia series *Altered Carbon* [2018]), Martha Higareda, the first-billed star in the ensemble cast of *Vive por mí*, stakes a claim to being one of the best-known celebrities in her home country. According to IMCINE's handbook, she rated 4th in the top-20 actors for 2016, attracting over five million admissions for just one title. High school comedy *No manches Frida* (Nacho G. Velilla, 2016 [the title is so idiomatic it appears to have no English version]), for which Higareda earned a producer credit, was the second-highest grossing local film of the year. Higareda's rivals achieved higher ratings only cumulatively with two or three releases (Secretaría de Cultura and IMCINE 2017, 109).

The central contradiction (or "productive polysemy") of Higareda's persona is that she is both the unthreatening girl next door (journalists often comment on her shortness of stature) and a canny businesswoman (depicted as carefully calculating her career). Unlike most of the stars treated previously in this book, Higareda is a veteran of the acting academy of Televisa not Argos, thus suggesting a mainstream destination from the outset. After serving as a TV presenter on the heritage channel, she broke through with feature film *Amar te duele* ("Love Hurts," Fernando Sariñana, 2002), where she played, in what would prove a typical role, a rich girl romancing a poor boy. Showing some versatility in *Niñas mal* ("Bad Girls") for the same director in 2007, Higareda played another privileged daughter, but this time a tattooed rebel, albeit with a heart of gold.

Although both films proved box office successes, it was not until 2014 that she established herself as a phenomenon by making an assured contribution to the romantic comedy genre sweeping Mexico. *Cásese quien pueda* (Marco Polo Constandse, "Get Married If You Can," 2014) cast her as a rich spoiled girl from the capital once more, about to marry her (faithless) dream lover. By a series of farcical mishaps, she ends up in muddy, rural Chiapas, where she falls, slowly but inevitably, for a selfless doctor and exchanges metropolitan haute couture for pseudo-indigenous costume.

The self-deprecating tone of this comedy of embarrassment becomes more surprising when we discover that, eclipsing its first-time director, Higareda was the one true auteur of *Cásese*, taking credits as screenwriter and producer as well as casting her real-life sister in the main supporting role as the hapless heroine's sensible sibling. In *No manches Frida* too, Higareda would combine a self-belittling role within the picture (as a nerdish schoolteacher disrespected and, finally, seduced by a macho imposter) with a controlling one outside it (unlike Higareda, the cocky male lead Omar Chaparro was not one of the producers).

Let us look at the remarkably consistent, but internally contradictory, Higareda press profile. An early interview shows her at age 18 girlishly chewing on her scarf (Flores 2002). Contradicting the image and said to be "satisfied by what she has achieved," Higareda recounts how she rejected the role of Gael García's girlfriend in *Y tu mamá también* (2001), telling powerful director Alfonso Cuarón that she would not play a fully nude scene. She attributes what success she has achieved so far to "perseverance" and is well aware that her first (delayed) leading part (in *Amar te duele*) may prove to be a "turning point in her career."

The theme of subsequent interviews is also a professional one: that, in spite of her origins in TV, she is "happier" in the cinema that is her "passion" (Barbosa Herrera 2003, 2004), as it permits her properly to prepare her part and "get to know her character." And if, when she has five film credits, the press calls her a "lucky girl" (Zúñiga 2004), still she is shown thinking professionally once more of her career development: the precarious cinema industry in Mexico does not provide "a living" and must be supplemented by TV and advertising (Martínez Enríquez 2004). Soon Higareda is described at the time as someone who "knows what she wants" and as a "woman" (no longer a "girl") who "struggles to make her dreams come true" (Cigarroa 2003). Rejecting both nude scenes (once more) and motherhood (Arellano Merino 2008), she insists rather on the necessity of ambition (Fuentes 2008). It is a steely determination belied by her charming and unthreatening performances on screen.

The professional aim is borne out by much subsequent press coverage announcing her incursions into screenwriting and producing, even as they are illustrated by pictures of her winsome smile and cascading curls (Huerta 2008, 2009). By 2010 the so-called new face of the cinema (in fact, now with a career spanning a decade) has achieved a rare goal of combining "beauty and talent" to "forge a solid career" (Espinoza 2010). Likewise Higareda is said to have the "vision of an entrepreneur" (Silva 2010) even as (in the case of *Cásese quien pueda*) she "promotes her own family" (Guerrero and García 2011). In real life, we are told, she "prefers to be the maid of honor," playing a supporting role at her sister's wedding while she concentrates on being a "workaholic" in her favored professional life (Castillo 2014). Self-deprecatingly once more the diminutive actress is said to "identify with Tinkerbell," a character she is voicing for an animated feature (Cabrera 2009). It is telling and unusual that Higareda here successfully polices the public/private divide ubiquitous in star profiles, keeping the focus on sibling loyalty rather than the conventional fields of romantic partnership or maternal devotion.

While to most Mexicans Higareda is ubiquitous and her image thus taken for granted (her ads for ecologically friendly BioExpert shampoo are unavoidable on free-to-air TV), one should not underestimate her unique achievement: combining physical attractiveness with commercial astuteness in a way that is neither demeaning to professional women nor disturbing to her mass audience.

Yet, identified as she is with comedy, Higareda's choice of relentlessly grim drama *Vive sin mí* just months after the commercial triumph of romantic farce *Cásese quien pueda* is surely no accident. Higareda's character in *Vive sin mí* is, as we have seen, yet another wealthy daughter, initially sensible and vulnerable, but latterly obsessive in her quest for a transplant. The part breaks radically with the tone of Higareda's previous roles on screen but draws still on aspects of her media persona off screen, alluding to the driven businesswoman behind the frothy fun. Indeed certain scenes read as a self-reflexive commentary on the demands of stardom: Higareda's normally dowdy character is pressurized to wear a glamorous scarlet gown to a fancy party (and, in an example of misleading marketing, is featured in that low-cut gown on the film's poster).

According to the inverted economy of the rules of art familiar from Bourdieu (1992), to lose the popular audience is to gain critical acclaim. The fact that *Vive sin mí* was barely seen in theaters, unlike Higareda's mainstream successes, thus does no harm to her bid here for a measure of cultural distinction which will add artistic luster to her mass appeal. And the network narrative remains a relatively prestigious film genre in Mexico, given its special local genealogy. There is also, as we have also seen, a troubling in-betweenness to Higareda's character in *Vive sin mí*, who, as her obsession with gaining a transplant culminates in literal ambulance chasing, can be only intermittently sympathetic. The film's albeit superficial attention to social problems in Mexico City, which are of course absent in the rom-coms that Higareda writes, produces, and headlines, also makes her presence in it yet more remarkable.

Pace the barely seen scarlet gown, Higareda's newly unglamorous image in *Vive sin mí*, coupled with the film's consistently dramatic tone, transform an ensemble feature into a disguised personal statement from one of Mexico's most popular stars, one that reinforces the film's final titles unapologetically promoting organ donation to its Mexican audience. The network narrative can thus be read as a kind of essay film within the fictional mode, even as here in a relatively failed form. And as such it can also be seen as a key step in a so-called lucky girl's bid to craft and control an enduring and substantial career as an independent woman in an unwelcoming Mexican media industry.

On the eve of the 2018 presidential elections (July 1), Martha Higareda retweeted to her 899K followers @marthahigareda a message from her fellow actress and rom-com rival Fernanda Castillo. It asked voters to remember that ten months earlier their fellow citizens were pulling political rivals out of the postearthquake rubble. The hashtags in the tweet read #Méxicosomostodos and #MéxicoUnido.

Yet, in the bitterly fought electoral contest, Mexico did not belong to everyone and was not united. In those same elections, María Rojo, most recently the star of *Sincronía*, stood as candidate of Leftist coalition Morena for mayor of Coyoacán, a wealthy southern borough of Mexico City. When she lost to the also Leftist PRD (a party to which she herself had belonged for decades), she contested the results, alleging amongst other things "gender violence" against her person (ADNPolítico 2018). Where Martha Higareda has recently combined stardom with entrepreneurship, María Rojo, then, has during a much longer period negotiated a joint career as respected actor and controversial Leftist politician. And both actors have been dismissed, in a tellingly patronizing motif, for their small stature (Illustration 10.2).

Even with over 100 acting credits over some 50 years (she has none as writer or producer), certain titles stand out. Rojo has consistently made landmark films for prestigious directors: *Las Poquianchis* (1976), a grim tale of forced prostitution and murder, was with Felipe Cazals, and *Rojo amanecer* ("Red Dawn," Jorge Fons, 1989) was the first mainstream film to treat the Tlatelolco massacre of 1968. She made minimalist dramas with fearless nude scenes in gay auteur Jaime Humberto Hermosillo's *Intimidades de un cuarto de baño* ("Bathroom Intimacies," 1991) and *La tarea* ("Homework," also 1991). It is interesting to note here that where, decades later, Higareda's enduring rejection of nude scenes was presented as part of her professional agency and control over her career, Rojo's acceptance of them in an earlier era (in spite of a face and physique that were not considered conventionally attractive) was judged proof of her commitment to her craft in a modern, radical cinema (and indeed theater) (Ortiz C 1992).

Illustration 10.2 María Rojo in *Sincronía* (Blim, 2017)

Rojo has also favored rare female directors: in the much loved *Danzón* (María Novaro, 1991), she played a Mexico City telephone operator who escapes to tropical Veracruz; in *Nadie te oye: perfume de violetas* ("Violet Perfume: No One Is Listening," Maryse Sistach, 2001), she was the unsympathetic mother of a troubled teen. Most relevant to *Sincronía* is her presence in the ensemble cast of a network narrative that predated *Amores perros*: Jorge Fons' *El Callejón de los Milagros* ("Midaq Alley," 1995).

While these features are familiar to foreign academics who have often studied them, Mexican audiences may remember Rojo more for her parallel career on television. Here she often chose female-centered narratives allegedly based on real events: *Nosotras las mujeres* ("We Women," Televisa, 1981), *Ellas, inocentes o culpables* ("Women, Innocent or Guilty," Azteca, 2000), *Lo que callamos las mujeres* ("What We Women Keep Quiet," Azteca, 2001). In one of her episodes of *Mujeres asesinas* ("Women Killers," Televisa, 2008), she even played a working-class cook who filled tamales with flesh taken from the corpse of the sexual abuser she has murdered. Rojo has thus combined challenging and unsympathetic roles with more audience-friendly material, but rarely in contradiction with her outspoken Leftist and feminist views. It is a strategy not easy to reconcile with powerful and politically compromised employers such as Televisa.

Her very extensive press profile in the Cineteca archive reveals an image that crystalized early on, but does not go uncontested. The year 1991 was something of an annus mirabilis for Rojo, who received many awards and tributes that year, especially for *Danzón*. Yet even in that year she was branded in an anonymous magazine piece both "the best of actresses" and the "most annoying" or "tiresome" ("pesada," Anonymous 1991). In the previous decade, she had supported her vision for the Mexican movie industry during its worse financial and artistic crisis, advocating for student and experimental film (Ayala 1985), predicting the "end of Mexican cinema" (Vélez 1986) at the hands of bureaucracy and lack of resources, and claiming "good cinema" could also be made at a "low cost" (Anonymous 1986). She herself was seen as a rare special case, however. A contemporary article claimed of the always-hardworking actor: "The crisis in Mexican cinema has not affected María Rojo" (Anonymous 1987a). We learn also that at this time she "refuses to make commercial cinema" (Anonymous 1987b) and "emphasizes films based on historical figures" (Vélez 1987).

By the end of the decade, Rojo is yet more specific in her denunciations of the industry in which she worked: attacking exhibitors for their lack of interest in screening "Mexican quality film" (Anonymous 1988), denouncing the travails of "cinema in a time of elections" (Vélez 1988), and claiming Mexican cinema needs more "freedom of expression" (Vega 1989). This political vision is also feminist, demanding an "opening in national cinema for the incorporation of women" (Áviles Duarte 1990). Such demands, perceived as "tiresome," created a backlash. One open "letter to María" published in the new Leftist daily *La Jornada*, which one would assume to be sympathetic to her positions, was written by a male ex-fan who claimed highhandedly that after a lengthy cinematic affair with the diva he "no longer loved her" (Roura 1991).

Like Martha Higareda, then, the young María Rojo sought to stake out a lengthy career through perseverance: "The important thing is to keep up the place that you have managed to achieve with so much effort" (Gallegos C. 1995). Unlike Higareda, however, Rojo went into politics herself, even sponsoring as a senator of a new Cinema Law ("Ley de Cinematografía") that addressed not just production but also distribution as priorities (Anonymous 2010). The accompanying picture in his article shows her in a striking floor-length dress and captioned "actress and Senator." Even there, then, her film career is seen as coming first.

Although, like Higareda once more, Rojo presents herself as in control of her career ("María Rojo does what she wants," Franco 2012), unlike Higareda she has no hesitation in revealing her resentments. One typical headline reads, implausibly: "María Rojo lacks recognition at home" (Franco 2013). The most extended and detailed interview I have seen, for magazine *Emeequis* (Rivera 2015), weaves all these threads into a coherent, but ambivalent, narrative. Thus Rojo presents herself as a "woman of the generation of 1968" (even claiming to be present at the Tlatelolco massacre), who wanted freedom, a career, and political activism, but is now left with regrets for neglecting her child and not "living [her own] life." Her roles as sexually active or rebellious women correspond to some extent to her own life (she says she has been "much loved"), although this agency or autonomy is contrasted with personal tragedy: her first husband, the "love of [her] life," died young of cancer. Yet, beyond disguised autobiography, she also carried out meticulous research for films such as *Las Poquianchis*, where her character could hardly be more distant from her own life, even visiting the real-life murderess in prison. And being a rare "Left-wing actress" brings its "demons." She says that she has been loved in the industry but also "badly treated" by it.

As a "committed actress" Rojo says that, looking back over a long career, she is embarrassed by no role she has played. Yet she distances herself from Mexican film tradition, attacking the cinema of the Golden Age and in particular Dolores del Río for being "lies": no real woman in Xochimilco ever looked like the ethereal diva in *María Candelaria* (Emilio Fernández, 1944). At once realist in her performances and activist in her politics, finally Rojo is disappointed by both the current Mexican cinema which, she says, is so ambivalent in its attitude to her, and the Left, which has also let her down by not keeping to its ideals. Still however she can take the credit for increased production in Mexico: since her Cinema Law passed, the country has gone from 7 to 70 features a year.

Where Higareda the entrepreneur produced personal projects within mainstream cinema, then, Rojo the politician promoted the collective enterprise of a national cinema that could support her favored art and auteur film. And where Higareda crafted a self-deprecating and attractive persona that sought to seduce and not to challenge a mass male audience, Rojo created the image of a "great actress" who was also tiresome, railing against the cultural establishment of which she was a part even as she was awarded multiple prizes and homages.

One little studied aspect of her career as a "diva" is her alternation of film and TV roles. *Sincronía*, as a streaming series that draws both on network narrative and essay film, serves here as a kind of synthesis of her professional life. The theme of forced sex work has been one treated by Rojo since at least hallowed auteur film *Las Poquianchis* in 1976. Yet it, and the related topic of gender violence (which, as we saw, she even invoked to contest the result of the recent local elections), is a constant in her work in television series on female "cases from real life" over three decades.

Rojo's press persona and familiar career trajectory thus interact, as ever, with her on-screen role. The "diva" of Mexican cinema here becomes, most appropriately, the "Madame" of Televisa's first streaming drama. And the contradictions of the character are also those of the actor. Madame (who has no personal name) is as professionally driven as the María who, according to the *Emeequis* interview, got her first big break as a small child by secretly memorizing a rival infant actor's role. Implacable in the workplace, Madame/María is also privately vulnerable, even sentimental, weeping bitterly over the dead prostitute she herself has entrapped (in the interview, María also weeps when told by her son that, obsessed with her career as she was, she was never truly his mother).

Martha Higareda is the klutzy entrepreneur, combining dizzy romance with hard-headed business. María Rojo, on the other hand, is the sentimental professional, mixing secret maternal tears ("What Women Don't Say") with a very visible and authoritative role as a public legislator. This is both the kind of disjunction or in-betweenness typical of the essay film and the mode of tricky interconnection familiar from the network narrative. As in the case of the other actors treated in this book, both women lay claim to professional trajectories that deserve to be prized and praised beyond the popular press profiles on which they have so tirelessly collaborated.

References

ADNPolítico. 2018. Morena impugnará elección en Coyoacán; María Rojo denuncia coacción del voto. *ADNPolítico*, July 5. https://adnpolitico.com/cdmx/2018/07/05/morena-impugnara-la-eleccion-en-coyoacan-maria-rojo-denuncia-coaccion-del-voto. Accessed 7 Aug 2018.

Anonymous. 1986. María Rojo film en Tlaxcala. Sí se puede hacer un buen cine a bajo costo. *El Sol de México*, February 11: no page.

———. 1987a. La crisis del cine mexicano no ha afectado a María Rojo. *El Heraldo*, April 26. Sección Espectáculos: no page.

———. 1987b. María Rojo se niega a hacer cine comercial. *El Día*, October 2. Sección Espectáculos: no page.

———. 1988. Existe gran desinterés de los exhibidores en proyectar cine mexicano de calidad: María Rojo. *Excelsior*, July 19: no page.

———. 1991. María Rojo la mejor de las actrices. La más pesada también. *Revista Fama*, October 31: 6.

———. 2010. Busca nuevo pacto para cine mexicano. *El Universal*, November 18. Sección Kiosko: 12.

Arellano Merino, Fabián. 2008. Martha Higareda se niega al desnudo y a la maternidad. *Ovaciones*, June 6. Sección Reflector: 5.

Áviles Duarte, Abel. 1990. Hay apertura en el cine nacional para la incorporación de la mujer. *Excelsior*, April 9: no page.

Ayala, Cervantes. 1985. Aseguró la actriz María Rojo: El cine experimental y estudiantil sufren en mayor la consecuencias de la crisis económica. *Excelsior*, March 29: 8.

Barbosa Herrera, Adriana. 2003. Martha Higareda, más cómoda en el cine. *Excelsior*, October 17. Sección Espectáculos: 4.

———. 2004. Martha Higareda: El cine, mi pasión. *Excelsior*, January 18. Sección Espectáculos: 1.

Bourdieu, Pierre. 1992. *The Rules of Art: Genesis and Structure of the Literary Field*. Stanford: Stanford University Press.

Cabrera, Omar. 2009. Se identifica Martha con Pulgarcita. *Reforma*, March 22. Sección Gente: 11.

Castillo, Ana Luisa. 2014. Prefiere ser dama de honor. *Excelsior*, July 31. Seccción Teve: 16.

Cigarroa, Iván. 2003. Sabe lo que quiere: Marta [sic] Higareda aseguró que luego de grabar '7 días,' se ha vuelto una mujer que lucha pro alcanzar sus sueños. *El Diario*, October 3. Sección: 1er Mundo Gráfico: 4F.

Cueva, Álvaro. 2017. La nueva mina de oro de Televisa. *Milenio*, March 1. http://www.milenio.com/firmas/alvaro_cueva_elpozodelosdeseosreprimidos/mina_de_oro-televisa-blim-serie-sincronia-milenio_18_912088791.html. Accessed 29 July 2018.

Espinoza, Verónica. 2010. El nuevo rostro del cine: la belleza y talento de Martha Higareda la han llevado a forjar, poco a poco, una sólida carrera. *Reforma*, July 21. Sección Circo: 6.

Flores, Leda. 2002. Martha Higareda: Le satisfacen sus logros. *Reforma*, October 18. Sección Gente: 26.

Franco R. 2012. María Rojo hace lo que quiere. *Excelsior*, March 14. Sección Función: 6.

———. 2013. A María Rojo le falta reconocimiento en casa. *Excelsior*, December 2. Sección Función: 10.

Fuentes, Martín. 2008. Martha Higareda: Hay que tener ambición. *Milenio*, July 3. Sección Hey: 2.

Gallegos C., José Luis. 1995. Lo importante es conservar el sitio que se ha obtenido con esfuerzo, dice María Rojo. No source, July 2: no page.

Guerrero, Jovana, and Diana García. 2011. Martha Higareda impulsa a su familia. *Excelsior*, March 3. Sección Teve: 33.

Huerta, César. 2008. Higareda: ahora será productora. *El Universal*, December 22. Sección Espectáculos: 1.

———. 2009. Higareda escribe, actúa y produce. *ElUniversal*, April 4. Sección Espectáculos: 15.

Kerr, Paul. 2010. *Babel*'s Network Narrative: Packaging a Globalized Art Cinema. *Transnational Cinemas* 1: 37–51.

Martínez Enríquez, Victoria. 2004. 'El cine no da para vivir': Higareda. *La Crónica de Hoy*, September 6. Sección Espectáculos: 39.

Ortiz C., Marisela. 1992. No tengo ningún prejuicio para desnudarme, afirma María Rojo. *Novedades*, July 7. Sección Espectáculos: 1.
Rascaroli, Laura. 2017. *How the Essay Film Thinks*. Oxford: Oxford University Press.
Rivera, Guillermo. 2015. María Rojo: 'Ser actriz de izquierda tiene sus demonios.' *Emeequis*, July 20: 14–20
Roura, Víctor. 1991. Carta a María. *La Jornada*, June 11. Sección Cultura: 33.
Secretaría de Cultura and IMCINE. 2017. *Anuario estadístico de cine mexicano 2016*. Mexico City: IMCINE.
Silva G., Gustavo. 2010. Higareda es una mujer con visión empresarial. *El Universal*, November 4. Sección Kiosko: 9.
TeVeAdictos. 2017. Trailer, *Sincronía*. https://www.youtube.com/watch?v=OPjG66rO6j0. Accessed 29 July 2018.
Vega, Juan Antonio. 1989. El cine mexicano requiere de más libertad de expresión: María Rojo. *Nacional*, February 23. Seccion Espectáculos: no page.
Vélez, María Luisa. 1986. María Rojo predice el fin del cine mexicano. *Novedades*, February 7. Sección Espectáculos: no page.
———. 1987. María Rojo insiste en cine a base de personajes históricos. *Novedades*, December 6. Sección Espectáculos: no page.
———. 1988. El cine en época de elecciones, según análisis de María Rojo. *Novedades*, July 19. Sección Espectáculos: no page.
Zúñiga, Félix. 2004. Martha Higareda, una chica con suerte. *Eso*, February 5. Sección Espectáculos: 8B.

11

Conclusion: Netflix and the New Telenovela

On August 10, 2018, Netflix presented with great fanfare its third series made in Mexico: *La Casa de las Flores* (it streamed simultaneously in the USA as *The House of Flowers*). According to Álvaro Cueva, the major Mexican TV critic whom I have cited frequently in this book, this dramedy made innovations in three areas: in genre (the revision of the now-exhausted traditional melodrama), in social topics (the presence of a mature adulteress and of bisexual and transgender characters), and in aesthetics (the appeal to a lush "Almodóvarian" style by a director, Manolo Caro, with a track record in feature film and legitimate theater) (Cueva 2018a).

La Casa de las Flores also boasted a self-conscious and ironic reference to traditional telenovela in the person of its star, the much-loved Verónica Castro. Once the heroine of classic serials such as *Los ricos también lloran* (*The Rich Also Cry* [Televisa, 1979]), Castro was now placed in the unaccustomed context of a series that Netflix presented as newly transgressive. Rumor had it that the veteran actress was not happy with her character's habitual drug use.

Although the new project might seem to be another step forward in multiplatform media in Mexico, no one seemed to notice that Netflix's series had been anticipated in the three areas mentioned above by telenovelas broadcast on network television and produced by the independent Argos as long ago as the 1990s. The latter was a corpus of TV drama infused with the explicitly Leftist political perspective of Argos' founder Epigmenio Ibarra, the producer of women's prison drama *Capadocia*, which I studied in Chap. 5.

One precedent for *La Casa de las Flores* is *Mirada de mujer* ("A Woman's Look," 1997–98), whose polemical premise was of a middle-class middle-aged housewife's affair with a much younger man. Argos' show (like Netflix's

20 years later) was a resounding critical and commercial success. Guillermo Orozco, Mexico's most distinguished academic commentator in TV studies, names it a "new Mexican telenovela" in both form and content (Orozco 2011, 211), while Rubén Jara, founder of IBOPE (Mexico's main market research company), claims that this was the telenovela that left the deepest imprint in the public's memory (Jara 2011). What is more, *Mirada de mujer* was the most viewed serial in Mexico over a period of some 12 years.

Mirada de mujer is also notable in that the mass audience it attracted came from the higher social classes (ABC+), those who now subscribe to Netflix. These viewers had already grown resistant to the less challenging charms of old school telenovela, which targeted a public of low socioeconomic level and high adherence to traditional gender roles. According to Jara once more, *telenovela* fans of the 1990s identified themselves as members of traditional Catholic families featuring high rates of babies, pregnant women, and men who admitted to "hating housework" (Jara 2011, 146). It is no coincidence, then, that this "traditionalism of the Mexican family" (Jara's phrase) was precisely the butt of the new telenovela of Argos (as later that of Netflix), which sought a more sophisticated "quality" audience by attacking social conventions.

Mirada de mujer's domestic setting is highly conflicted. The couple have three children, two girls and a boy, all with distinct problems. One daughter has an eating disorder, while the other is obsessed with her legal career (soon she will have to cope with unwanted pregnancy). The son, meanwhile, is an idealistic musician, overattached to the mother who believes him to be gay. Later episodes will explore such topics as HIV-AIDS and abortion, previously unseen on Mexican television.

Netflix's *La Casa de las Flores*' recasts this innovative heritage telenovela for the streaming era. Aiming for a tone of shockingly dark comedy, the opening sequence of the first episode shows a fancy party held by a bourgeois family where the spurned lover of the wealthy patriarch hangs herself from the ceiling. Benefiting from Netflix's generous budget, the domestic setting here is much more lavish and stylish than in *Mirada de mujer*, with lush floral motifs featuring throughout the brightly colored decor and wardrobe.

Although the tone of Netflix's series is more playful than that of Argos' telenovela, the family's children (two female and one male, once more) are as troubled as their predecessors. The gay son is in the closet (after experimenting with threesomes, he will finally come out as bisexual). One daughter is separated from a husband who will prove in a later episode to be a trans woman (albeit played by a cisgender man). Another arrives at the opening party with an Afro-American fiancé in tow, to the consternation of her conservative mother.

11 Conclusion: Netflix and the New Telenovela 197

La Casa de las Flores' 13 highly colored episodes allude lightly to social issues such as racism that were treated more seriously two decades earlier in *Mirada de mujer*, where an Afro-Mexican girlfriend caused genuine conflict in the bourgeois family. By now, however, such themes are overfamiliar. And when it is revealed that the husband who is adulterous (like the patriarch in *Mirada de mujer*) secretly owns a drag bar, named like the family florist business "The House of Flowers," the series' tone comes too close for comfort to early Almodóvar. Mexican creator Manolo Caro (a director well known in Mexican cinema for his rather conventional romantic comedies) signals this allegiance to the Spanish master by featuring campy pop hits from Spain on his soundtrack and by casting a Spanish star, Paco León, as the trans woman married to a Mexican matriarch.

Mexican TV audiences should be more aware, then, that the supposedly transgressive elements of Netflix's *La Casa de las Flores*, widely feted by current viewers and reviewers, were in fact already present in the "new telenovelas" of Argos and Azteca. These had pioneered the transformation of the heritage genre, the appeal to controversial social issues, and a renewed and invigorated aesthetics. And, there is one very precise precedent to Netflix's show that I have not yet mentioned: by the final episodes of *Mirada de mujer*, the newly divorced housewife has founded a florist business, her very own "house of flowers."

Argos employed the emergence of broadcaster Azteca, the then-new national rival to Televisa, to establish itself as Mexico's key independent television producer of the 1990s and beyond. Netflix is using the more recent advent of streaming platforms to attempt precisely the same aim today. Time will tell if the US newcomer proves as innovative and enduring in Spanish-language production as its long-lasting Mexican rival. But the global reach of Netflix already makes its as yet reduced number of very visible Mexican series much more accessible to international fans and scholars alike than broadcast television.

However the vast and underappreciated universe of free-to-air TV continues to entertain mass Mexican audiences, many without access to broadband, as it has for some 70 years. As the streaming giant becomes more dominant, it thus risks distorting both popular and academic perspectives, especially outside Mexico. There can be little doubt that the much despised *La rosa de Guadalupe* plays a much greater role in the daily life of the Mexican masses than the much heralded *La Casa de las Flores*.

In 2018 once more Netflix produced a feature film that also raised new questions around distribution. Alfonso Cuarón's *Roma*, an epic personal essay shot in glorious black and white and named for the *colonia* that had been hit so hard by the twin earthquakes, had been excluded from Cannes for failing to yield to the French festival's guidelines on theatrical exhibition. But later it was to win Best Picture or "Golden Lion" at Venice. As the film premiered hesitantly around the world, it gave rise to polemics around access in various territories, nowhere more so than in Mexico itself. Dominant exhibitor Cinépolis refused to show the film in its theaters when Netflix would not agree to the hitherto universal "window" of a three-month exclusively theatrical run before its streaming premiere.

In a statement whose full text was tweeted by film critic Arturo Aguilar (@aguilararturo, November 22, 2018), the Mexican company wrote that they had been negotiating with the Americans for six months without success. And that if Netflix were to agree to the "window" delay, they would not only screen the film in theaters in 75 cities around Mexico, but also donate 50% of the box office to charities helping domestic workers like those memorialized in Cuarón's film. This conflict was yet more surprising as *Roma* had been the opening film at the Morelia International Film Festival, which is sponsored by Cinépolis, and which had hosted events featuring the director Cuarón and the exhibitor's CEO Alejandro Ramírez side by side (@Alejandro_Ramz, October 25, 2018). The most anticipated local film of the year was available on only 50 screens throughout the nation.

This was thus a time of change with a vengeance in multiplatform media in Mexico, one heightened by the lengthy transition to the regime of a new President. Andrés Manuel López Obrador, like his predecessors, was expected to name his own appointees to lead film and television institutions such as IMCINE and the Cineteca.

Meanwhile feature film followed trends tracked by this book. The sex work docs I cite here were supplemented by *Casa Roshell* (Camila José Donoso, 2017), a documentary on a little-known subculture of self-identified heterosexual transvestites, who offer their straight-acting clients sexual favors. And the posthomophobic comedies I examined were complemented by what might be called postfeminist comedies. One was *Una mujer sin filtro* ("No Filter," 2018), the new title from Nicolás López of *Hazlo como un hombre* and another remake of the director's own Chilean originals. This time the format was a romantic comedy without the romance, as the highly stressed heroine ends up rejecting not only her boorish macho of a husband but also the sensitive ex-boyfriend waiting patiently in the wings. In the final sequence, she drives out of a chaotic Mexico City happy to be free at last from male entanglements.

In new TV fiction, meanwhile, the women's prison now seemed ubiquitous. All four of the controversial serials with which the new Azteca "surprised" free-to-air audiences in 2017 featured episodes in the location (*El Sol de México* 2017). And if many miniseries on the lives of singing stars or historical figures filled the gap in the schedule left by traditional telenovela, anthology dramas continued to hold sway earlier in the evening.

New platforms offered new contents beyond *La Casa de las Flores*. Netflix's sequel series *Narcos: México* received excellent reviews at home, surprisingly so since local critics have often attacked television for morbidly exploiting violence (Cueva 2018b). And the convergence between film and TV was confirmed in the continuing career of the prolific Eugenio Derbez, Mexico's most popular comedian in both media. His most recent bilingual crossover features were *How To Be A Latin Lover* (Ken Marino, 2017) and *Overboard* (Abby Kohn, 2018). Derbez continued to executively produce for Televisa new episodes of *Vecinos* ("Neighbors," 2005–08, 2017–18), a Mexican remake of a Spanish comedy format, and to appear in reruns of his bizarre original sitcom *La familia P. Luche* ("The P. Lush Family," Televisa, 2002–12). Meanwhile all of the many and varied stars treated in this book continued careers that are mostly invisible to Anglo-American audiences but central to audiovisual culture on screens big and small in their home country.

One special case of Richard Dyer's "structured polysemy" (or multiple conflicting meanings) is that of Karla Souza, the protagonist of some of the biggest box office comedies in the history of Mexican cinema as well as a high-profile US network TV series. Souza had long collaborated with director-producer Gustavo Loza, who has made such varied titles treated in this book as *Run Coyote Run* and *Sincronía*. When Souza revealed in interview that she had been raped early in her career by a (unnamed) filmmaker, Televisa announced that they were suspending their collaboration with Loza (he denied the insinuated allegation and his sitcom *40 y 20*, with its guest star ex-*vedette* Wanda Seux, made a belated return to the broadcaster in 2018) (*Excelsior* 2018). As Souza never confirmed the identity of her abuser, Mexico's #MeToo thus had an abortive and inconclusive beginning and the movement was not taken up by other high-profile women actors. Meanwhile Souza's very visible star profile over several media, characterized by both independent career women and ditzy single girls, was colored by a new and disturbing semiotic association.

Finally, then, the interconnected fields of cinema, television, and transmedia have clearly grown and changed in Mexico over the last decade and future audiovisual trends are by no means predictable. Still it will remain vital for scholars to combine industrial analysis with close readings of significant texts on all screens and to combine general media studies with local reporting if we are to measure up to the rich potential of Mexican multicultural media.

References

Cueva, Álvaro. 2018a. Crítica a *La Casa de las Flores*. *Milenio*, August 10. http://www.milenio.com/opinion/alvaro-cueva/el-pozo-de-los-deseos-reprimidos/critica-a-la-casa-de-las-flores

———. 2018b. *Narcos: México*, de Netflix. *Milenio*, November 16. http://www.milenio.com/opinion/alvaro-cueva/el-pozo-de-los-deseos-reprimidos/narcos-mexico-de-netflix

El Sol de México. 2017. TV Azteca sorprendió este 2017 con cuatro polémicas telenovelas. December 25. https://www.elsoldemexico.com.mx/gossip/tv-azteca-sorprendio-este-2017-con-cuatro-polemicas-telenovelas-544851.html

Excelsior. 2018. Gustavo Loza rechaza ser violador de Karla Souza. February 21. https://www.excelsior.com.mx/funcion/2018/02/21/1221791

Jara, Rubén. 2011. Telenovela y rating: matrimonio indisoluble. In *Telenovelas en México: nuestras íntimas extrañas*, ed. Camila González, 125–160. Mexico City: Delphi.

Orozco, Guillermo. 2011. Entre espectáculo, mercado y política. In *Telenovelas en México: nuestras íntimas extrañas*, ed. Camila González, 185–218. Mexico City: Delphi.

Index

A

Abarca, Ricardo, 115, 118, 119
Almodóvar, Pedro, 16, 127, 197
Amazon Prime, 3, 69, 102, 169
Ambulante documentary festival, 152
Angélica María, 4, 131, 133, 146, 147
Años de Fierro, Los ("The Years of Fierro"), 17
Antena 3, 3, 15, 65, 68, 69, 83
Anthology dramas, 3, 77–96, 139, 179, 199
Argos TV, 65, 67, 69, 70, 72, 74, 99, 112, 163, 184, 195–197
"Aristemo," 93
Astorga, Paula, v, 20, 21
Azteca, 3, 21, 39, 67, 68, 106, 154, 179, 188, 197

B

Becker, Kuno, 158, 159
Bellas de noche ("Beauties of the Night"), 2, 27–43
Blim, 4, 108, 115, 173, 180, 181, 188
Bondoni, Joaquín, 93
Bourdieu, Pierre, 51, 64, 168, 169, 186
Buonanno, Milly, 63–65, 68–70, 101

C

Canal Once, 24, 109, 110, 181
Capadocia, 3, 63–74, 99, 195
Caro, Manolo, 195, 197
Casa de las Flores, La ("The House of Flowers"), 5, 195–197, 199
Casa del Cine, La, 27, 153
Castro, Verónica, 134, 195
Catholicism, 25, 78, 86, 89, 95, 110, 166, 181, 196
Centro de Capacitación Cinematográfica, 2, 13–26
Chapoy, Pati, 39, 41
Cinemex, 21, 154, 160, 161
Cinépolis, 21, 24, 198
Cineteca Nacional, 2, 19–26, 35, 38–40, 57, 137
Cine Tonalá, 153, 154
Club de Cuervos, 37, 99, 111, 112
Como dice el dicho ("As the Saying Goes"), 3, 77–96, 139, 146

Cuarón, Alfonso, 5, 23, 151, 152, 164, 185, 197, 198
Cuates de Australia ("Drought"), 22
Cueva, Álvaro, 79, 80, 95, 96, 104, 153, 180, 195, 199
Cuevas, María José, v, 2, 27–34, 36, 38–40

D

Day of the Dead, 4, 5, 127–147
de la Peña, Chema, 4, 173, 177–180
de la Reguera, Ana, 3, 50, 66, 68, 70–74
Derbez, Aislinn, 48, 50, 52, 58
Derbez, Eugenio, 4, 110, 128, 129, 152, 199
Día de la unión, El ("The Day of Union"), 158–160
Documentaries
  años de Fierro, Los, 17
  Bellas de noche, 2, 27
  Cuates de Australia, 22
  Plaza de la Soledad, 2
Dyer, Richard, 6, 58, 113, 134, 167, 199

E

Earthquakes
  1985, 30, 155, 156, 158
  2017, 1, 4, 6, 77, 151–156
Écija, Daniel, 69
Espectro ("Demon Inside"), 4, 127–130
Essay film, 1, 5, 173–191

F

Fiesco, Roberto, 16, 45, 96
Film festivals
  Ambulante, 162
  Guadalajara, 5, 13–26
  Morelia, 21, 24, 112, 152
  San Sebastián, 5, 13–26

40 y 20 ("40 and 20 [years old]"), 37, 38, 108, 199
Fox Networks Group Latin America, 102, 104, 114, 117

G

Garcés, Mauricio, 46, 48
García Bernal, Gael, 4, 8, 14, 70, 104, 152, 162–169
Gay men, 23, 138
Globomedia, 68, 69
Goded, Maya, v, 2, 27, 31–35, 43
González, Everardo, 22, 24
González: falsos profetas ("González"), 25
Guadalajara International Film Festival, 13–19

H

Hazlo como hombre ("Do It Like An Hombre"), 3, 45–59
HBO, 15, 67, 69, 70, 74, 120
  HBO Latin America, 3, 65, 66, 99
Heredia, Dolores, 3, 66, 68, 70–74
Higareda, Martha, 5, 8, 111, 173, 178, 179, 184–191
Homophobia, 14, 45, 46, 49, 50
  See also Post-homophobia
Homosexuality
  acceptance of, 94
  initiation into, 83, 91
  and youth, 87
Hopewell, John, 13–15, 70, 104–106, 108
Hoy, 4, 37, 144, 152, 161, 162

I

Ibarra, Epigmenio, 3, 58, 67, 69, 195
Iñárritu, Alejandro G., 5, 24, 164, 173, 175–179
Instagram, 139, 140, 144, 147, 169

K

Kerr, Paul, 175–177, 180–182

L

Lacalle, Charo, 81–83, 87, 92–95
Lefebvre, Henri, 59
Lesbianism, 129
López, Nicolás, 3, 46, 51, 198
Los Ángeles, 17–19, 22, 99, 129
Loza, Gustavo, 37, 57, 99, 103, 104, 106–122, 173, 182, 199
Lucerito, 7
Luna, Diego, 4, 8, 70, 111, 152, 162–169

M

Macho, 3, 34, 45–59, 73, 85, 86, 89, 110, 118, 140, 146, 185, 198
May, Lyn, 3, 28, 29, 35–43
Me gusta pero me asusta ("I Like Him But He Scares Me"), 154
Méndez, Luis Gerardo, 3, 99, 106–113
Mexico City
  and aftermath of earthquake, 6
  as film location, 53
Mi corazón es tuyo ("My Heart Is Yours"), 131, 141
Mi marido tiene más familia ("My Husband Has Another Family"), 93
Mirada de mujer ("A Woman's Look"), 195–197
Modisto de señoras ("Ladies' Dressmaker"), 45, 47
Monsiváis, Carlos, 6, 155, 156
Morelia International Film Festival, 24, 109, 112, 152, 198
Morín, Polo, 4, 8, 80, 111, 132–147
Museo de Memoria y Tolerancia, 156

N

Netflix, 4, 5, 27, 37, 65, 99, 102, 111, 112, 120, 162, 169, 181, 184, 195–199
Network narrative, 1, 4, 5, 106, 108, 173–191
New platforms, 5, 96, 99–122, 199
Norteado ("Northless"), 109, 116
No se aceptan devoluciones ("Instructions Not Included"), 4, 128–130
Nosotros los Nobles ("The Noble Family"), 110–112

O

Ochmann, Mauricio, 3, 52, 56–58
Orozco, Guillermo, vi, 100, 101, 121, 196

P

Parodiando: Noche de trajes ("Taking Off Evening Dress"), 4, 131–133, 138
Plaza de la Soledad ("Solitude Square"), 2, 27
Poniatowska, Elena, 155, 156
Post-Homophobia, 45
  See also Homophobia
Princesa Yamal, 28–30, 39
Puño de hierro, El ("The Iron Fist"), 18

Q

¿*Qué culpa tiene el niño?* ("Don't Blame the Kid"), 107, 108, 115, 118, 182

R

Rascaroli, Laura, 173–176, 180, 183
Rodarte, Miguel, 3, 47, 48, 56–58, 108
Rojo, María, 5, 8, 173, 179, 181, 182, 184–191
Roma, 5, 70, 151, 153, 154, 197, 198

Rosa de Guadalupe, La ("The Rose of Guadalupe"), 3, 77–96, 139, 140, 143, 197
Run, Coyote, Run, 3, 4, 99–122, 199

S

Salvando al soldado Pérez ("Saving Private Pérez"), 48, 56
San Sebastián International Film Festival, 13–19
Serrano, Antonio, 3, 35, 45–47, 56
Seux, Wanda, 3, 28, 30, 35–43, 108, 199
Sex scandals, 111
Sex work, 33, 35, 143, 154, 190, 198
Sincronía ("Synchronicity"), 4, 5, 108, 115, 173–191, 199
"Sismos 1985/2017" ("Earthquakes 1985/2017"), 156
Social media, *see* Instagram; Twitter
Solórzano, Fernanda, v–vi, 152
Souza, Karla, 5, 108, 112, 118, 199
Stanwyck, Barbara, 36, 38, 42
Star Studies
  and mature women, 30, 42
  and Mexico, 6–8
  and Richard Dyer, 6
  and social media, 1, 6, 8, 134
Streaming series, 169, 173–191
Streaming services
  Amazon Prime, 3, 169
  Blim, 180, 181
  Netflix, 5, 99, 169, 181

T

Telemundo, 57, 65, 67, 72
Televisa ("Las Estrellas"), 3–5, 7, 21, 27, 37, 40, 41, 46, 48, 56, 57, 67, 77–80, 83, 86, 88, 92–95, 105, 106, 108, 110, 116, 122, 128–133, 138, 139, 141, 143, 144, 151–154, 157, 161, 162, 166, 173, 180–182, 184, 188, 190, 195, 197, 199
Television broadcasters
  Antena 3, 3, 15, 83
  Azteca, 3, 71, 106, 130, 151, 163, 179, 197, 198
  Canal Once, 24, 110, 181
  Telemundo, 78
  Televisa, 3, 4, 27, 37, 130, 132, 133, 144
  Univision, 132
Television pedagogy, 100
Television production companies
  Argos, 70, 99, 112, 195
  Globomedia, 74
Tívoli, 40
Torres, Harold, 2, 4, 8, 25, 99, 104, 106–113, 116, 118, 120
TVNotas, 152, 161–163
TVyNovelas, 95, 133, 152, 161
Twitter, 38, 39, 77, 94, 110, 139, 140, 144–147, 151–153

U

Univision, 78, 129

V

Variety, 13, 15, 21, 104, 108, 129
Vedettes, 3, 27–39, 42, 43, 108, 140
Vega, Paz, 127, 128
Venga la alegría, 152
Vis a vis ("Locked Up"), 3, 63–74
Vive por mí ("Live For Me"), 4, 173–191

W

Women in prison (WIP) television drama, 3, 5, 63–74

Y

Youth television, 82, 95

Z

Zabludovsky, Jacobo, 157, 159

GPSR Compliance
The European Union's (EU) General Product Safety Regulation (GPSR) is a set of rules that requires consumer products to be safe and our obligations to ensure this.

If you have any concerns about our products, you can contact us on

ProductSafety@springernature.com

In case Publisher is established outside the EU, the EU authorized representative is:

Springer Nature Customer Service Center GmbH
Europaplatz 3
69115 Heidelberg, Germany

www.ingramcontent.com/pod-product-compliance
Lightning Source LLC
LaVergne TN
LVHW020330260326
834688LV00037B/950